D0449247

SOCIAL BLUEPRINTS

SOCIAL BLUEPRINTS

CONCEPTUAL FOUNDATIONS
OF SOCIOLOGY

DAVID K. BROWN
Illinois State University

New York   Oxford
OXFORD UNIVERSITY PRESS
2004

Oxford University Press

Oxford   New York
Auckland   Bangkok   Buenos Aires   Cape Town   Chennai
Dar es Salaam   Delhi   Hong Kong   Istanbul   Karachi   Kolkata
Kuala Lumpur   Madrid   Melbourne   Mexico City   Mumbai
Nairobi   São Paulo   Shanghai   Taipei   Tokyo   Toronto

Copyright © 2004 by Oxford University Press, Inc.

Published by Oxford University Press, Inc.
198 Madison Avenue, New York, New York 10016
www.oup.com

Oxford is a registered trademark of Oxford University Press

All rights reserved. No part of this publication may be reproduced,
stored in a retrieval system, or transmitted, in any form or by any means,
electronic, mechanical, photocopying, recording, or otherwise,
without the prior permission of Oxford University Press.

Library of Congress Cataloging-in-Publication Data
Brown, David K., 1955–
    Social blueprints : conceptual foundations of sociology / David K. Brown.
        p. cm.
    Includes bibliographical references and index.
    ISBN 0-19-516226-9 (alk. paper)
    1. Sociology.   I. Title.
    HM586.B76 2004
    301–dc22   2003066179

Printing number: 9 8 7 6 5 4 3 2 1

Printed in the United States of America
on acid-free paper

For my mother
Rita Brown
for helping and letting me grow up

CONTENTS

Preface **xi**

Acknowledgments **xv**

1 INDIVIDUALITY, SOCIETY, AND IDENTITY: CORNERSTONES OF SOCIOLOGICAL REASONING 1

Introduction **1**

Vivifying the Mundane: The Sociological Imagination **5**

The Sociological Imagination: C. Wright Mills **5**

Individual Problems Versus Social Problems **7**

The Sociology of Celebrities: Individuals in Social Context **11**

The American Preoccupation with Individualism in Cultural, Political, and Economic Life **16**

The Sociology of Identities **22**

Individuals as Webs of Group Affiliation **22**

Social Identities: Repertoire Selection, Multiple Consciousness, and Ambiguity **25**

The Contested Terrain of Sociological Knowledge **30**

Some Cautionary Notes About Sociology Versus Psychology **31**

The Reality of the Social: Social Facts **32**

The Gulf Between Fact and Value Statements **34**

Muddying the Waters: The Politics of Social Knowledge **38**

Conclusion **41**

Suggestions for Further Study **43**

2 SOCIAL THEORIES: THEIR INTERPLAY AND CONTRADICTIONS 45

The Nature and Relevance of Social Theories 45
Theories as Paradigms 46
Theoretical Reasoning: Induction and Deduction 47
Four Broad Types of Social Theory 48

Rational Choice Theories: Individuals Pursuing Interests 50
Where Do Desires Come From? 53
The Free-Rider Problem: Are Rational People Honest? 56
Do People Choose to Be Unequal? 58

Functional Theories: Harmony and Necessary Differences in Social Organization 59
Basic Functionalist Imagery 60
Is Social Inequality Simply Necessary? 64

Symbolic Interactionist and Social Constructionist Theories: Interaction, Meaning, and Everyday Life 64
Mind, Self, and Society 66
Modern Symbolic Interactionism 67
Symbolic Interactionism/Constructionism: Are the Trees Hiding the Forest? 74

Conflict Theories: Arenas of Power and Inequality 75
The Interplay of Conflict Theory with Other Perspectives 77
Karl Marx' Enduring Legacy 79
Max Weber's Multidimensional Conflict Theory 84
Conflict Theories: Too Much Pessimism, or Sober Realism? 93

Conclusion 94

Suggestions for Further Study 95

3 CULTURE, STRUCTURE, AND INTERACTION: UNRAVELING THE FIBERS OF SOCIAL LIFE 97

Introduction 97

Distinguishing Social Structure, Culture, and Social Interaction 98

Social Structural Determinism, Cultural Autonomy, and Human Agency 101

    Beyond Good and Evil: Religion as an Emblem of Society 103

    Beyond Cold Hard Cash: The Sociology of Money 108

Understanding Culture and Social Power 112

    Cashing in on Culture: The Flow of Cultural, Social, and Economic Capital 114

    Roads Between High Culture and Popular Culture 117

    Interpreting Pink Flamingos: Everyday Expressions of Social Positions 119

    "Lions and Tigers and Bears—Oh My!" The Cultural and Political Construction of Social Problems 122

Cultural Production, Distribution, and Interpretation 127

    A Basic Model of Cultural Production Processes 129

    Making Chili Peppers: Organizational Processes in the Rise of a Band 132

    Pets or Meat? The Interpretation of Cultural Products 137

Conclusion 140

Suggestions for Further Study 141

4   POWER AND AUTHORITY: IN SOCIAL MOVEMENTS, STATES, AND ORGANIZATIONS 143

The Sociological Perspective on Power 143

    The Power Prism and Its Refractions: An Analytical Tool 144

Social Power and Social Movements 147

    Reading Power into Political Protests 152

Power, States, and Legitimacy 159

    Spreading Social Power in Authoritarian Regimes 160

    Theaters of War: The Social Construction of State Legitimacy 163

Power in Organizations 171

    Power and Control in Workplaces 173

Bureaucratic Organizations and Abstract
Social Power 183
The Symbolic Architecture of Organizational Power 185

Conclusion 192

Suggestions for Further Study 192

5 GLOBALIZATION: CONCEPTUALIZING
   TWENTY-FIRST-CENTURY SOCIAL CHANGE 194

Introduction 194

Globalization: How Global, How New? 195

Economic and Political Globalization 197

The Ideological and Policy Basis of the New World
Order: Neoliberalism and Its Critics 199
The Global Power of Transnational Corporations 204
International Governmental and Nongovernmental
Organizations: International Monetary Fund, World
Bank, World Trade Organization, and the G-8 209
Bittersweet Chocolate: Child Slave Labor in
West Africa 213
So Long Nation, Hello Corporation? 214
International Social Movements 216
Mexico: Poverty and Protest in a "Model" Free
Trade Nation 219

Cultural Globalization 223

Limiting Factors Concerning Cultural Globalization 224
Global Consumerism: You Gotta Shop Around,
Even If It's All the Same 228
Global Tourism: Cultural Freedom, Structural
Constraints, and Exploitation 233

Conclusion 238

Suggestions for Further Study 242

References 243
Index 251

PREFACE

Sociology challenges people to think in new ways about the world, and perhaps even to act differently. When sociologists examine social issues, they often ask different questions and provide more critical and controversial answers than conventional wisdom offers. For many people, sociology courses are departure points for different and exciting trajectories of thought that change their outlooks on life forever. The goal of this book is to enable you to imagine the social worlds that envelop you in new and complex ways.

Where does one begin when embarking on the study of a new field? One of the ironic difficulties involved in learning sociology is that the varied subject matter of the field is so intriguing that it is easy to get caught up in it and miss the core ideas that span all of these topics. If one fails to note and understand the basic concepts and theories of a field, it becomes very difficult to move ahead to more challenging materials or to apply knowledge to new areas. It took me a very long time to begin to cull from my studies the central conceptual and theoretical lessons of sociological thought. However, there may be a more expedient path to mastery of these key ideas.

This book is my best effort to make essential social processes more discernable for others, without sacrificing the sophisticated analysis and critical challenges to popular thinking that make sociology the vibrant field that it is. In doing so, I learned a lot myself. If the book is challenging, and I think that it is, that is not because I want to dazzle you with intellectual trickery, but because society itself is much more complicated than we generally are led to believe by the media, politicians, and other authorities.

The first steps in learning a new field are always the hardest, and it is no different with sociology. One of the best ways to tap into the considerable knowledge that sociologists have about the puzzles of social existence is to consider the basic conceptual and theoretical foundations of their discipline. This is what *Social Blueprints* is all about. A toolkit of core ideas is contained in the chapters that follow, along with what I hope you find to be an interesting mode of presentation of these building blocks of sociology. Familiarity with these foundations will enable you to explore additional sociological studies on topics that most concern you.

In writing this book, I used a broad range of examples of social issues in order to enliven the discussion. The goal was not, however, to cover all of the topical areas that larger, standard textbooks treat. Rather, pivotal concepts such as power, culture, interaction, identity, and social structure that overarch all sociological subject areas highlight social mechanisms that apply across groups, issues, history, and places. The most fundamental sets of concepts of the book appear in the chapter titles: individuality, society, and identity (Chapter 1); social theories (Chapter 2); culture, structure, and interaction (Chapter 3); power and authority (Chapter 4); and globalization (Chapter 5). Within each chapter, there are many further concepts (bolded in the text) that stem from these fundamental ones.

There are three other orienting themes to the book that I want to call your attention to. First, you will find a repeated pattern of consideration of three interrelated realms of society—the economic, the political, and the cultural. These three templates can be applied to all social phenomena in order to reveal different dimensions of society. Second, I have called attention to social inequalities in each chapter because these issues are of great concern to the vast majority of sociologists. The conceptual and theoretical focus of the book is not an advocacy of isolationism in the cloisters of academia, but rather a call to informed engagement in the social world. Finally, I have sought, where possible, to suggest constructive bridges between various perspectives within sociology rather than to set them up as mutually exclusive viewpoints.

As you proceed, I encourage you to be an active reader, rather than a passive receptor of information. Sociological thinking is more complex than simple memorization of terms and definitions. Close attention should be paid to how concepts are applied in the book's examples and to the relationships that are drawn between concepts. Some of the examples used are drawn from personal experiences. I mention these cases not because I have led a particularly interesting life, but because I want to encourage you to carry the messages of sociology to your own life. In considering all of these examples, your attention should be focused on the key concepts at work in each case, rather than on the descriptive matter of the examples.

While the optimal way to read the book is the way in which it is presented here, I have written the chapters so that they can be read in a different order without confusion. The only exception is Chapter 5, on globalization, which covers the perplexing issue of global social change and therefore assumes familiarity with much of what precedes it.

Sociologists don't have all of the answers about how to build a perfect society, but they do have blueprints of the current one that I will share with you in what follows. Sociology is by its nature and calling a liberating discipline, and it is my desire that this book will have a similar effect on you as a reader. Whether this reading is your first exposure to sociology or an extension of prior inquiry, I appreciate your willingness to venture into a project that far too few people—even educated ones—ever undertake. The rewards of sociological awareness will be well worth the investment.

David K. Brown
Bloomington, Illinois

ACKNOWLEDGMENTS

Books are cultural products with long strings of social influence that extend from their authors. This book began as I formalized lecture material from my large introduction to sociology course at the University of Illinois–Urbana and came to a conclusion making a trial run of the contents with my students at Illinois State University. These students and graduate assistants endured the organization of my thoughts, while I learned from their struggles with the material. I am grateful to all of them, especially to Angela Caldwell, Laura Chambers, Ashley McKinney, Diana Mincyte, Diane Muehl, and Grant Shoffstall for their efforts to make my thinking more comprehensible.

Colleagues and reviewers at these and other institutions served as able gatekeepers who with their suggestions made sure that the end product was less my own and more a collective contribution to sociology. If the book has any shortcomings, they surely are more a consequence of my obstinate foolishness than their bad advice. Frank Beck, Dan Chambliss, Tom Cushman, Virginia Gill, Jeremy Hein, Bob Heiner, Peter Kivisto, Kent Sandstrom, Ira Silver, and James Witte deserve credit for some of the better elements found in what you see before you. Peter Labella, Sean Mahoney, Brian Kinsey, and others at Oxford University Press provided the outstanding guidance, support, and tolerance as this work moved toward publication. Great publishers make all of our jobs easier, and the people at Oxford fall into this category.

My deepest gratitude goes to Michelle Byers, who carefully read the entire unfolding manuscript and offered countless suggestions along the way that were often maddeningly on target, the way that only a teacher and companion in life could do. Much is sacrificed that can never be recouped in writing a book, but as a token of my appreciation, I owe her an inestimable number of meals and walks in the country, and many hours of pensive listening to trifling frustrations of the sort that not just authors are prone to suffer.

SOCIAL BLUEPRINTS

CHAPTER 1

Individuality, Society, and Identity

Cornerstones of Sociological Reasoning

"You're free to choose—be yourself," we are constantly told. Is this idea really true? This opening chapter will acquaint you with basic differences between individualistic and sociological thought. To be sociologically aware, you need to bracket away the deeply entrenched tendency to think of everything in terms of isolated "individuals" who think and act wholly on their own. Individuals actually are more complex than they may seem at first sight—they are themselves very "social" due to group influences. Social realities are fundamentally different from individual actions and thoughts and therefore require a separate mode of analysis than individual psychology offers. Sociological thinking also is different from mere opinion because sociology is based on the facts of social existence rather than the peculiar values that people hold.

INTRODUCTION

Chicago, Illinois, is an incredible city. Situated on the shores of Lake Michigan, its skyline and lakefront parks are among the most spectacular sights of their kind in the world. The architecture of the city is astounding, boasting some of the best works of modern masters such as Frank Lloyd Wright, Louis Sullivan, and Mies van der Rohe. Chicago is the transportation and industrial hub of middle America, with a rich history of railway, canal, financial, commercial, and manufacturing enterprises. The many and diverse ethnic neighborhoods of the city form a tapestry of global cultures. There are great universities (including the University of Chicago and Northwestern University), fascinating museums and art galleries, a vibrant music and theater scene, zoos and botanical gardens, and professional sports teams–virtually everything that one would expect to find in a world-class city. At night, the city throbs with energy, for there are attrac-

1

tions that serve all tastes. Past the city limits, suburbs sprawl for fifty or more miles along and away from the lake. Beyond the suburbs lie the black and fertile farmland of America's heartland, and the speckling of small towns that serve the rural hinterland population.

I grew up in one of these little towns about seventy-five miles from the downtown "Loop" district of Chicago. Amazingly, I visited the city only a handful of times during my youth—to see baseball games with my father at the Chicago Cubs' Wrigley Field, and once on a school field trip to the Museum of Science and Industry on the south side of the city. I recall being spellbound by the massive buildings and electrified by throngs of people who seemed to be present everywhere. This decidedly different world that I had seen only on television was awesome to me when I experienced it in person. The most puzzling things to me during these visits were the miles and miles of dilapidated tenement buildings that we passed along the freeway, and the people in the streets who obviously lived in them. There was, and remains, a drearier side of Chicago—its poverty-stricken areas. While my family was not rich (my father was a bricklayer, and we were working-class people) and there were poor people in my community, I had never before seen the geography of poverty so clearly massed before me. I could tell, even at an early age, that these were difficult places to live in.

At about the same time in my life, I also remember watching a television special that depicted the life of a poor man from Chicago who lived in rundown, outmoded housing that was rat infested. He attended in his youth cold, miserable, lead-painted, filthy public schools that were filled with violence. The man experienced street crime and drug culture as facts of daily existence, and was chronically unemployed. His face was hardened and disfigured, and his body was scarred; he was a supremely scary sight to me—almost a monster of sorts. I related the story to what I had seen with my own eyes in Chicago, and it made me think, "Why doesn't this man just *leave* that situation—get *out*?" I had heard others from my town say the same thing in other contexts. After all, I thought, there was plenty of room in my town and it was far away from all of that hardship—why not just come *here*? I concluded, again with others, that it must have been a decision that this poor man made for himself to stay, that it was part of his "mind set."

My early understanding of this example was very individual-based, rather than sociological. Later in life, I moved to Chicago myself. By then, I was a graduate student in sociology at Northwestern University, just north of the city limits in the suburb of Evanston. I lived in the city because I couldn't afford the high rental prices in Evanston. Daily life in the city was an awakening for me that was very exciting, but sometimes frightening as well. I once was chased up a stairwell by a man who wanted to beat me with a crowbar. Break-ins were routine events in my building. A neighbor was confined to a wheelchair with oxygen respirator tanks from a brutal beating she suffered at the hands of an intruder. Just blocks away, a mass murderer was arrested for raping young boys, chopping up their bodies with a chain saw, and throwing their bagged-up remains into the alley dumpster. I rode the elevated subway north to school in Evanston, and then after school took it south to my workplace where I got off at the station that served the infamous and crime-ridden Robert Taylor housing project. As I milled through the crowds there, it was as though the man in the news story from my youth now confronted me face-to-face each day. The poverty was still there, stark and horrifying, but I had learned some things in sociology by then that changed my thinking about the sources and sustenance of poverty. I also came to a better understanding of why that man in the newscast did not just pull up stakes and move to my idyllic little town in downstate Illinois.

Previously, I was looking at poverty and its solution from a purely individual standpoint—that man should have simply done something to change his lot in life. It wasn't that easy. As it turns out, the television man was a black man, but he might just as well have been an immigrant Pole, an American Indian, or a Hispanic person. The fact was that my hometown was all white and full of racism. So were other affluent areas of Chicago and the suburbs. A poor black man walking the streets of my hometown, looking for a job and place to live, quickly would have been accosted by the local police and ushered out of town. Importantly, this man's poverty was shared with many others in his situation as a minority group member, and as a relative newcomer to the city (a first-generation migrant from southern plantations, in this case) who had suffered the brunt of factory closings in the city. His educational credentials were meager and did not allow him the same level of mobility and comfort that I had in moving to his city. The dead-end jobs that were available to him offered such low wages relative to the high cost of living in the city that he remained in poverty even when he did work full time. Small wonder then, in this situation, that people resorted to crime to get some taste of the things that others had. And when they did, the police were always there within shouting distance to roust up the criminals and send them to jail, even as landlords went unregulated and unpunished for charging exorbitant rents for unsafe dwellings that violated public health laws. This man also had no car. The elevated train and city bus system were his only modes of transit to look for jobs and new places to live, and the cost of public transit limited his range of opportunities even within this option. In order to survive, this man depended on his family and friends, and he was expected when appropriate circumstances arose to share his meager resources within this network. These strong social ties also were common among the many global immigrants to Chicago. My outside world would have been as unnerving to this man in the absence of friends as his urban world was to me. Schools in his neighborhood were inadequate because local taxes pay for schools, and there was little tax base to support better schools. On nearly all of these counts, this man and I differed not so much because we were different as "individuals," but because he and I experienced life in different groups and the distinctive social processes associated with them. I eventually moved back to my hometown for a period of time. After all, my social ties were there. But I was a different person than I was in my youth, and the difference had more to do with my sociological understanding of the world than with the simple fact that I was older.

You don't necessarily have to live directly within another group to gain new viewpoints about the varieties of social existence. I had read a number of sociological studies of urban street corner society, including Elliot Liebow's *Tally's Corner* (1967), which more or less prepped me for my experiences in Chicago. Mitchell Dunier's recent books *Slim's Table* (1992) and *Sidewalk* (1999) offer similar insights about urban life today. As a prominent sociologist once said, "One need not have *been* Caesar in order to *understand* Caesar." Sociological study offers a reasonable proxy for actual social experience that is both enlightening and liberating. This chapter explores some first steps in this direction.

VIVIFYING THE MUNDANE:
THE SOCIOLOGICAL IMAGINATION

Sociology is more than a collection of prior research with its many established facts and explanations of various facets of social life. Perhaps even more importantly, sociology is a distinctive *perspective* that radically changes how we understand the ordinary world that buzzes around us day after day. To practice sociology is to see things very differently from the way that mass media, politicians, and popular culture typically present them to us. Indeed, as we shall see, sociology is a different form of consciousness. Properly understood, sociology will fundamentally change you as a person just as much as a religious conversion or adoption of a radical philosophy might alter your perspective. The difference is that sociology has an empirical basis that stands at the foundation of this change of worldview.

The Sociological Imagination: C. Wright Mills

One of the more enduring contributions to the sociological perspective came in the 1950s from a sociologist named C. Wright Mills (1916–1962). Mills, an American, was a radical, free spirit who rode BMW motorcycles and was intimidating both in his physical stature and his piercing intellect. He challenged nearly every major societal center of power in the conservative age of the 1950s—government, the military, and big business. These challenges came both in his scholarly writing and his social activism. Despite his renegade spirit, Mills understood that he and others were products of larger societal forces, not just independent individuals.

One of the keys to truly critical thinking, Mills (1959) argued, was the cultivation of a **sociological imagination**. By this term, he meant two ways that individuals are shaped by society, as shown in Figure 1.1.

First, Mills argued that we need to liberate ourselves from the chains of **individualism**—the tendency to place primacy on individuals rather than societal forces—so that we can see our personal troubles, successes, choices, opportunities, and general experiences as part of wider *societal forces*, that is, to recognize the "public issues" that lie behind our private experiences as shared circumstances with others. Second, we should be attentive to the *historical context* of our lives because freedom and constraint in making choices are conditioned by the era that we live in.

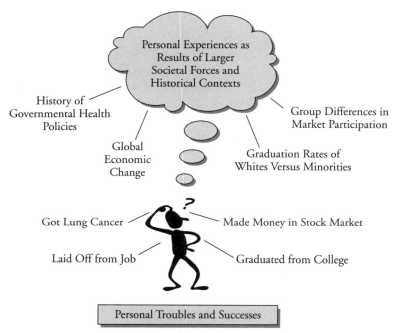

Figure 1.1   Development of the Sociological Imagination

One's individual suffering as a victim of cigarette-induced lung cancer, for example, can be seen against the larger social and historical backdrop of power and public policy. While one certainly makes choices about smoking, the actions of the tobacco industry, the mass media, the medical establishment, and government regulatory agencies historically painted the choice to smoke cigarettes not only as a safe one, but also as a glamorous activity that enhanced one's social status. Thus the private trouble of cancer can be informed by the sociological imagination. This perspective applies not just to misfortunes, but also to successes. To take a different sort of example, we can come to view our achievements in schooling not simply as "individual achievements," but also as results of our relative privileges in terms of level of parental involvement in advocacy of hard work in school, our early access to quality schools versus underfunded, poorly equipped ones, the availability of peers who serve as role models, and most generally as results of our membership in racial, class, and gender groups that tend to receive different forms of educational experience. These sobering thoughts are what the sociological imagination is all about. Mills is saying that both our successes and others' failures are influenced by sociological factors. Moreover, he felt that there was a definite moral and ethical obligation for people to acknowledge these forces, and to act compassionately toward underprivileged groups in the political sphere, that is, in the creation of public policies that address inequalities.

Individual Problems Versus Social Problems

Let us take an example from popular culture to further expand on differences between individualistic logic and the sociological imagination. In Joel Schumacher's 1993 film *Falling Down*, actor Michael Douglas plays a character who suddenly "snaps" and vents his anger toward society. Even if you did not see the film, one can readily empathize and appreciate the situation that gave rise to Douglas' tirade. As the film opens, Douglas is stuck in a snarl of freeway traffic on a terribly hot afternoon. He has just been laid off from his job at a defense manufacturing plant. Traffic is going nowhere as he observes all manner of people and vehicles waiting out the congestion. Douglas is sweating and irritated. After honking his horn in despair and cursing at motorists, Douglas peers at the world above the freeway. He suddenly gets out of his car and simply leaves it to further mangle traffic as he scales the freeway embankment to enter the streets above—he's "going home." Now in the bustle of urban life, Douglas experiences further frustrations in trying to get change to call his ex-wife from a local convenience store owner who speaks little English. He lashes out, blaming minorities for his troubles throughout the film. When Douglas gets hungry and enters a fast food restaurant, he quickly becomes infuriated that he cannot special order his meal—the establishment's rules forbid alterations to the posted menu items. Enraged, Douglas blasts away with a stolen gun at the restaurant crowd en route to a series of ever more violent encounters with the social order.

Luckily, most of us do not go to the extremes that Douglas did in *Falling Down*, but most of us similarly have experienced the constraints of society as isolated, frustrated individuals. Anyone who has tried to contact the phone company and been forced through a maze of menu selections only to be put on hold in the end, readily can empathize with Michael Douglas' situation. Filmmakers know that this is the case, and that is how they so successfully play on our individual anxieties in producing hit movies. Few popular films portray sophisticated social visions of the world of the kind that a sociological imagination might engender.

Imagine a different theme to the traffic jam and restaurant fiasco, or to your own outrage in similar circumstances. While the net result might still be one of frustration about the world, a sociological eye to such events at least reveals more than simple irrationality in the social order, and suggests more than just psychological empathy ("Can't we all just get along?") as a solution to our problems. First of all, traffic jams are imminently social and historical phenomena. Some countries, such as the United States, have greater difficulty with traffic than others because they lack adequate mass transit. U.S. mass transit is quite primitive by the standards of other industrialized countries. In the United States, early twentieth-century forms of mass transit, such as electric railways, were abandoned in favor of automobiles and highway construction because U.S. motor companies that sought sales and profits from cars influenced governmental transportation policy toward highway construction. The inevitable problem of traffic congestion, not to mention the inherently more dangerous mode of individual locomotion, is a peripheral concern. Michael Douglas thus was stuck in history as much as in his present predicament.

Auto manufacturers also spawned through their advertising and other mass media a veritable cultural "love affair" between Americans and their cars that is unrivaled in the world. It is common to hear people describe their vehicles in such sociological terms as "manly," "sexy," "cool," "family," or "sport" vehicles. Different groups drive different kinds of cars and see them as status symbols. People even come to hate certain cars because of the groups that automobiles represent. Much of our personal and social identity is wrapped up in these machines. It is no wonder that tempers flare in traffic jams where strangers, symbolically represented only by the cars they drive, confront a large-scale social malady as isolated individuals. "Road rage," which *Falling Down* drew much publicity to as a modern panic, is a social creation, not an individual psychological disorder.

Given these social problems, it is rather ironic that Americans still see automobiles as symbols of their freedom to move about in utter privacy. People go in substantial debt to buy cars, and incur untold costs in fuel, maintenance, and insurance to enjoy this so-called freedom. As Steven Nock (1993) observed in his research on privacy and surveillance in America, young people particularly relish the independence that cars afford them from life at home with their parents, and most generally the freedom cars bring from adult surveillance. The car is a private place, and the driver's license is a gateway to individual autonomy. Having a car in American culture became a key asset in love and sexuality, as so many films about the topic abundantly demonstrate. In a very similar way, cellular phones today carry this symbolism of freedom, even though the government may eventually link cell phone use to satellite surveillance imagery that could trace our every move, place us at crime scenes, and be sold to businesses that could call us with advertising gimmicks as we pass by their stores!

Michael Douglas' restaurant scene also could speak volumes to the sociological imagination, were it not cast in such individualistic terms as a mere psychotic episode. The automobile had ripple effects throughout American social institutions, including the many businesses that sprang up alongside U.S. highways. Motels, drive-in theaters, quick-stop gas stations, and of course fast food restaurants with drive-up windows all were designed to facilitate the fast and impersonal pace of American life that the automobile created. It is doubly frustrating to move sluggishly along in traffic that is supposed to be efficient, and then to see our freedom further limited when we pull off at fast food establishments that are too slow, provide us with inadequate choices, and give us the same impersonal human interactions that we experience in our cars.

In order to further our efficiency in other areas of life, restaurants such as McDonald's adopted a model of organization that fit the needs of a frantically paced society. As sociologist Robin Leidner (1993) illuminated in her in-depth study of the McDonald's corporation, eating at these establishments is a means to other ends, such as getting to work on time, or rapidly traversing interstate highways on vacations. As such, the emphasis in fast food restaurants is on standardized, predictable products, and corresponding socialization of restaurant workers *and customers* to efficient, impersonal behavior in the preparation, ordering, and eating of food. McDonald's actually maintains its own accredited management training university, Hamburger University, to instruct managers worldwide in the exact same principles of "hamburgerology." Truly loyal managers are said to have "ketchup in their veins." There is no room for special orders, fraternization with customers, or leisurely dining here. Rather, we see only the veneer of choices and sociability in standardized "value meals," and thinly veiled promotional responses of pseudo-cordiality from employees, such as "Would you care for fries with your Big Mac?" Savvy, hurried customers even try to amplify the efficiency of the process by anticipating these queries and saying as they order, "Big Mac, no fries."

Other fast food restaurants, for example, Taco Bell, Kentucky Fried Chicken, and Arby's, offer different foods but organize production and consumption in largely the same manner as McDonald's. There is a great deal of interorganizational modeling along central product themes, such as Southwestern variants of chicken, hamburgers, sandwiches, and so on. Some restaurants are given a "local theme" in their interior decorations to offset the overwhelming anonymity of the organizational design. On-site children's playgrounds are other common sales gimmicks that seek to add a family atmosphere. As George Ritzer (2000) has observed, the fast food model of business has spread to many other areas of social life. In everything from housing and education to mass media, replication and efficiency come to predominate as organizing principles of what Ritzer calls the **McDonaldization of society**.

The very mechanization and routinization of tasks that restaurants and other businesses have undertaken makes workers very replaceable, for there is little real expertise required in their jobs—even soft drinks are poured to specified levels by machines, if the task is not relegated to the customer at separate soft drink stations. As a consequence of this deskilling of labor, these companies can hire and replace low-wage, low-skill workers as they please, while maintaining product consistency and high profits. Service workers of this type have little reason actually to care about their customers, so the organization's forced façade of friendliness from workers is quite understandable in this circumstance. In addition, service workers at different establishments (McDonald's and Burger King, for example) fail to *see* their plight as a common one, instead viewing their job situations much as Michael Douglas saw his job layoff and the rest of his world—as individual misfortunes.

American mass media and political rhetoric are replete with the kinds of individualistic messages that the *Falling Down* example illustrates. Countless films have reinforced our erroneous beliefs that "hero" teachers or school principals can single-handedly change the social structural problems of U.S. education. Individual movie cops routinely bring down entire corrupt political machines. Evil empires fall as one gallant soldier goes behind enemy lines to wreak havoc on the bad guys. Individual viewers can live out their fantasy resistance to the absurdities of the social order by watching fictional or even actual (e.g., on the nightly news) individuals go berserk. Our politicians all too often echo these same myths about individual efficacy in their recommendations for societal betterment. These stories are great fantasies, of course, but the lesson of the sociological imagination is that real life is fraught with a host of seldom-noted social and historical complexities that make actual social change and public policy reform endeavors of great nuance.

The Sociology of Celebrities: Individuals in Social Context

There can be no doubt that Americans deeply value the notion of individuality. It is embedded in our Constitution, in our beliefs about the sources of success and failure in our lives, and in our attachment to heroic individuals who strike out on their own against social conventions. Most Americans consider themselves to be individuals more than members of groups. It is a virtue in the United States to be different from others, and a sign of weakness merely to follow along with others in groups. This rabid individualism is noteworthy because Americans, perhaps more than any other people, devalue loyalty to groups in favor of what they at least perceive as being individuals. Nowhere is this individuality more pronounced than in Americans' admiration of celebrities, yet as Joshua Gamson (1994) has persuasively argued, celebrities are deeply social in nature.

Just think for a moment of who comes to mind when you think of truly individual celebrities. These people would be individuals whose freedom we admire as they "buck the system," so to speak. Perhaps you thought of Minnesota's former pro wrestler governor, Jesse "The Body" Ventura, who ran and won as a freewheeling independent candidate? Surely this man, who regularly insults members of the press corps and speaks his mind, is the epitome of individualism. Or maybe the renegade-style singer Madonna best serves as your model of rugged individualism? There are many other celebrities who fit this billing. Many Americans would rank Dennis Rodman high on their scales of individualism. Rodman is the former pro basketball player whose antics on and off the court capture the popular idea of individuality as utterly unfettered expression of free will against the constraint of social norms. Dennis Rodman is different, most people would agree.

In the 1990s, Dennis Rodman was a member of the Chicago Bulls team (along with Michael Jordan and Scottie Pippen) that won several National Basketball Association (NBA) championships. Rodman's forte was rebounding the ball, but his technical prowess in this facet of the game was much overshadowed by his reputation as a dirty player who taunted the opposition, the referees, and even spectators on occasion. Even his own teammates and coach learned to tolerate his extravagant lifestyle. In appearance, Rodman was equally striking. His upper body was covered with tattoos, his hair was dyed in an ever-changing variety of rainbow colors and designs (leopard spots, "smiley faces," and other unusual fashion statements), and he wore multiple earrings.

Off the court, Dennis Rodman also was a dazzling figure. His sex and party lives were notorious. He cross-dressed and bragged of his partying and sexual stamina. Pearl Jam and Smashing Pumpkins were his favorite rock bands. Rodman was involved in a brief relationship with singer Madonna (individualism times two!), was married for a short while to the *Baywatch* television show star Carmen Electra, and for an equally short time was married to model Annie Banks. At one point, Rodman teamed up with pro wrestler Hulk Hogan for a tag team match. He played in several films and wrote an autobiography entitled *Bad as I Wanna Be* that made the *New York Times* best sellers list. Again, Dennis Rodman was not an ordinary basketball player.

One bit of conventional wisdom about the sources of Rodman's behavior was that "he just wanted attention," that is, he had some kind of psychological problem that drove him to extremes. It is impossible to assess the validity of this claim, but a second charge— "He was doing it for the money"—at least had the force of evidence

Even in this case of apparently radical individualism, doesn't the oddity of the matter rest on Dennis Rodman's and our recognition of a dominant social norm—that bridal attire is appropriate for women? Even breaking social conventions assumes knowledge of them. (© Mitchell Gerber/CORBIS)

behind it. Less obvious, and more revealing, is a sociological perspective on Rodman's supposed individuality that greatly tempers the whole idea that he was radically dissociated from the mainstream of society.

Perhaps if we back up a little bit in Dennis Rodman's life we can begin to piece together how this latter claim may be so. Rodman was born and raised in an all-female household in the poverty-stricken housing projects of Dallas, Texas. Dennis was very thin in build as a youth and did not play organized basketball. His two sisters, however, were all-American basketball athletes. Rodman enjoyed playing pinball, and his friends nicknamed him "The Worm" for the way that he wriggled while playing the game. Rodman showed little sign of the successes that were in his future at this time. He wondered if he was gay very early in life, foreshadowing his later traversing of sexual boundaries. After graduating from high school, Dennis worked at various low-paying jobs that gave him little socialization to the proper lifestyle of the wealthy—a lifestyle that would continue to elude him in later years. Rodman also began to grow in physique after graduation. He eventually enrolled in a community college and began playing organized basketball at that late date. He had no prior socialization to the etiquette of the organized game, only street basketball. Rodman transferred to a four-year college where he became a star player who was drafted by the Detroit Pistons of the NBA.

While Rodman was with the Pistons, he was a modest scorer and a tenacious defensive player. The Pistons were a championship team while Rodman was there. His coach, Chuck Daly, was a father figure, a presence Rodman had never previously enjoyed in his life. The Pistons were notorious for their "bad boy" tactics on the court and Rodman picked up this new identity more from the team than from some personal disposition for dirty play. In time, Rodman became dispensable and was traded to the San Antonio Spurs where he had problems getting along with the struggling team. The Spurs traded him to the Bulls who wanted Rodman to be a rebounder. To dramatize the transition, Rodman developed a very nonchalant free throw shooting style that underscored his diminished role as an offensive basketball player. Many of the odd, identity-forming behaviors that Dennis Rodman developed at this time may be understood as compensation for his being relegated to a low-status role alongside superstars such as Michael Jordan. There were powerful social forces at work that encouraged his adoption of strange behaviors.

Even these aberrant behaviors hardly were shattering breaks with the existing social order. Rodman's first tattoos were merely depictions of his wife and child—these are not exactly statements of resistance to dominant norms. Moreover, tattoos, body piercing, and neon-colored hair dyes had been resurrected from older traditions to become rather standard fare among the younger generation by this time. In the social context of pro basketball, however, these things really stood out. Then too, there had been plenty of flaky players in the past—including Phil Jackson, Rodman's coach with the Bulls.

What may have been different was that Dennis Rodman was a *black player* in a nonconformist role.

The same relative lack of personal originality can be said about Rodman's sexual and partying demeanor. Many players, of course, had been party lovers in the past. Rodman's sexuality in terms of cross-dressing hardly would have been unique if he were not, again, a pro basketball player. His public affairs with women were utterly unoriginal, even in the basketball world, except for the fact that he was with *white women*, which again in the conservative bubble of pro basketball was even less acceptable than in the wider society.

Once he attained great popularity, "Dennis Rodman" the icon and media image quickly became a thoroughly standardized commodity in the larger capitalist society that he lived in. Consumers gobbled up number 91 jerseys, organized fan clubs and Dennis Rodman websites, bought his book, watched him on talk shows, and even bought his "hair secrets" from an "official" website. How much more mainstream can one get?

It also is worth bearing in mind in Dennis Rodman's case and others that even conscious efforts to break the rules at least represent affirmations of the *existence* of such rules, and so constitute an ongoing social relationship with authorities in society. It is impossible to do wrong without at once reinforcing what is right. Some societies (the United States versus China) and even sectors of societies (pro wrestling versus basketball) are more tolerant of these seemingly odd behaviors than others, which introduces yet another social contingency to the concept of individualism.

This critique of unbridled individual personalities does not end with the subject of strange or antisocial people. It applies equally well to our understanding of charismatic individual leaders such as India's Mahatma Gandhi, U.S. Senator Hillary Clinton, and Brazil's Eva ("Evita") Peron. The ability of such individuals to motivate others extends beyond their personalities to a wide array of favorable social and historical circumstances. Likewise, the entire phenomenon of individual genius and creativity, as expressed in the works of dominant philosophers such as Kant and Hegel in Germany, scientific giants Albert Einstein and Marie Curie, musical legends Ludwig van Beethoven and Ella Fitzgerald, entrepreneurs Martha Stewart and Bill Gates, or film stars Halle Berry and Wesley Snipes, needs to be understood against a larger social and historical backdrop of factors that enabled their successes, along with factors that made the worthy contributions of their competitors mere obscurities in history. Individuals are born into more or less opportune historical eras and social contexts for particular forms of genius and creativity to emerge. Even given such opportunities, some people are better equipped to strike up beneficial relationships with others who can advance their ideas and creations through complex societal institutions, and ultimately into societal prominence, while other people lack these connections. I will explore these matters more in Chapter 3 as organizational determinants of popular cultural products, such as rock music.

For now, I recognize that influential individuals exist, but it is the task of sociology to bring to light the social circumstances and processes that create notable and less notable individuals. Sociology thus brings some measure of humility to the erroneous, if not pompous, notion that individuals alone are infinitely capable of achieving their own will.

The American Preoccupation with Individualism in Cultural, Political, and Economic Life

America's fascination with the idea of unfettered, free-thinking individuals is evident in much of our everyday lives, even though we seldom pause to notice this influence. Individualism pervades nearly all of our social institutions—the mass media, political discourse, and economic thought (Lipset 1996). Even our favorite mythologies, such as the rogue western cowboy, extol the virtues of the individual (Wright 2001). It may be useful to consider a few examples from cultural, political, and economic institutions—the three major realms of social life.

Individualism in Culture.   Education is a cultural institution, so let's begin there. Even as you read these words, many readers are participating in an individualistic process. I don't mean simply that you are reading alone. Rather, if you are a student, you likely will be tested on what you read here, and that test will purport to measure your individual competence and mastery of the content of this book. So what? you might ask. Let me suggest a couple of ironies about this situation. First of all, your individual ability to understand this book may not be "individual" at all. Some readers may have had a prior sociology course, while others have not. Furthermore, that difference may have depended on the availability of such a course in readers' high schools, which itself may be a consequence of the relative wealth of school districts and their ability to provide broad course offerings. For these reasons, some readers are socially, rather than individually, more prepared to comprehend the book, and to do well on exams. Some people go to what conventionally are called "bad" schools. It is interesting to note that even when Americans acknowledge "good" and "bad" schools, they may view the solution to the problem of bad schools to be the provision of individual vouchers that supposedly will allow parents and children to "choose" to attend a better school (regardless of the fact that it may be located miles away, and that some groups may be more knowledgeable about the quality of schools than others).

A second contradiction between individual and social reasoning is that our educational system requires "individual" competencies in testing in the first place. We know that teamwork often is what is desired in real life, and that job recruiters value this ability. In fact, many people advocate school sports programs as training in teamwork (although there remains a penchant for calculating statistics of individual performance). It might make more sense to have group cooperation in educational testing, but the ideology of educational individualism stands at odds with the profoundly social character of the world, and regards cooperation as cheating.

Political Individualism.   Beliefs in individualism reign over our political system, as well. In the contested presidential election of 2000, George W. Bush, Al Gore, and the rest of the nation were dumbfounded by the virtual tie that resulted from the voting process. News reporters seemed capable only of extolling the virtues of individual-based democracy in the midst of this crisis—"one person, one vote," they repeatedly observed in arguing that the tie showed that each individual vote "makes a difference." Unfortunately, the media failed to attribute equal emphasis to the fact that in sparsely populated states such as South Dakota the electoral college (which determines the winner) actually allotted a greater ratio of electoral votes to the population than in heavily populated states such as California, New York, Pennsylvania, and Illinois. Apparently, people are worth some decimal amount *more* than one vote if they live in South

Dakota. Nor did these news commentators seem to realize that people commonly vote as members of groups—Jews, females, African Americans, union members, millionaires, and so on—that hardly suggests purely individual choices in the election process. Moreover, the media utterly failed to bring to light the fact that our supposedly individual choices largely were limited to two candidates whose political parties provided huge amounts of financial and other resources that made them more highly visible than third party candidates, and that made them seem to most Americans the only two reasonable choices available. It would seem at the very least that our power of individual choice in elections is severely limited by these kinds of societal forces.

Consider the U.S. census as another example of political individualism. Every ten years, the U.S. Census Bureau counts and surveys the U.S. population. The results are tabulated to show all manner of social groupings, including simple numbers of people who reside in cities, districts, states, and so forth. The census is important because governmental resources are allocated partly on the basis of how many people live in given areas. There are, of course, inaccuracies that are expected in such a large endeavor. The interesting thing is that scientific experts in social statistical analysis of this sort *know* within a small margin of error how many people of various social types (e.g., poor, homeless, children) will be undercounted in various places by virtue of a variety of reliable information sources outside the census itself. Undercounting occurs more frequently in poorer than in richer locales for a variety of reasons, including lower respondent rates among the poor to written surveys. In principle, Census Bureau experts are capable of making far more accurate statistical estimates of populations than the census results themselves provide, but they don't do it. Why not? Margo Anderson and Stephen Feinberg (1999) investigated the politics of the census. The answer they found told that politicians who represent the interests of wealthier groups do not want accurate (i.e., higher) representation of poorer groups because that would take away government resources from richer areas. They block the advancement of scientific analysis in public policy by arguing in antiquarian and individualistic fashion that a virtual head count (really, a counting of returned surveys) is the only acceptable means of counting people.

Another key political function is the administration of criminal law. In America, it is indicative of our faith in nonpublic control of life that even our prison system rapidly is becoming privatized, in other words, owned and operated by private corporations, rather than the government. Today, individuals actually can privately invest in the stock market in companies that specialize in the incarceration of our citizens! Americans view crime as purely individual malfeasance, even though they know deep in their hearts that crime is deeply rooted in social existence. The wealthy are responsible for many atrocities that are not prosecuted or punished. Crime, as it is viewed in America, very significantly overlaps with poor people's actions, that is, as "street crime" as opposed to white-collar crimes, such as embezzlement and fraud. Our prisons are disproportionately populated with minority group members, not just random individuals. Nevertheless, we tend to view criminal acts as purely individual choices to do the wrong things, and to punish harshly such actions in an effort to deter other evildoers. We view crime as cold, calculating actions of bad individuals, as the wildly popular television show *COPS* suggests in its opening, reggae beat jingle: "Bad boys, bad boys—what'cha gonna do . . . what'cha gonna do when they come for you?" In the face of overwhelming evidence that there is something social about crime, we continue to think of it as a purely individual phenomenon.

Economic Individualism.   Many people view the U.S. economy in an analogous way. In economic life, most Americans are firm believers in the prevailing lore of classical economic theory—that individuals participate in "markets" for goods and services as utterly individual sellers and buyers, and that laws of supply and demand determine pricing. Assuming the existence of such laws, markets would be "self-correcting" mechanisms that work best when left to the individual choices of participants, rather than being regulated in any way by government. According to this perspective, the market itself produces the most socially desirable outcomes. Sociologists have countered this simplistic vision with harsh criticisms that markets themselves are manipulated by powerful groups who monopolize supplies and cooperate in cartels (thereby eliminating the price competition that is said to drive markets), and who create demand among consumers for products through advertising and limitation of available goods and services.

Pricing in the oil industry is one of many examples that pit individualistic economic thinking against a more sociologically informed understanding of economic life. For classical economists (and for the majority of politicians and media pundits who echo their views), rising gas prices are simply the result of changes in supply and/or demand for products. For example, in the winter of 2000–2001, U.S. natural gas prices for home heating doubled, and in some places tripled, from the price of a year earlier. Why? Conventional economic explanations merely said that oil companies had not produced as much gas as before (supply was short), and the unseasonably cold winter had increased demand for gas. Consumers were given a typically individualistic bit of advice—their best course of action was to curtail their demand by turning down their thermostats and adding insulation to their homes. Gas companies told the truly needy that they could soften the blow of skyrocketing costs for a basic human need by spreading their gas costs across the summer months.

Nowhere in the popular press did consumers hear a sociologically informed voice that might have posed new questions. For example, why was productivity curtailed in the first place? In fact, a small group of producers that monopolized the gas industry agreed not to produce oil precisely in order to create scarcity (many would argue that there was an adequate supply in underground storage facilities, anyway). It was not surprising that dissent and intervention failed to emerge from politicians, for the largest natural gas producer—Enron Corporation—was the top contributor to that year's presidential campaign of George W. Bush and had on its board of directors a number of former staff members of former president George Bush. By late 2001, Enron had dissolved, scattered its profits, and come under congressional investigation in a monumental investor fraud case. By and large, Americans simply came to accept the "fact" of high gas prices as a natural outcome of individual actions in the economic market.

In much the same way, market oligopolies (control by a few cooperating firms) in health care, transportation, and products as diverse as tobacco, beer, lightbulbs, refrigerators, clocks, and coffins are obscured by popular beliefs that independent, individual competition and consumer choices guide economic affairs. "Supply and demand" remains the mantra of popular economic consciousness despite compelling evidence that this most basic tenet of economic thought is deeply flawed and in need of sociological supplementation.

Poverty policy also has taken on a "pull yourself up by your own bootstraps" character in recent years that suggests that poverty is just an individual failing, or worse yet, the result of individual psychological states of laziness and unwillingness to work. Modern "welfare to work" initiatives that seek to move people out of poverty merely by changing their outlook on life are expressions of this sentiment. This "War on the Poor," as Herbert Gans (1995) called it, is in stark contrast to prior policies, such as the "War on Poverty" of the 1960s, that understood the root of poverty to lie in large-scale economic processes that wealthy, powerful groups manipulated to their advantage, and to the disadvantage of the poor. The most influential of these powerful groups then and now are huge corporations that perhaps tellingly are defined as mere "individuals," rather than as groups, in the U.S. legal system (which makes it more difficult for government to intervene in regulating corporate actions). Prior poverty policies were informed by an understanding that the vast majority of the poor were not poor by choice, but rather were poor due to social forces that were beyond their control. Moreover, as sociologist Jill Quadagno reports in her *The Color of Welfare* (1994), popular opinion about welfare has shifted from the idea of welfare as an "entitlement" when whites were perceived as the primary recipients of benefits, to more recent views of welfare as "handouts" when blacks and other minorities gained their share of such public relief (which still remains much less overall than welfare payments to whites).

Just as poverty relief is under attack today, so too are affirmative action policies decried by some critics simply as a form of group favoritism or "reverse discrimination." This latter view obscures the group-level fact of the enduring effects of past and present discrimination against minority groups and women. Discrimination has long-term effects that stretch across generations. Whether current affirmative action policy is the correct way to address these social problems is debatable, but the *social* nature of the problems themselves is clear.

The net result of this individualizing motif by conservatives in U.S. public affairs—cultural, political, and economic—has been increasing popular distrust and disfavor of so-called big government regulation of society (even though the United States already has a smaller role for government than other industrialized nations), where people opt instead for greater individual competition in a variety of economic markets, for example, health care, work, transportation, communications, and insurance. Since Americans cannot adequately envision the social basis for their relative poverty or affluence, they cannot understand the viability of social solutions to their problems.

THE SOCIOLOGY OF IDENTITIES

Even though individualism is a defining feature of the modern world, it is possible to question the very *existence* of individuals as entities that are separate from groups. There can be no question that modern people are more different from one another than their forebears who tended to be rather homogenous members of traditional communities. As so many late nineteenth-century observers noted (classical sociologists Emile Durkheim, Karl Marx, Max Weber, and Ferdinand Tonnies, to name a few), a transition occurred from relatively undifferentiated, egalitarian, agrarian communities of like-minded people to the modern, complex division of occupational labor and accompanying divergence of values, beliefs, and practices. The question that we need to address concerns the source of differences between individuals in the modern case—is it based purely on a new individual psychology, or is it essentially a social phenomenon?

Individuals as Webs of Group Affiliation

The great German sociologist and philosopher Georg Simmel (1858–1918) offered a devastating critique of naïve, psychological conceptualizations of the individual that has guided much contemporary thought about individual identities. Simmel was a wonderfully creative, eclectic thinker who influenced widespread areas of sociological thought. Simmel (1908) began his discussion of individuals with the popular notion of individuality as uniqueness, or "being different" from others. My guess is that this idea of being different from others stands at the foundation of many people's understanding and positive evaluation of being an individual today. For Simmel though, these differences in individuals are in fact largely the result of the different groups that we belong to, and which intersect within ourselves. He called these complex relationships **webs of group affiliation**. Simmel envisioned the social basis for individual differences as shown in Figure 1.2.

In order to understand Simmel's argument, imagine yourself and any other person—a friend, your teacher, your worst enemy, or a stranger. Now, think of all the groups in which you *share* membership with the other person. Suppose, for example, that two people are both upper middle class, work in the same occupation of teaching, belong to the same age group of thirty-somethings, are Catholic by religious affiliation, vote Democrat politically, and are Americans by nationality. None of these group affiliations create individual differences between these two people.

Next, contemplate each group affiliation that differentiates you from the person that you had in mind above. What different groups do you each belong to? In the example I gave, suppose that the two

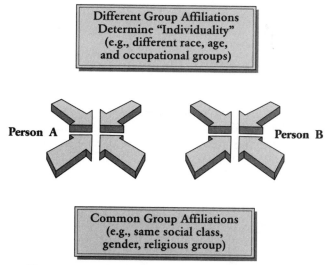

Figure 1.2   Individuals as Webs of Group Affiliations

people differ in gender, where one is male and the other is female. In racial/ethnic heritage, one is Puerto Rican and the other Asian. In region of residence, one is from a northeastern inner city and the other is from a farm in Texas. In education, one was trained in philosophy, whereas the other studied business administration. Continue with all such group membership differences.

Simmel's point was that the lion's share of what we typically regard as individuality actually is attributable to the norms, values, beliefs, tastes, customs, and so forth that we absorb in our interactions with *different groups*, that is, in varying webs of group affiliation. We shall look more closely at exactly how these traits get conveyed in subsequent chapters. For now, it is worth noting that taken to its logical conclusion, the vast majority of what we think and do, from our tastes in home décor to our stand on affirmative action policies, is a product of the groups that we associate with. What remains in terms of purely individual psychological differences, or personality, is very small by comparison.

Again, in traditional societies, all people tended to belong to the same groups (kin, religion, occupation, etc.), with only age and gender to differentiate them. Individuality thereby was limited, and indeed devalued, as a personal trait—loyalty to common groups was stressed. In modern societies, we have much greater differentiation from person to person in terms of their varying webs of group affiliation, thus we have more—and more highly esteemed—individualism (again, understood as a social phenomenon).

When one thinks about it, there is much commonsense confirmation of what Simmel was talking about. For example, when we walk down the street, or when we interact with strangers in any setting, what do we first see in people—individual personalities, or the groups that they seem to belong to (e.g., race, gender, or age)? Do we view their clothing as individual tastes, or as expressions of group memberships (businesspeople, students, working class, etc.)? What do our loved ones first ask about a guest whom we are going to invite home for dinner—the person's personality traits, or their social affiliations? As a matter of fact, it might be just as revealing to attempt *not* seeing groups in our observations about strangers. Can we choose to ignore these realities? Probably not, which lends great credence to Simmel's argument.

Social Identities: Repertoire Selection, Multiple Consciousness, and Ambiguity

Simmel's basic ideas about individuals being sets of groups within them has its counterpart in much contemporary analysis of the social dynamics of people's **identities**. Identities are ways that people use their affiliations with groups to come to an understanding of themselves as individuals. Among the many groups that intersect within us, some social identities may rise to particular prominence over others as **master statuses**. Age, race/ethnicity, and gender frequently take on this enhanced importance in everyday interactions. Young people are viewed first and foremost as "young" in their interactions with adults. Immigrants to new lands may experience heightened awareness and significance of their racial, ethnic, and/or national identities as they interact with natives of the new land. Women in male-dominated workplaces often find their gender identities accentuated.

Identity Selection.   In each of the above examples, outsiders (older people, natives, men) select and impose increased significance and meaning to one among the many social identities of the parties mentioned. In many cases, this kind of imposition of identity is linked to discrimination, power, and inequality between groups. It is important to realize, however, the active and self-interested role that individuals and groups *themselves* may take in advancing or suppressing one or more social identities over others within their **identity repertoires**. Immigrant groups in U.S. history have self-consciously sought to obscure their ethnic affiliations precisely in order to avoid discriminatory treatment by natives. Many celebrities, for example, changed their original, ethnically identifiable names to more common "American" names, for example, Pat Benatar (Patricia Adrejewski), Martin Sheen (Ramon Estevez), Alan Alda (Alphonso D'Abruzzo), Kirk Douglas (Issur Danielovitch), Bob Dylan (Robert Zimmerman), and Winona Ryder (Winona Horowitz). In a similar way, Robert Granfield (1991) found that working-class students in elite schools frequently covered up their working-class culture in order to blend in better with students from upper social classes.

Conversely, people may choose to highlight one or another identity in order to gain the benefits of interaction with others. In a job interview, for example, one might be tempted to call attention to one's loyalty to an educational alma mater if the interviewer went to the same school. It is convenient for people of mixed Irish and German ancestry to "be Irish" on St. Patrick's Day and to "be German" during Oktoberfest. Latino politicians may stress their ethnic heritage while on the campaign trail among local constituencies, but maintain that they are "Americans like everyone else" as they interact with predominantly white members of city hall. These selective identity practices are very common throughout social life, and provide an important, dynamic element to Simmel's original ideas about webs of group affiliation.

One quick note about identities in the modern world is in order. As Manuel Castells (1997) has observed, collective identities have reemerged in recent decades in response to the decline of national identities, as for example in the reemergence of ethnic cultures in the territories of the former Soviet Union. Global economic and political trends have had a strong influence on identity formation in recent years, as well. I will return to these fascinating issues in the final chapter of the book.

Multiple Identity Consciousness.   Identities may be even more complex when people experience social life not as the intersection of discrete groups that they belong to, but as a sort of hybridization of two or more group memberships. Writing about the social experiences of African Americans around the turn of the twentieth century, the sociologist W. E. B. DuBois (1889) spoke of the **double consciousness** that they experienced being at once "American" and "black." DuBois saw the inherent tension between these two identities, where African Americans were not fully "American" (given the political and economic discrimination they faced), but rather experienced their identity as a tenuous fusion between national and racial identity. DuBois favored neither assimilation nor racial nationalism, but rather a dual identity for African Americans.

In other global contexts, this double consciousness has given rise to horrific violence. One need only think of modern cases of warfare and genocidal ethnic cleansing in various teetering nations to see the import of DuBois' early work. In the former Yugoslavia, ethnic Serbs and Croatians no longer accepted their previously imposed common national identity as dual consciousness after the breakdown of the national government. A striking case of this same process of ethnic fragmentation took place in Indonesia. Perhaps surprising to many people, this Southeast Asian country is the world's fourth most populous nation with 225 million people. Indonesia is composed of more than 6,000 islands (the largest of which are Java, Sumatra, Borneo, New Guinea, and Sulawesi) that span an area 3,200 miles long between the Pacific and Indian oceans. These islands declared independence from European colonial rule and nationhood in 1949. Until recent economic problems ended his rule, President Suharto's brutal military regime (his administration murdered 1 million supposed dissidents in a matter of months in the mid-1960s) maintained some semblance of national identity among the 300 ethnic groups with different languages and various religious groups that make up Indonesia. Today, the future of this nation is very much in doubt because the national consciousness of competing ethnic groups has waned and given way to violent ethnic and religious struggle. After protracted conflicts with the national military, East Timor voted for independence in 1999. Overcrowding on some islands and labor needs on others were dealt with by a national relocation policy that placed various ethnic groups in direct interaction and competition. A brutal slaughter that involved numerous beheadings came in 2001 as a result of such conflicts between native Christian Dayak and immigrant Muslim Madurese ethnic groups in Borneo. Similar, if less spectacular, struggles have marred the double consciousness of people in many other regions of Indonesia. The difficult project of nationalism and empire building in world history (e.g., the Roman and Ottoman empires, various Chinese dynasties, the Soviet Union, the U.S. Civil War, India and Pakistan, and many other cases on each continent) offers ample cases of successful and less successful attempts to fuse group identities of the kind that DuBois had in mind.

The idea of double consciousness also has modern parallels in race and gender studies, as for example in the works of sociologists Patricia Hill Collins (1991) and bell hooks (1989), who have argued that the experiences of black females must be understood as identities that are distinct from those of black males. That is, to be black for females is a fundamentally different experience of "being black" from what black males experience in terms of race. Black female labor market experiences, interactions with the criminal justice system, and political agendas, for instance, vary from the experiences of black males. By the same token, being middle class is a fundamentally different experience for all blacks than for whites because of the intersection of race and class (Patillo-McCoy 1999). The general social experience of being female varies as well, hence feminism has different meanings for women of working-class versus upper-middle-class, lesbian versus straight, Mexican-American versus Korean-American, and teenage versus middle-aged groups. The intersection of "female" with other group affiliations fundamentally alters the meaning of being female as such. Country singer Dolly Parton's media identity, for example, is a complex fusion of gender, class, and regional forces (Wilson 1995). Judith Butler's (1989) path-breaking analysis of the ambiguity and politics of sexuality showed the fluidity of gender identities as such. Much the same can be said concerning the hybridization of social experiences of masculinity along class, racial/ethnic, and age lines. From this standpoint, identities are quite malleable, as multiple combinations of group experiences actually alter the original composition of each social element.

Teenage Angst as Identity Ambiguity and Crisis.   In some instances, social identities may be ambiguous. Aging through the course of one's life offers a prime example of this phenomenon in American society. Aging is a biological fact, but the meanings associated with different age groups are rather arbitrary definitions of age that vary across societies and history. Teenage adolescence in modern societies is an interesting case of a historically constructed, ambiguous social identity that exists between "childhood" and "adulthood."

During the early industrial era, adolescence simply did not exist as a socially recognized age group. Children moved directly into adulthood as exploited workers in factories, mines, and other industrial enterprises. Moreover, the acceptable age for marriage and childbearing was much younger than today, basically at or just before reproductive maturity. As technological innovations eased the demand for child labor in factories, children entering adulthood became defined as "unfit" for work and entry to "adulthood," and thus experienced an identity crisis as an unemployable age group. The universal societal solution to this transformation of age identity was the development of compulsory schooling in an expanding educational system.

Schooling today maintains much of this function of limiting adults' labor market competition with youths, while providing youths with a social identity of being in incubation for adulthood. Schooling can be understood as a lengthy **rite of passage** between the statuses of child and adult. Rites of passage mark social transitions, such as marriages, baptisms, retirements, and graduations.

As David Elkind (1997) and Jonathon Epstein (1997) have noted, teenagers occupy an inherently ambiguous and crisis-ridden identity. Adolescence has been for many individuals a time of "searching" for coherent social identities. In other words, adolescence has never been a fully satisfactory invention as a social identity. Teens are largely excluded from rewarding and influential economic and political roles in society, and they are the butt of much cultural criticism in terms of their habits. This rather anguish-filled period of life has found its expression in a variety of historical identity-searching practices among teens. The "bobby-soxer," "greaser," and "beatnik" subcultures of the 1950s; the "hippie," "freak," "disco," and "rocker" subcultures of the 1960s and 1970s; and the "club," "raver," "jock," "geek," "goth," "metal head," "grunge," and "gang banger" identities of youth culture in recent years are notable examples of this pattern of social behavior.

While these pursuits invariably have been seen by youths as pure expressions of their individuality, a more penetrating sociological analysis reveals that others have done, and are doing, similar things. These and other identities are fundamentally social in nature. Just as newcomers to a city are anxious to join clubs and civic organizations in order to establish an identity in a new place, and just as retirees who are forced out of their prior work identities sometimes frantically seek out new groups, so adolescents often vacillate among memberships in a variety of identity-forming groups. It is a sociological phenomenon, not some peculiar psychology of adolescents as such, that drives this anxiety and desire to have social attachments.

From this perspective, it is not surprising that youth cultures often take on the character of cultures of resistance and rejection of the dominant values of the social identities that frame their experiences as adolescents. Parents are symbols of childhood, and grown-ups in general are representations of the adult threshold that adolescents know they eventually must cross into, even though they currently are barred from entry. The worlds of childhood and adult-

The goth look in youth culture is in some ways an expression of the social position of adolescence and young adulthood. Much like other historical adolescent and young adult fashions, goth is neither for children nor mature adults. In fact, it is an explicit rejection of traditional adult fashion. Clearly, dressing goth, or many other ways, is more than just a reflection of one's individual taste—after all, many other people dress roughly the same. We do of course make choices in our dress, but these choices are typically limited to a specific range of options that match our social standing. (© Terry Doyle/Getty Images, Inc.)

hood are frequent objects of youths' derision. Predictably though, most adolescent identities are short-lived and are supplanted by a variety of adult identities (e.g., mother, father, lawyer, alderman) in due time.

THE CONTESTED TERRAIN OF SOCIOLOGICAL KNOWLEDGE

By now, the differences between individual and group-level reasoning should be getting clearer to you. In subsequent chapters, we shall explore in greater detail a number of further conceptual and theoretical nuances of sociological thinking. Before that, though, there are some preliminary considerations about the nature of social knowledge that require discussion. We need to address two questions: Do groups actually *exist* as legitimate objects of study, and if so, is it possible to develop valid, unbiased accounts of social life? There is considerable contemporary debate, especially about the second question, that students of sociology need to be aware of. In essence, we need to assess the prospects for a science of human life.

Some Cautionary Notes About Sociology Versus Psychology

This book explores the possibilities and limits of a science of human existence. Can we reach valid conclusions about the causes of people's actions, the meanings of human events, and the determinants of various beliefs and thoughts? If so, there would be profound ramifications of such a body of knowledge for our understanding of societies: economy and work; politics, crime, and global relations; mass media, culture, and education.

Just imagine it—a science of human behavior. Maybe we could fashion a better, utopian world if only we knew what makes people tick. Before we get carried away, though, a few caveats are advisable. When most people conjecture about a science of people, they immediately begin thinking in terms of some set of universal principles of individual psychology, in other words, about basic mental triggers that guide human actions. Behavioral psychology dominates popular conceptions of the prospects for a human science. This branch of psychology has had its own utopian visions about social engineering. B. F. Skinner's wistful book *Walden Two* (1948), for example, was an influential early application of behavior modification principles to societal modeling. These ideas have become entrenched in modern thinking about a variety of social policies that address crime, education, poverty, and other pressing issues.

Let me be emphatic in saying that this type of thinking is *not* what sociology is all about—indeed, psychological propositions often are diametrically opposed to sociological insights. Sociologists and psychologists seek to explain different things (groups for sociologists, individuals for psychologists), but even when they focus on the same topic (e.g., individuals), their perspectives more often than not clash. Perhaps it is no accident that college departments of sociology and psychology sometimes are housed in separate buildings.

In any case, the student who has studied (or currently is studying) psychology needs to be very careful to distinguish between these two perspectives, even if popular opinion holds that they are closely related.

The main obstacle that people encounter in understanding sociology is thinking of people as individuals, rather than as members of various groups. The understanding of human events and actions as the sum total of individual choices involved in these events and actions, and the assumption that people's beliefs and thoughts are purely individual mental states, block fundamental sociological insights about human interactions, social settings, and shared modes of cognition. We should not underestimate the constraints that such individualistic thinking may already have placed on our ability to envision the social in everyday life. Oddly enough, individualism as a belief system itself is a social force that our society and its various institutions impose on people. One of the goals of this chapter then, is to loosen the hold that individualistic thinking—including the effects of psychology as a discipline—has on readers, and thereby to open pathways for better sociological reasoning.

The Reality of the Social: Social Facts

Most people do not doubt that individuals exist (Georg Simmel, mentioned earlier, was one important exception), but the question remains, do *groups* exist? In order to have a science of sociology, groups must be **empirical** (knowable through basic human senses, such as observation) phenomena, not just figments of our imagination. The problem is not so trivial as it might at first seem, for individual people are directly observable in ways that larger groups (e.g., political parties, social classes, ethnic groups, or religious groups) often are not. How do we know that such groups are real, that is, apart from the observable individuals who make them up?

One classic solution to this problem was advanced in the infancy of sociology's disciplinary development by the influential French sociologist Emile Durkheim (1858–1917). Durkheim was seeking to establish sociology as a distinct, scientific field of study in the French universities at a time when psychology and biology already held considerable legitimacy as competitor academic disciplines that claimed to explain human behavior. In order to justify the necessity of a science of the social, Durkheim (1895) had to establish that **social facts** were *sui generis* realities—they were phenomena that were independent from, and irreducible to, other modes of comprehension of humans (i.e., psychological and biological explanations). He believed that groups were more than, and essentially different from, the sum total of individual experiences within them.

Durkheim outlined several points in his argument for the primacy of social facts. Groups, he argued, are indeed observable—at least in part. One can empirically study, say, "Catholics," in their weekly congregations, in parochial schools, at gatherings for visits by the Pope, and in their homes, even if not all Catholics are physically co-present in a given place. Real things, as opposed to imaginary things, also persist over time. Social groups meet this criterion as well, for one can find groups in the same places, doing the same things, at regular intervals. Durkheim's most forceful argument for the empirical reality of groups was his observation that groups must be real and separable from individual experiences because *groups exercise coercive power over the individuals within them.* Membership in a group such as a fraternity, for example, makes individuals alter their behaviors and beliefs in accordance with the norms and values of fraternity culture. The coercive power and reality of groups is evident in the fact that people cannot simply "think away" the influence of groups—again, they are not imaginary things. Just as a brick wall demonstrates its reality by resisting our will when we try to walk through it, so memberships in racial, gender, and age groups are realities that are imposed on people even when they desire not to be seen as members. As individuals, we are part of these groups, yet they have an existence that stretches beyond our immediate experiences and persists after we die or otherwise leave the group. We "carry" the reality of the group with us as a guide to action and thought, even when the group is not physically gathered together. Durkheim distinguished between cohesive social groups, mere aggregates of people (e.g., strangers at an airport), and analytical categories of people (e.g., all individuals with black hair). Unlike aggregates and categories, social groups have a consciousness of kind, or as Durkheim put it, **collective consciousness**, that is analogous to a group mind that influences how members think and act. Real groups think of themselves as groups.

In his attempts to justify sociological inquiry, Durkheim was unrelenting in his attacks on individualistic thinking. One need not utterly deny the existence of individuals, as Durkheim and Simmel tended to do, to accept the basic precept concerning the reality of social phenomena. Groups exist, but there still is the sticky issue of the validity of our knowledge about them. After all, people who attempt to study groups themselves are not isolated individuals, but rather members of social groups. If we are to remain consistent with prior discussions, these groups presumably exert considerable, bias-producing pressure on analysts of society. Does this fact not make valid sociological knowledge a contradiction in terms? This is a profound question that has troubled social thinkers for many years. It is time to turn the sociological lens on ourselves as social thinkers for a moment.

The Gulf Between Fact and Value Statements

A very common critique of the idea of sociology as science is that everyone has individual opinions about society, so it is impossible to have a social science. One hears this sort of argument very frequently in references to sociology by ordinary people and by the mass media. The basic line is that sociological knowledge is only true for the person speaking because it is based on the values held by researchers. Sociology, according to this viewpoint, is simple advocacy of personal positions about the social world. The fact that there are disagreements among social scientists themselves sometimes is held up as further evidence of the purely opinionated nature of the endeavor. These popular critics of sociology sometimes couple this problem with observations about the variability and supposed unpredictability of humans. The supposed unpredictability of humans in this argument rests on a misplaced notion of individuals doing things on their own. We already have seen numerous replies to this simplistic idea in this chapter. Sociologists actually are less interested in predicting *individuals'* actions and beliefs, than in explaining (often after the fact) common *patterns* of behavior and belief, that is, in explaining group-level phenomena. Again, there can be no question but that group-level differences (e.g., racial/

ethnic, gender, age, social class) exist—there are variations in voting, tastes in music, crime rates, occupational pursuits, church attendance, attitudes toward abortion, and many other behaviors. Precisely these *variations* are required in scientific explanations (recall "variables" in scientific method!), so it is rather ignorant to point to the mere fact of human differences as a stumbling block for scientific inquiry. Not "every individual" in a group always behaves exactly as sociologists might expect, but the overwhelming reality of patterned behavior is the object of sociological analysis, not individual outlying cases that may themselves be determined by other social forces. If we find that 98 percent of the members of a teamsters union local votes Democratic, we tend to accept that as a worthwhile social fact and not worry too much about what (perhaps social forces) makes 2 percent of the group act differently.

The idea that sociologists merely espouse their personal opinions likewise is a rather simplistic critique of the discipline. Even if sociology were just opinions, one would need to reckon with the fact that such supposed opinions don't vary infinitely, that is, from individual to individual—entire *groups* of sociologists disagree with other sociologists about which explanations of human behavior are on the mark. In these debates, the evidentiary materials that are brought forward in support of one position or another typically are empirical facts. Sociologists, like other scientists, look to verifiable observations about group attributes (not simple parroting of their "opinions") to advance their research claims. Disagreements in science get referred back to the field of empirical evidence. At the very least, sociologists who claim scientific status for their research are obeying the same rules and rhetoric of science that other scientists subscribe to. One might even argue that disagreement in science is a sign of health in a discipline because it forces researchers to revert back to facts to prove their claims. Natural scientists have made some of their biggest mistakes by being in total agreement with one theory, for example, when everyone in physics believed that the planets revolved around Earth, or when biologists uniformly got it wrong by thinking that human health was guided by a proper balance between three essential body fluids (this agreement gave rise to the practice of bloodletting in "scientific" medicine). In sociology, there are a number of competing theories, or "paradigms" (see Chapter 2), that have maintained healthy, empirically based dialogue within the discipline.

Part of the problem with perceptions of sociology may be that many people fail to see that there is a logical gulf between **statements of facts** and **evaluative statements**. The statement "Female lawyers' earnings *are* less on average than male lawyers' earnings" is a factual claim—it can be proven correct or incorrect with reference to empirical evidence. By contrast, the statement that "Female lawyers *should be* paid the same as male lawyers" is an evaluative statement that one either agrees with or not, based on personal values. One cannot prove an evaluative claim in the same way that one can prove a factual claim. Likewise, it is impossible to use facts to establish values. Facts and values are fundamentally different assertions, although they are bound up in complex ways in most actual scientific practice. Figure 1.3 displays the framing of factual scientific knowledge by value-based processes that guide the initiation of research and value-guided implementation of scientific knowledge. Atomic research is a case in point. The decision to pursue atomic research was a choice that was informed by specific *values,* held by government officials, private corporate leaders, media-influenced

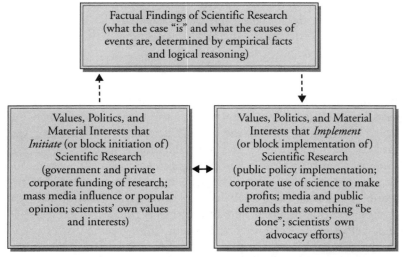

Figure 1.3   The Framing of Factual Knowledge by Politics and Values

citizens, and scholarly advocates of such an undertaking, that, to illustrate, it might be useful or profitable in some way. The ability to produce the atomic bomb came as a result of getting certain *facts* straight in the scientific community. The decision to use the bomb during World War II again had to be based on values advanced by specific groups—in other words, should we bomb Hiroshima? There were, to be sure, other factual consequences of the bombing decision that were taken into account (the war would end sooner, saving American lives that were valued), but it remained a value-based decision to do the deed.

Sometimes facts get ignored, and values prevail. Diane Vaughan's *The Challenger Launch Decision* (1996) studied the decision to launch the space shuttle *Challenger* that exploded just after liftoff, killing all aboard. She discovered that the shuttle launch decision was made despite available factual evidence that there was something wrong with the craft. Because authorities had become accustomed to ignoring scientists' factually based red flags about safety, they easily succumbed to political pressures to get the ship in the air. Sociologists similarly produce factual knowledge that may or may not find its way into value-based public or private decision making. Science and advocacy are, at least in principle, separate realms. In sociology, it often is a political and value-driven process that generates funds for particular kinds of research. If the National Science Foundation makes available millions of dollars to study the social causes of school violence, it is because authorities in government, and perhaps a variety of other groups such as teachers' unions and network news producers, have deemed such research "valuable"—it "should be" done. Doing the research in a scientific manner requires factual evidence and logical reasoning about which of the possible causal variables "is" the cause of school violence. Subsequent implementation of corrective social policies geared toward curtailing school violence based on scientific research once again can only be guided by social values—in other words, that school violence "should" be stopped.

The point here, and one that students of sociology must understand, is that there is a formal difference between saying that something "is" the case (factual statements) and saying that something "ought to be" the case (value statements). The former is the language of science, while the latter is the rhetoric of ideology, material interests, and belief.

Muddying the Waters: The Politics of Social Knowledge

The preceding discussion was an effort to answer relatively simple objections to the validity of sociological knowledge. You may already have anticipated that these debates get more complex, and more contentious. Science is not, and never has been, a purely individual pursuit. At the very least, science is *framed* by social and political value choices, as we have just seen. Some foes of science even go so far as to say that science *essentially is* a political endeavor.

It should come as a surprise to no one that bad science, based on factual and logical fallacies, often has been sponsored and used by powerful groups to legitimize their political agendas and to exploit entire groups of people. A good example of this tendency was psychologists Richard Herrnstein and Charles Murray's book, *The Bell Curve* (1994), which resurrected and popularized early twentieth-century eugenics thought about the genetic inheritance of intelligence. The authors relied on a research methodology that was rather badly flawed (including the use of an antiquated I.Q. test that originally was used by the military to exclude minorities from service, and hackneyed individualistic logic throughout the work). Within academic communities, the book was widely criticized, even by psychologists. The authors' political agenda was clear—to use "science" to "prove" the inherent inferiority of minority racial groups, and in particular blacks. The book was wildly popular in reinforcing racist beliefs about intelligence, despite concerted efforts within the scholarly community (especially Fischer et al. 1996) to point out its many faults as a scientific work.

The history of social thought is strewn with many cases of this kind. Much nineteenth-century sociology displayed a blind optimism in its many renditions of a theory of inevitable "social progress." Narratives that passed for science spoke about "stages" of societal development, where human improvement was held to be guided by the insights of science and reason. Science hailed itself savior of the world. Again, science served greater ideological purposes than explanatory ones. There undoubtedly remain contemporary heirs to the prophets of progress in the many scholars and bureaucrats today who boast of the computer age and its application of information technologies to human affairs as the dawning of a rosy new future.

There are more thoroughgoing critiques of science, though. More sophisticated critics of science have argued that even *within* the confines of scientific communities, political processes bias the kinds of knowledge produced. Radical critics of science hold that science fundamentally is about social oppression and deception, and that the elementary building blocks of science—objectivity, facts, causal logic, and theoretical generalizations—are fraught with arbitrary power and social inequality. Declaring the "modern" era of science and reason to be a passing mythology, "postmodern" perspectives across many disciplines have challenged the primacy of the scientific mode of inquiry about the social world.

One critique of scientific pretense to objective truths argues essentially that scientific truths are at least partly, and sometimes wholly, fictional accounts of what is going on in a given subject area; groups of scientists merely come to agree that these accounts are facts, and they convince others outside their community of the same beliefs. Agreement in science takes place within relatively small groups who are insulated from scrutiny by the wider scientific community. The **social construction of science** perspective studies how scientists interact among themselves and their subjects (natural or social phenomena) to form collective judgments about realities (see further discussion of social constructionism in Chapter 2). Andrew Pickering's book *Constructing Quarks* (1999), for example, examined how physicists came to believe in the existence of certain subatomic particles (e.g., quarks), and how they convinced others of the truth of their findings. Similar processes occur in the social sciences. Edward Saïd's influential work *Orientalism* (1978), for instance, was a devastating critique of Western social science's erroneous assumptions about the uniform, and fundamental differences between Western and Eastern societies and cultures. If the balance of so-called scientific work and truths indeed can be shown to be tilted toward mere collective fiction, rather than truly objective facts (i.e., claims that a large and diverse community of scholars actually have empirically tested), the legitimacy of the scientific enterprise would be dealt a severe blow.

Another criticism of scientific sociology holds that any attempt to attribute causal or other supposedly objective meanings to social phenomena is inherently misleading and politically disenfranchising of human subjects. According to **standpoint sociology**, the task of sociology is not scientific analysis, but political empowerment of underprivileged groups. Dorothy Smith, for instance, in her *The Conceptual Practices of Power: Toward a Feminist Sociology of Knowledge* (1990), and Donna Haraway in her *Primate Visions* (1989), each outlined the need for a new sociology that would be a vehicle for expression of women's distinctive standpoint on a variety of social issues. Steven Seidman's *Queer Theory/Sociology* (1996) addresses similar shortcomings in the discipline's treatment of gay and lesbian standpoints. The poor, racial and ethnic minorities, women, the working class, sexual minorities, ability groups, and others have been ignored in the history of sociology because the discipline was dominated by upper-class white males of Western European descent who spoke mainly to the issues that served their interests, and who spoke the language of power through a causal scientific medium. For standpoint sociologists, objective sociology would be one that gave "voice" to powerless groups so that they could express their lived experiences to wider audiences. These voices themselves are valid, and need no further scientific dressing up to justify their being heard. Standpoint sociology builds on the notion of identities discussed above, suggesting that there should be as many "sociologies" as there are distinctive social identities.

What are we to make of these criticisms of science? These objections rightly argue that science is itself a product of society and history—the sociological imagination does apply to sociology itself. Methodological and epistemological (the philosophical theory of truth and knowledge) controversies of this type stretch back to the very origins of social science. Sociology needs to be self-reflective in order to avoid bias and complacency in its conclusions. Like other disciplines, sociology has learned much from its mistakes, and hopefully it will continue to do so in the future.

It would be shortsighted, however, to assume that historical and contemporary instances of bad science, mistaken consensus, and group-based bias in sociological research utterly invalidate the discipline. There simply is too much good sociological research that has been done to "throw the baby out with the bath water," as the saying goes. Disagreements in sociology and elsewhere still evoke reference to the empirical world as the primary judge of the validity of research, which suggests the enduring value of scientific analysis.

When we learn from Kathryn Edin and Laura Lein's (1997) painstaking sociological research that single mothers who are recipients of welfare relief are in fact very rational and frugal managers of small budgets, rather than being the spendthrifts that popular opinion makes them out to be, this knowledge is worthwhile—it is not simply a "standpoint" or "construction." When the breakdown of the Soviet Union was shown by Randall Collins' (1986) rigorous comparisons with the decline of other historical empires to have had economic, military, and social sources that had little to do with communist political ideology, we learned something that defies everyday fictions that hold communism itself to have been the undoing of the Soviet Union. Sociology serves a significant, beneficial "debunking" function in dispelling popular myths about groups and societies.

Specific sociological research initiatives necessarily focus on particular groups and issues, to the relative neglect of others who may be more or less associated with a given topic. It would be a hopeless exercise to reproduce each and every social experience and identity associated with any complex social phenomenon. These conventional exclusions do not in themselves invalidate the circumscribed findings of research, any more than simple efforts to be inclusive of as many parties as possible make for worthwhile insights about the social world. It is systematic, thoroughgoing neglect of key social actors (e.g., women in history) that sociology must seek to avoid. Sociology should not be excused for its failures, but relative to other disciplines, sociology has done a rather good job of correcting for such faults.

CONCLUSION

If this chapter has succeeded in its mission, readers should have had some questions cross their minds about who they are from a sociological viewpoint. As individuals, we are mere bodies that act, think, and experience the world around us. When all is said and done, individuals as such are rather uninteresting entities, except to themselves of course. It is the social world that breathes life into individuals, making them behave and think in patterned ways as men, women, doctors, students, politicians, widows, and athletes. These social groups speak and act through the individuals whom they inhabit. For the most part, people's sociological selves remain unexamined, though

massively formative, elements of their consciousness. Sociological
study is a time and a way to give pause for reflection about these hidden social forces. With practice and consistency, it is possible to illuminate "the social" as a recognizable spectrum in one's everyday
experiences, and to act and think accordingly.

There is an unmistakable political and moral dimension to the
call for recognition of the sociological components of human life.
Groups will exist and exert their decisive forces in society whether
we recognize them as groups or not. Individualistic thinking—which
dominates so much mass media, political discourse, economic policy making, and everyday reasoning—largely obscures these social realities from our consciousness. The principal producers of
misleading individualistic interpretations of societal issues are politically and economically powerful groups because it serves their interests not to have less powerful groups see the social determinants
of their subordinate positions. These same powerful groups seldom
are strong advocates of research and teaching of sociology for the obvious reason that troubling sociological findings may expose the social dimensions of their power. While power analysis is not all that
sociologists do, sociology indeed has long been a rather lonely academic advocate of probing research concerning underprivileged
groups and their relation to powerful groups and institutions. Sociology "speaks truth to power," as the now popular phrase goes.

Partly as a consequence of sociology's steadfast efforts to lay bare
the machinations of social power, the discipline has been a favorite,
if undeserving, target of much derision concerning the rigor and
scientific status of its undertakings. Sociology, critics lament, is an as-
semblage of value-laden opinions that hardly merit serious consideration in public policy, workplaces, and other centers of decision
making. This critique is unduly harsh, as I have suggested above, because other sciences are equally beset with troublesome value-related
and political issues. It is important to bear in mind that social research that attains scientifically valid conclusions about societal issues does not automatically translate into practical implementation
of these findings by politicians, corporate CEOs, media executives,
educational administrators, or other authorities whose interests may
be better served by believable fabrications than by disconcerting factual truths. Science and politics are separate spheres in many cases,

and it can be a very frustrating experience to see sound sociological knowledge lay fallow in the minds and actions of authorities who shape our social world.

The individual, the social, and identities are indispensable concepts in sociological reasoning. We shall see them arise again as we move on to other key elements of sociological thinking. In the next chapter, several theoretical perspectives in sociology will be explored. These broad perspectives on social organization utilize multiple sociological concepts, including the ones discussed in this chapter, to model how societies work.

SUGGESTIONS FOR FURTHER STUDY

Joshua Gamson. 1994. *Claims to Fame: Celebrities in Contemporary America.* Berkeley: University of California Press.

Celebrities, such as Dennis Rodman (discussed in this chapter), are interesting, but they are not merely unique individuals. Gamson relates the equally fascinating social processes that create fame in America.

Robert N. Bellah, Richard Madsen, William M. Sullivan, Ann Swidler, and Steven M. Tipton. 1985. *Habits of the Heart: Individualism and Commitment in American Life.* Berkeley: University of California Press.

This now classic work details a variety of disturbing consequences of American individualism, including the decline of attachments to communities and voluntary associations.

Mary Patillo-McCoy. 1999. *Black Picket Fences: Privilege and Peril Among the Black Middle Class.* Chicago: University of Chicago Press.

bell hooks, 2000. *Where We Stand: Class Matters.* Boston: South End Press.

The identity dilemmas of middle-class blacks, sandwiched between ongoing racial prejudice and discrimination and improved economic standing, is explored with great subtlety in these two books.

David Elkind. 1997. *All Grown Up and No Place to Go: Teenagers in Crisis.* Cambridge, MA: Perseus.

Jonathon Epstein. 1997. *Youth Culture: Identity in a Postmodern World.* Oxford: Blackwell.

Teenage identity crisis and the deeper meanings of various youth cultures as responses to this situation are discussed with clarity, empathy, and insight in these two works.

Lillian Rubin. 1994. *Families on the Fault Line: America's Working Class Speaks About the Family, the Economy, Race, and Ethnicity.* New York: HarperCollins.

Based on revealing interviews that are excerpted in this book, Rubin examines how and why ordinary Americans often fail to see the essential sociological forces that create their problems.

W. Richard Stephens. 1998. *Careers in Sociology.* 2nd ed. Boston: Allyn and Bacon.

This book is a good beginning resource for the jobs available to sociology majors. See also the American Sociological Association website, below.

Philadelphia. 1993. 125 min. Directed by Jonathan Demme.
Tom Hanks and Denzel Washington star in this film that depicts one man's development of awareness of AIDS as a social, rather than individual problem.

American Sociological Association. Online: www.asanet.org.
This website houses materials of the national association for sociology. It provides a wealth of information and links about sociology, including student and career information. Regional and state sociology associations and websites of individual university departments of sociology are additional resources to explore.

CHAPTER 2

Social Theories

Their Interplay and Contradictions

"That's all fine in theory," people sometimes remark in a sarcastic way. In sociology, as in other fields, many students initially find concepts and theories uninteresting and divorced from the worlds they feel they know. What are these concepts and theories for? Are they really necessary? The truth is that people always use theories, even if they don't realize it. This chapter is an attempt to show the utility of concepts and theories as they relate to everyday life. One must know basic social theories in order to understand the shorthand that sociological authors use in their writings. Social theories are interrelated sets of concepts that seek to make sense of social facts so as to show how the social world operates. There are four general theoretical perspectives that you will learn in this chapter: rational choice, functionalism, symbolic interactionism/constructionism, and conflict. Within each theoretical perspective, there also are important variants that need to be noted. It will be important to learn the areas of debate and overlap between these orientations because while they are different, they are not mutually exclusive.

THE NATURE AND RELEVANCE OF SOCIAL THEORIES

The reason why concepts and theories are necessary, worth the trouble of learning, and even exciting is because they open windows. Theories point beyond immediate stories and examples to a whole range of similar cases. Once one understands the basic mechanisms of sociology as expressed in its central concepts and theories, one becomes capable of interpreting a vast array of personal experiences in a new light. Without such a master plan, each new experience can present itself as something utterly unique, which of course is not the case. Theories and concepts are sensible ways of processing the huge, confusing amount of information that one experiences in the social world. Imagine how difficult it would be to operate a personal computer if every time you tried you had to start from scratch in terms of basic assumptions such as the function of the mouse, the procedure for finding documents, and the command for Internet access. This knowledge is not inherently interesting, but it is a prerequisite for accessing all of those things that are quite intriguing. So, one does not have to become a sociology "geek," but do not expect to understand sociology without coming to terms with the equivalent of its basic operating language.

Theories as Paradigms

In his great book *The Structure of Scientific Revolutions* (1970), philosopher Thomas Kuhn shook the academic world by arguing that "truth" in science was a product of prevailing historical and social forces in academia. Kuhn used the example of the development of the science of physics. Truth, he argued, was merely a stationary moment in the flux of changing accepted wisdom, rather than a reflection of objective reality about the universe. Scientific theories of the physical world were similar to religious worldviews—they only revealed of "reality" what was possible within the confines of their conceptual biases and assumptions *about* reality. So long as physicists conceived Earth as the planetary hub of the solar system (rather than the Sun, for example), the movement of celestial bodies remained a troubling mystery. The theory of the Earth-centered universe constituted what Kuhn termed a **paradigm**—an accepted explanation of a variety of facts. Changes in paradigms were produced by particularly troubling, inexplicable, facts—Kuhn called them "anomalies"—that did not fit the existing paradigm. These anomalies thus demanded new explanations.

Social theory has experienced the emergence and passing of a number of paradigms over its relatively brief history. Kuhn was concerned with fundamental theoretical breaks with past thought in physics ("revolutions"); social theory has proceeded in more cumulative fashion, discarding elements of past theories, rather than the whole thing. It will be useful to think of the social theories presented in this chapter as paradigms in the sense that the basic assumptions of particular theories do tend to limit their power of revelation. A theory that assumes only harmony and cooperation will be ill-equipped to handle the apparent anomaly of power and conflict, whereas a theory of total, "all against all" conflict will have trouble explaining selfless, altruistic behavior. For this reason, we shall stress the **interplay of theories** as a way of capitalizing on the strengths, and minimizing the weaknesses of various perspectives.

Theoretical Reasoning: Induction and Deduction

Think of theories as *explanations* of variations in social events, rather than as purely abstract "up in the clouds" speculations. In our efforts to arrive at such explanations, philosophers of science speak of two interrelated modes of theoretical reasoning, **inductive** and **deductive reasoning**. In both types of thinking, there is a relationship between theory and empirical observations, or facts. Inductive reasoning attempts to induce explanations from a given set of facts, whereas deductive reasoning seeks to deduce (or "test") facts that logically derive from the theory if it were true. Most science, social or otherwise, involves a circulation of these two kinds of reasoning in the research process. We usually have some pretty good hunches about why certain events occur (deduction), we modify our explanations as we observe more facts (induction), we test further predictions that follow from our fine-tuning of theories (back to deduction), and so forth. This cyclical nature of theoretical thinking is represented in Figure 2.1.

Some recent research on teen pregnancy affords a good example of this process. Sociologist Kristen Luker (1996) wanted to know why the mass media and politicians had become so concerned about this social problem in the 1990s. One hypothesis that held much popular currency was that teen pregnancy was "on the rise" at this

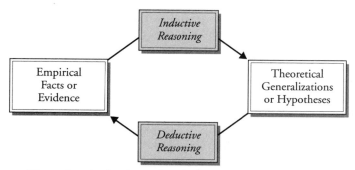

Figure 2.1 Inductive and Deductive Theoretical Reasoning

time, and so gained attention. Using deductive reasoning, she tested this notion to see if indeed the hysteria over teen pregnancy was a simple reaction to increasing incidence of the behavior. Luker quickly discovered that the facts did not match the theory—the rate of teen pregnancy had not significantly changed over the period of time in question. Next, Luker delved a little more into the facts, hoping to generate a better explanation (induction). She wondered if the real issue was just "unwed motherhood," and discovered that the problem, if defined that way, displayed an interesting result: There had in fact been a significant rise in the rate of unwed motherhood, but it was among the age group 20–34, not teenagers—a very interesting fact. Luker also noticed that particular social groups of teens—minorities—were the primary objects of public concern. Again, this was interesting, and suggestive of a different explanation for the concern. We cannot explore all of the nuances of Luker's findings here, but her explorations in the two forms of theoretical reasoning eventually led her to the conclusion that the attention given to teen pregnancy at this point in history was a result of the efforts of powerful groups to stigmatize young minority females. Powerful groups feared that these women were usurping national wealth through abuse of the welfare system. There was no real increase in the number of "babies having babies," however.

Luker's foray into the politics of social problems was greatly assisted by her prior familiarity with two broad types of social theory—conflict theory, which stresses the importance of social power, and social constructionist theory, which focuses on how such powerful groups can influence other people's perceptions of social events. Other researchers have used such theoretical perspectives to explain topics as varied as "wars" on crime, anti-alcohol movements, political scandals, and environmental activism.

Four Broad Types of Social Theory

Theories are just the result of good sociological inquiry. They are starting and ending points of our studies. There are many theories in sociology, corresponding to the wide variety of subjects that the discipline covers. In the sections that follow, four general types of theory are discussed: **rational choice, functional, symbolic interactionist/ constructionist,** and **conflict theories**. There are many variants that I will discuss within each type that will require close attention. The goal here is to gain a basic understanding of these four modes of sociological explanation, and to see how these theories complement and/or contradict one another. Table 2.1 summarizes some major differences between these theories that I will explore as I proceed.

One dimension that social theories vary on is their level of analysis of social life. **Micro-sociological theories** analyze the social world at the level of day-to-day social interactions between people. Observations of the actual behavior of clients at a particular coffee shop would be a good example of this level of analysis. The intimate knowledge gained from such close-up study can be quite valuable, but it is difficult to analyze all such establishments in existence in this manner. For this reason, **macro-sociological theories** focus on larger-scale social phenomena, or social structures, in an attempt to generalize beyond particular cases. In the above example, a macro-sociological approach might look at sales figures for U.S. coffee shops as a whole, or salaries of workers in this sector of the economy to get at the larger picture. Of course, by doing so, macro-level theories may miss exactly what micro-level analysis reveals. Therefore, the interplay between the two levels of analysis—and theories that focus at particular levels of analysis—is extremely important to note.

TABLE 2.1 Four Sociological Theories Compared

	Rational Choice	Functional	Symbolic Interactionist/ Constructionist	Conflict
Level of Analysis	micro	macro	micro	micro + macro
Sources of Social Order	rational contracts between cooperating individuals	interdependence of social structures and common culture	accepted cultural meanings of interactions	stable power structures and legitimate authority
Sources of Inequalities	individuals' choices and resources	differences that are necessary for a functional society	accepted cultural meanings of interactions	unequal social power

A second major variation in social theories concerns the nature and significance of social interactions, social structures, and culture within each theory. I will have much more to say about these concepts as I proceed and in Chapter 3, but for now note that micro-level theories tend to focus on face-to-face social interactions, while macro-level theories tend to pay greater attention to larger social structures, and that the role of culture and meaning differs among social theories.

Finally, theories differ in their explanations of and relative focus on social order, harmony and solidarity versus social inequality, discord and conflict. Some theories shed greater light on what holds societies together, while others illuminate social power and societal conflict.

As you assess each theory, bear in mind that their worth should be judged in terms of their ability to explain the facts at hand, not in terms of your own personal position about the world each theory depicts. For example, conflict theories stress the role of social power—a phenomenon that you may find abhorrent. The task is not to find a theory that matches your values and tastes, but to evaluate each theory in terms of how much of the things to be explained—the stubborn, sometimes harsh realities of society and culture—actually get explained.

RATIONAL CHOICE THEORIES: INDIVIDUALS PURSUING INTERESTS

U.S. citizens tend to pride themselves in the idea that they are free thinking, unconstrained actors—they tend to believe that they are individuals. Americans are not utterly unique in this belief in the freedom of the individual (after all, they inherited these ideas largely from European philosophical and religious traditions of the Enlightenment), but their degree of faith in individualism is rather notorious.

Americans often imagine that society and its component groups are the result of rational individual decisions and actions made under conditions relatively unconstrained by outside forces. **Rationality** is action that is self-interested and efficient in achieving stated goals. Rational behavior is calculated action in the sense that people evaluate available alternative ways (means) to attain given goals (ends). The assumption is that people have specific desires that they rationally seek to have fulfilled. People are constrained in these pursuits by their limited resources for achieving given goals. Groups form when people with similar interests band together. This means–ends rationality is the hallmark of rationalist interpretations of social life, including an influential social scientific theory known as **rational choice theory**. The basic elements of this theory are depicted in Figure 2.2.

Rational choice theorists argue that groups, organizations, institutions, and whole societies develop when individuals pursue common interests. From this perspective, lawyers for example, would constitute a group of individuals who made choices that led to their placement in the legal profession. In education, rational choice analysts view students at a given college or university similarly as a group of those individuals who, after careful consideration of alternatives, chose to attend the school. Sometimes rational choice thought surfaces in people's everyday attempts to make sense of their lives. For example, if a poorly paid secretary reasons that she or

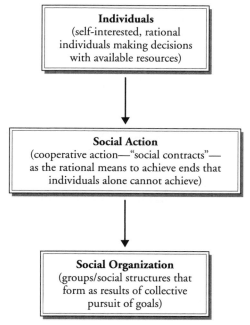

Figure 2.2   Rational Choice Model of Social Organization

he is in that line of work because of early individual choices that led to the current position, this thinking unwittingly employs rational choice logic. According to rational choice theory, these lawyers, students, and secretaries form groups because they individually have made choices that were in their interest, and they have rationally pursued and achieved them.

One readily can imagine that this theory sees humans as economically optimizing creatures. Indeed, it is in the discipline of economics that rational choice perspectives have held their greatest influence—much greater than in sociology. The very idea of "free economic markets" emerged from rationalist thought, and has dominated conservative economic policy for over two centuries. The postulate of the free market is one where people freely invest capital, rent property, seek employment, sell goods and services, loan and borrow money, and so on, based on their pursuit of self-interest. The capitalist economy as such, eighteenth-century economist Adam Smith (1776) argued, simply was the sum total of individuals who "chose" to participate in it based on their self-interest. Moreover, Smith felt that laws of supply and demand—ultimately based on individual choices to produce and consume—would produce an optimal and fair standard of living for all involved in the economy.

The rational choice vision of social organization is one that has tended to view society as a set of individual decision makers who, when they do unite as groups, do so because such cooperation is in the individual interests of all concerned. That is, people form groups to accomplish ends that they cannot achieve on their own. Social organization (groups, organizations, institutions, societies) is the outcome of what philosopher Jean-Jacques Rousseau (1712–1778) termed **social contracts**—agreements that two or more people faithfully will work together, fulfilling their respective duties, toward the achievement of some common goal. Even though everyone in a particular social contract may not perform the same tasks, or even get the same measure of gains over costs of participation, all see their self-interests served in sufficient measure to justify continued allegiance to the group. In this view, society is held together by the fact that each individual calculates and realizes that faithful participation pays off well enough, and that going it alone will not achieve our individual goals.

The rational choice model is alive and well in both academic and popular thought (Coleman 1990). Much of its vitality undoubtedly owes to its resonance with everyday notions of individual freedom and reason. Rational choice theory should be given credit as a theory that gives just due to micro-level determinants of social action—individuals involved in shaping themselves and the world around them through the pursuit of self-interest. There is, in short, a good deal of no-nonsense attention to well-established human propensities in this theory.

One wonders, though, if the heavy focus of this perspective on such cherished values as individuality, freedom, and reason does not obscure as much as it reveals about actual human behavior and societal organization. Maybe there is some wishful thinking that has worked its way into the paradigm. There are three basic questions that rational choice thinkers have had difficulty reckoning with. Perhaps some of them already have crossed your mind. First, are individuals really so calculating in their actions, and if not, why not? Second, if individuals are rational and self-interested, why wouldn't they do the most cost/benefit effective ("rational") thing in their group interactions—cheat other members by not fulfilling their duties in the social contract, while still collecting the benefits of others' efforts? Finally, doesn't the difference in resources between people in terms of their wealth, power, and prestige *itself* deserve explanation? Moreover, why do these differences display such a markedly *social* character, for example, in terms of class, race/ethnicity, gender, and age? A closer look at each of these questions follows.

Where Do Desires Come From?

How often, and how consistently, do people actually enact the sort of planned behavior that rational choice theorists depict as the primary basis of human societies? While people certainly do try to act in their own interests on a regular basis, it would appear that they nevertheless could be quite nonrational in such actions.

Consumer behavior offers a good example of this propensity. Demand for products and services stands at the very base of the hypothesized rational economy of rational choice thinkers. Yet, consider how people buy automobiles, the purchase that is second only to home buying as a costly and consequential decision. First of all, what creates people's desire for a new car, in other words, where does the goal come from? Material need? Perhaps in some cases, but how many people just get rid of perfectly serviceable cars in order to have "new" ones? The same might be said for clothing, another essential material need. Back to cars though, does the desire for a new car come purely from within the individual, or is it also imposed by advertisements and envy of others with new cars? We might even ask why people buy specific models of cars. In the 1950s, fuel-inefficient, long cars with huge tail fins were popular, but it is hard to imagine

In the late 1950s, American consumers' fascination with the "jet age" spread to their love affair with automobiles. Here, a service station attendant gleefully pumps Texaco "Sky Chief" fuel into a woman's car that has twin tail fins reminiscent of an aircraft. Millions of dollars were made in marketing such products. Was the inducement to buy these things founded on individuals' rational calculations of the best means to achieve some material need? Probably not, which suggests a shortcoming of rational choice theory, and the importance of cultural, emotional, and social power factors in explaining this and other kinds of human behavior. Consider people's recent demands for cellular phones and Nintendo games. Were these rational decisions of the kind that rational choice theory specifies? (© Charles E. Rotkin/CORBIS)

that individual consumers simply developed a demand for such ridiculous appearances. It seems far more likely that producers of automobiles created demand through advertising and other strategies. The gas-guzzling cars of the 1950s and 1960s lost popularity in the 1970s as smaller, more fuel-efficient cars were developed in apparently rational response to rising fuel costs that the OPEC oil embargo brought on. Once prices stabilized, though, many consumers quickly turned back to gas-guzzling "muscle" cars. More recently, the fad has been for gigantic and costly "sport utility vehicles" that offer little advantage on American highways and streets, save for their crash-worthiness in collisions with smaller cars (in which case, wouldn't a cement mixer truck be more rational?).

In other circumstances, people fail to behave rationally because it is too time consuming (costly in a different sense) to do so. Consider your last trip to a supermarket. Shopping would take hours if one actually were to compare on each item the various "price per ounce" labels that grocers so generously provide for our rational consideration. Add to price options the glut of nutritional information, sale items, and "Made in the U.S.A." considerations, and the burden of being rational rather quickly gives way to selections based on such nonrational criteria as brand reputation, package design tastes, and shelf height of the product. Not surprisingly, manufacturers and distributors devote serious attention to these advertising issues (Schudson 1984).

At other times, people lack adequate information to make rational decisions. This situation happens when alternative decisions exhibit no discernible differences in their consequences. If individuals simply do not *know or understand* the differences between three available computer systems, they are forced to choose based on nonrational considerations, including trust in others' advice, and copying others' decisions—both very *social* bases for action.

Most of the arguments that I just illustrated about *individuals'* nonrational tendencies can be extended to the lack of rationality in entire *groups'* actions, decisions, plans, and so on. In the business world, for example, models of management that posit simple goal seeking, efficiency-minded, egalitarian organizations suffer from a failure to recognize the profound social influences on organizations. These forces range from social power and resultant organizational inequalities to the infusion of nepotism, trust/distrust, tradition, and values in everyday business life. Management theory long has overemphasized the rational character of business enterprises as simple goal-seeking entities. Actually, such businesses may confront the same difficulties with being rational as individuals do—their goals are unclear, conflicting, or set by outsiders, and the efficient pursuit of goals is muddled with problems of accessing and processing good information. Hence, such organizations tend to invest a great deal of trust in other organizations, as for example when they copy other organizations' practices as solutions to problems.

Rationality also is limited by the simple fact that organizations are part of larger societal and cultural contexts. For example, many of the difficulties that national economic gurus have had in implementing global free trade agreements stem exactly from this kind of lack of recognition of the social character of business organizations, as they vary from nation to nation. Stubbornly preferring to imagine some abstract natural law of markets, free trade advocates all too often merely have accused recalcitrant nations of protectionism, rather than coming to terms with the historical embedding of economic markets in national cultures. It is impossible to understand the varied types of capitalist economies in such giants as Japan and China, let alone the developing economies of Taiwan and South Korea, without serious attention to social and cultural constraints on rational economic action in these countries. Moreover, this tendency is not an exotic "Eastern" phenomenon. Social permeation of markets has parallels throughout the world in Africa, South and Central America, the Mideast, Europe, and the United States (Carruthers and Babb 2000).

In widespread everyday circumstances, then, both individuals and the organizations they inhabit may fail to act rationally because (1) their goals are not firm or self-generated and (2) consideration of alternative means to goals that they do have is impossible or impractical. In many spheres of life, individuals rely on external, social influences to assist them with the entire decision-making process, from setting goals to choice of means to achieve them.

The Free-Rider Problem: Are Rational People Honest?

A second major problem with rational choice theories centers on the source of group solidarity proposed—contractual cooperation of like-minded individuals who seek to achieve ends that they cannot reach on their own. Again, such cooperation obviously happens, and is an influential part of social life. The question is how thoroughgoing is this rational, calculating, self-interested basis for social attachments.

In his great work *The Logic of Collective Action* (1965), political scientist Mancur Olson observed that this sort of rationalist view is inadequate for understanding collective action because it actually is more rational, from a purely cost/benefit standpoint, to cheat on other group members. By not cooperating, not doing one's share, and still cashing in on products of others' efforts (by cheating), people gain the most with the least cost. Olson used the example of a "pay according to ability to pay" public bus system to illustrate the shortcomings of rational choice explanations of group solidarity. The problem with such a bus system is that people routinely take advantage of such **public goods** by not contributing as much as they should. The bus system goes broke unless pure self-interest can be curbed with some infusion of a sense of "responsibility" among individuals that really is nonrational. No one will contribute if they suspect that others are cheating. Trust and loyalty that extends beyond self-interest must be established. The general difficulty that Olson identified has come to be called the **free-rider problem**. In many cases, self-interest alone cannot explain group cohesion. Cultural norms of a basically nonrational character frequently augment interests as solidarity-producing mechanisms.

Another example of the free-rider problem that many students are familiar with is the group-graded task, where some students are quite adept at getting the public good (the grade) by relying on the faithful efforts of others, while expending little or none of their own effort. Depending on what a student wants for a grade (the goal), it may be quite rational to get something for nothing, even if the grade will not be as high as if he or she contributed. This is very effective, rational behavior, however despised it may be in educational culture. As a matter of fact, we might surmise that the norms of educational culture that prohibit cheating exist precisely because the free-rider problem is so pronounced. Even larger social entities such as the government encounter the free-rider problem. Income tax payment, for example, is something that most people could cheat on with impunity. The chances of getting caught for underpayment, or not filing at all, are so slim that it is quite cost-effective to cheat. Yet, if everyone did so, the government would go broke. Perhaps that is why we encourage citizens to learn the "Pledge of Allegiance" as a nonrational, cultural device for preserving solidarity in the face of individual greed.

It appears that cooperative action in numerous situations may be guided as much by various types of values and morality that produce trust and loyalty, as by simple self-interest. Unfortunately, rational choice theorists often fail to mention such trust-building mechanisms, let alone analyze their nuances. For that type of insight, we must turn to other social theories that seriously examine the role of culture in uniting and dividing groups.

Do People Choose to Be Unequal?

Rational choice theorists do not focus on existing differences between people in terms of their wealth, power, and prestige—social inequalities. In contrast to some social theories that early on made claims that differences in individuals' "innate" abilities produced social differences (functionalism, to be discussed in the next section), rational choice theorists at least point to the influence of different choices on individuals' fates. This tactic may help us to explain why two equally poor children take different paths in life—an important contribution. However, the individualist underpinnings of the theory do little to help us understand why most poor children remain poor, and most rich children remain rich in later life. This silence of rational choice theory regarding social inequalities (as opposed to individual differences) is troubling. A social theory that does not explain key facets of the social has serious defects, to say the least.

It is a very disenchanted, technically efficient, and ultimately nonsocial world that rational choice thinkers ask us to imagine as the dominant empirical reality. Conspicuously absent from rational choice theory is a serious treatment of social power and its consequence—social inequality. From a historical perspective, modern civilization may very well be the most rationalized one to date, as Max Weber (discussed later in this chapter) sought to show in some of his writings. But Weber, perhaps the greatest social thinker of all time, was no fool. Weber knew that the very fact that modern people *conceived* their society to be purely based on rationality, individual choices, and fairness masked underlying realities of social power and inequality. Propagation of the illusion of rationality is a very effective way for powerful groups to make their subordinates think that existing social arrangements are fair, if not equal. Unfortunately, much rational choice thought has mistaken this power-driven rhetoric of rationality for an empirical fact. Rational choice theories share this failure to address power and inequality adequately with the next group of thinkers, the functionalists.

FUNCTIONAL THEORIES: HARMONY AND NECESSARY DIFFERENCES IN SOCIAL ORGANIZATION

In the early 1980s, Ronald Reagan took office as president of the United States. The Reagan administration initiated a series of economic and social policies that sought to rectify what the administration painted as an America that had lost its guiding cultural values. The catch phrase of the day was that "family values" had waned. American culture had become, as social critic Barbara Ehrenreich (1989) noted, "too permissive." Additionally, the Reaganites argued that this cultural demise had damaged the functioning of other social institutions, including the economy. In the ensuing years, "Reaganomics" cut myriad social welfare programs, while it reduced taxes and otherwise subsidized corporate wealth and profitability. Working-class people saw government assist corporations in breaking their unions, sending them on what would be a two-decade-long decline in their wages. All the while, politicians assured people that the road to their well-being was in "free market" capitalism, and that the primary social problems concerned cultural value issues. Wars on crime (not corporate crime, of course), drugs (not alcohol or cigarettes, which were produced by corporations), and welfare cheats (not handouts to the rich, though) were the order of the day.

This political strategy of blatantly favoring elites in economic matters, while telling the people that the real problems lie in declining cultural values, is one that the Bush Sr., Clinton, and Bush Jr. administrations alike would employ with great success in later years. The appeal of this rhetoric clearly lies not in its Republican or Democratic party proponents, but rather in what seems like a logical argument. Implicit in the argument noted above, that depraved culture is the cause of problems in other societal spheres, is a type of explanation known as a **functional explanation**. The implied

function of cultural values in this case is that they hold society together—such common values make things run smoothly in the rest
of society. Failure in one social sphere (values) has negative consequences in other social spheres. A healthy or functional social
arrangement, from this standpoint, is one that has cooperation between various societal parts, for example, cultural values, economy,
law, government, education, and so forth. By contrast, a social
arrangement that lacks such cooperative character is, by definition,
dysfunctional and in need of repair.

Once one can recognize the basic features of functionalist arguments, it becomes much easier to spot them, and to critically assess
their assumptions. This form of argument is pervasive in lay interpretations of the social world, at least in a crude form. Many people
regularly employ at least fragments of functionalist reasoning, without even knowing it. A closer look at the telltale elements of more
sophisticated formal theories of a functionalist nature is needed at
this point.

Basic Functionalist Imagery

Functionalism as a formal social theory arose at the same time that
the natural sciences were making their most revolutionary advances—in the nineteenth century. Probably the best known of these
early formulators of functionalist causal imagery was the English
social philosopher Herbert Spencer (1820–1903), who made the
now famous analogy that "society was as an organism." Spencer was
quite self-consciously borrowing the narrative structure of his arguments (the "story," if you will) from the biological sciences of his
day. Spencer did not borrow from Charles Darwin, though—later
nineteenth-century social thinkers would develop "social Darwinism," arguing that poor people should be left to perish so that the
natural law of the "survival of the fittest" would advance society as
a whole. Spencer's model instead built on the notion of biological
organisms as natural systems.

Recall for a moment that organism from elementary biology
classes, the paramecium. The paramecium is a relatively simple crea-
ture with a number of parts that work in unison for the benefit of
the organism as a whole. There are hair-like cilia for motion, food
and water vacuoles for digestion, and a nucleus that is the information center of the cell. Now, if one were to try to explain why the

paramecium has, say, cilia, an essentially functionalist argument would be that cilia exist to cooperate with other parts of the organism in order to ensure the optimal survival of the whole. One might also conjecture that if a given part of the organism were *not* as it is, negative consequences would follow for the organism as a whole—"that's how it is, so that's how is has to be." These are functionalist arguments—they "explain" a given state of affairs as "necessary" for the orderly functioning of an already specified set of normal (functional) relations between parts. So long as we accept as natural and necessary a given blueprint of the normal organism, it is easy to specify the meaning of various smaller parts of the plan. If, however, the natural state of the organism is *not* a given (i.e., if alternative blueprints are possible), the whole logic of the argument becomes suspect as a circular argument with assumptions that presuppose conclusions. This problem is exactly what one encounters when trying to extend the biological system analogy to societal systems.

The functionalist vision of social life makes the argument that society (the "whole") benefits from a particular, interdependent, functional arrangement of various societal subunits. Emile Durkheim (1858–1917), the great French sociologist, argued that societies are **social systems** that are bound together by **functional integration** between their parts. Societal subunits range from large **institutions** such as the economy, government, religion, education, and health care; to particular **organizations** within institutions, such as IBM Corporation, the Internal Revenue Service, the Catholic Church, Harvard University, or the American Medical Association; to the norm-governed patterns of behavior in specific **statuses** in organizations, such as manager, agent, priest, student, or doctor. These various levels of social organization are all parts of society as a whole. Figure 2.3 portrays such relationships between several important institutions and their subparts.

According to functionalism, there is a natural, functional state wherein these parts all work in cooperation with one another in an interdependent effort to serve the common good of the whole. One function of education, for example, is to provide individuals with job skills that are needed in another part of society, the economy. From this perspective, the way that education is organized—how it works from top to bottom, and all its policies—likewise should correspond to some optimal way of fulfilling a social function. Grad-

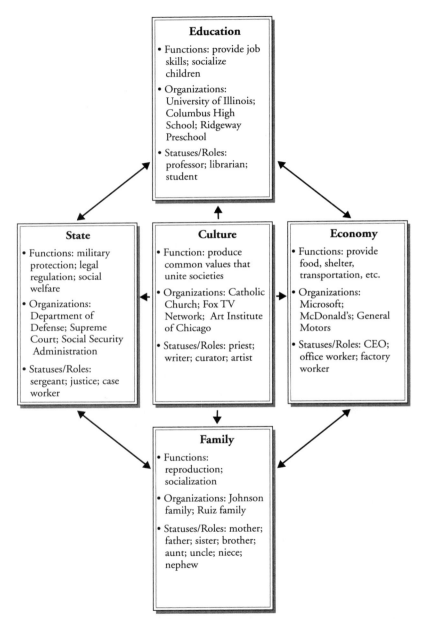

Figure 2.3 Functional Model of Societal Integration for Selected Institutions

ing, decision making, budgets, salaries, and so on, all should be explicable as a necessary way to fulfill educational functions. Consider politics and administration more generally. Functionalists see these parts as the brains of the social system, fulfilling needed regulatory functions, in addition to providing defense from enemies. The medical establishment contributes its part by attending to the health of societal members. All social organization purportedly is functional.

Functionalist logic holds that societies are organized as they are because such organization is necessary for optimal societal performance. Societies strive for an **equilibrium state**, where all social parts harmoniously fulfill their respective functions. *The argument further states that if social arrangements were not just as they are, negative consequences would result.* Thus, if education were not set up exactly as it is, the economy would suffer the repercussions of less adequately skilled individuals, and ultimately society as a whole would be negatively affected.

As if this scenario were not idyllic enough in its personification of society as a nearly conscious, smart system that promotes social order and prosperity for all, functionalists add to this ensemble further solidifying cultural institutions and their functions. Religion, the family, and in some regards the mass media and education develop and disseminate common beliefs and values that bond societal members together in symbolic unity (i.e., in addition to their interdependence with regard to material matters). Culture, then, is the glue that further binds societal parts, much as cytoplasm holds the paramecium together. I will return to this idea in Chapter 3, because there are some important, lasting insights in this element of functionalist thought, particularly in Emile Durkheim's analysis of religion and culture.

There is, of course, an inherent conservatism in this functionalist argument that things must be just as they are. Social change and alternative ways of getting tasks done are completely alien to this mode of thought. Also ignored is the entire matter of social inequality resulting from conflict and competition, which functionalists conveniently regard as temporary departures from the normal social order. What are we to make of persistent job competition, revolutions, genocide, religious wars, labor strikes, poverty, greedy billionaires, sabotage, cheating, and so on? Surely these are common enough phenomena that they are not just fleeting moments in an otherwise perfect world.

Is Social Inequality Simply Necessary?

It is one thing to observe that social inequalities always have and always will exist, but it is another matter to explain *why* this is the case. Within the functionalist framework, there is no mention of inequalities that result from simple greed of groups who have greater power than other groups to achieve their desires. Instead, rather obvious social differences in resources such as income, wealth, authority, and prestige are explained as "necessary" differences. How can it be justifiable that individuals who practice some occupations, such as lawyers, doctors, and corporate executives, are paid so much more than others, such as secretaries, factory workers, and clerks? The answer is simple for functionalists. First, some jobs are more important to society than others. Second, in order to get the most talented people to take positions of appropriately high value to society, rewards in these jobs must be high. In other words, if society did *not* arrange things this way, bad consequences would follow for society as a whole.

What appears at first to be a convincing argument begins to fall apart once we make a few troubling observations. What about the dismal salaries of teachers? Are teachers really less important to society than lawyers? What about nurses? Are they truly less important than doctors for our health care? Imagine the whole occupational structure of a nation. Is it actually the case that each job is rewarded in accordance with some verifiable functional formula? Then there are multi-billionaires such as Bill Gates, not to mention the inherited wealth of old families such as the Rockefellers and Vanderbilts. Is there really a functional explanation for such atrocious prosperity, or would we be better off factoring in the pursuit of power? That is what conflict theorists, discussed later in this chapter, do to account for these differences.

SYMBOLIC INTERACTIONIST AND SOCIAL CONSTRUCTIONIST THEORIES: INTERACTION, MEANING, AND EVERYDAY LIFE

Thus far, with rational choice and functional theories, we have seen arguments that speak of society and its constituent social structures as if they actually existed as independent realities. But who really has seen a whole society, or even an institution such as the state, the family, or education? These structures are **macro-level** phenomena that are not directly observable. Even social classes, a primary reference point for conflict theorists, surely are not observable in any simple sense. At best, we observe fragments of such structures in the everyday interactions of real people. For this reason, one branch of sociology, known as **symbolic interactionism** or **social constructionism**, explicitly developed as a **micro-level** mode of analysis. For these theorists, **social interactions** are the bedrock of sociological inquiry. Symbolic interactionists see the **cultural meanings** that emerge from social interactions as central sociological concerns. Collective perceptions of social realities are constructed within these everyday interactions. In some cases, symbolic interactionism even argues that social structures do not exist, in other words, that they merely are the sum total of everyday interactions between people. Some thinkers within this school would add to this point the idea that powerful social groups who control diverse kinds of social interactions are able to impose their visions of social reality on other less powerful groups. A closer look at this school of thought reveals a vibrant, sometimes startling, vision of social life that has become firmly entrenched alongside other types of sociological reasoning. There are several variants of this type of thought in the history and contemporary practice of sociology. The elementary assumptions of these types of sociology are shown in Figure 2.4.

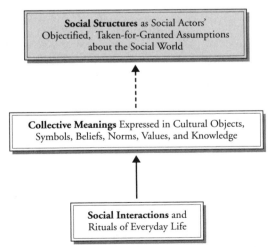

Figure 2.4   Symbolic Interaction and the Social Construction of Reality

Mind, Self, and Society

To see the origins of the symbolic interactionist perspective, we must back up to American sociology's early twentieth-century efforts to distance itself from the already flourishing discipline of psychology as a science of human behavior. As we shall see, sociology developed a science of the mind and thinking that radically differed from individual-based psychological treatments of the topic. One of psychology's assumptions was that humans possessed "selves" that were defined by individuals' law-like physiological, psychological, and developmental mechanisms. The self was a relatively independent unit. Furthermore, people's sense of self–of who they are–supposedly was to be understood through these same mechanisms. A number of early sociologists sought to legitimate their discipline by launching a frontal attack on this very building block of psychological thinking, arguing instead that the self fundamentally was a social creation.

Charles Horton Cooley (1864–1929), for example, studied the development of children (including his own) and argued that their sense of self was not achieved as a biological or individual psychological process, but rather took shape in interaction with others. For Cooley (1902), we never "know" ourselves except as a reflection of what others think about us, and how they act toward us–he termed this self a **looking glass self.**

An even more profoundly sociological early rendering of mental life was contained in the work of the philosopher/sociologist George Herbert Mead (1863–1931), who expanded the rather mundane debates about the social nature of the self to a full-blown sociology of conscience and thinking–a sociology of mind, as he called it. Mead (1934) understood and accepted Cooley's basic points about the reflective nature of the self. Mead's "I" as the impulsive self and "Me" as the socially reflective self were largely compatible with Cooley's ideas. Still, Mead felt that Cooley's model was too simplistic and mechanistic. Mead realized that Cooley's model of the self did little to explain how society and its component patterns of action (social structures) came about and were maintained over time.

One problem was that our visions of ourselves in the mirrors of others are not purely random–we tend to develop within our groups similar selves because the messages we read in others' reactions to us in fact have some consistency. We also develop and internalize a rather effective permanent self that no longer needs direct confirmation or condemnation from others. That is, we develop a social conscience, or what Mead called a sense of the **generalized other**. Our perceptions of appropriate roles of mother, father, and child as generalized others in the family institution are examples. We know these roles, and the relations between them in the abstract, more or less as "rules of the game" of family life. It is this mental state of acting in accordance with generalized others that *are* society and social structure in Mead's view. The abstraction or abbreviation society/social structure gains its specific reality in the micro-level fact that people carry around in their minds a socialized self, and act on its basis. Such patterned social interaction is the reality that lies beneath all of our references to abstract concepts such as families, states, classes, and organizations.

Mead's big idea was that society itself is a set of ideas that various people act upon, thereby forming a pattern of social interaction, that is, groups and social structures. One of Mead's contemporaries, William I. Thomas, echoed his insights in the now famous **Thomas theorem** that says, "If people believe things are real, they are real in their consequences," meaning that if people *think* that something is the case, and then come to act on that basis, the result (consequence) must be regarded as a reality, even if it derived from false assumptions. Robert K. Merton (1949) later formalized this notion as something called a **self-fulfilling prophecy**, a situation where people's initial thoughts ("prophesies") about the nature of social reality, when acted upon, *become* real. A good example of the points made by Thomas and Merton is the teacher who assumes that some students in a class are "smart" and others "dumb." If the teacher then assigns difficult materials to the supposedly smart students and easy material to the purportedly dumb students, the consequences of such actions fulfill the original prophecy over time—the students who are challenged learn, while the ones who are given simple materials stagnate.

Modern Symbolic Interactionism

The works of mid- and late-twentieth-century thinkers such as Herbert Blumer (1969), Howard S. Becker (1963, 1982), Harold

Garfinkel (1967), Erving Goffman (1959), Peter Berger and Thomas Luckman (1966), and Gary Alan Fine (1987, 1996, 1998) helped establish and forward symbolic interactionism as a research paradigm in American sociology. These and other researchers used the perspective to illuminate the collectively constructed meanings of such diverse matters as medical education, embarrassment, marijuana smoking, insane asylums, jury decisions, restaurant behavior, little league baseball, mushroom hunting, and art appreciation. A closer look at several of these modern examples of symbolic interactionist/constructionist thought shows the brilliance of this distinctive type of sociology.

Ethnomethodology.　Leave it to 1960s California to develop one of the most radical branches of social thought. Working out of the University of California at San Diego, and borrowing liberally from prior American and European social thought, Harold Garfinkel (1967) and his associates sought to demonstrate how people lived in social worlds that were largely composed of "taken-for-granted" assumptions about what is going on, and how we should act in various social situations. This taken-for-granted-ness was, in effect, the reality of social structure in these researchers' view. Garfinkel called his type of research **ethnomethodology**, as it sought to reveal the agreed-upon meanings that lie beneath all social existence.

　　Garfinkel's famous **breaching experiments** purposely arranged for his experimental collaborators to violate the assumptions that guide everyday interactions. Garfinkel had his associates (often graduate students) engage in behaviors that challenged the taken-for-granted social order, for instance by bartering on the price of milk at the supermarket, rather than just paying the listed price, or by acting overly polite to one's parents in saying "Yes, Sir" or "Please" all the time. These violations of the rules of everyday life yielded predictably unsettling results in the social situations in which they unfolded. In fact, the social order often broke down entirely as people got angry with the experimenters for not playing appropriate roles according to situations. This result, he felt, suggested the frailty of a social order that was based on mere collective assumptions about social reality. Social breakdowns are as much the result of failures to communicate common meaning as they are consequences of more tangible material issues between people.

Garfinkel also found that many of the conventions that we tend to take for rational and objective realities are in fact mere contrivances of people in situational interactions. His studies of decision making among jurists were a classic demonstration of this point. Jurists are given only the most vague instructions on how to render decisions, so they have to invent and interpret rules, and create a semblance of rationality in their deliberations. For Garfinkel, the jury is a model of much other social behavior insofar as human groups seldom have much to go on as they construct social meanings of what is going on in given situations. Board meetings of executives at Apple Computers, or coaching meetings prior to a professional game, would have the same chaotic character, until the members came to an agreement that particular lines of action were in fact the right things to do. People then justify their actions based on these arbitrary renderings of rational action. This kind of constructed rationality is quite different from the sort that rational choice theorists posit as the basis of society.

Becoming a Marijuana User: The Labeling Theory of Deviance and Crime.   Howard Becker's book *Outsiders* (1963) is another good example of modern interactionist thought. In it, he discusses how crime and deviance are social processes wherein people become deviant and have their deviant identities further reinforced through the definitions or "labels" that authorities impose on such people. In the 1950s, Becker was familiar with deviant lifestyles of Bohemian Chicago from his days as a jazz pianist. Now a sociologist, Becker wanted to come to a better understanding of deviance and criminality. One of his studies involved the deviant subculture of marijuana smoking. Based on his interviews and observations of actual behavior, Becker developed an interesting argument about becoming a marijuana user. Starting with the premise that the physiological effects of marijuana use were not objectively pleasurable (they initially were disorienting), Becker suggested a variety of **social rituals** (passing joints, holding in the smoke, proper use of paraphernalia) and peculiar language used in conjunction with pot smoking that helped novices to perceive the effects of smoking as pleasurable. Group interactions led novices to reinterpret physiological effects as "getting high," "rushing," "having the munchies," "coming down," and other insider interpretations of smoking. Becoming a marijuana user was an interactive process that gave rise to new cultural meanings of the practice.

In a similar way, one might argue that experiences as diverse as joining a religious group or a youth subculture such as "straight-edge," becoming a parachutist, appreciating particular foods and beverages, and declaring a major in a college subject are group interaction processes that impart peculiar cultural meanings to activities, objects, and experiences. Gary Fine's recent book *Morel Tales* (1998), for example, is a study of how people come to know the ins and outs of hunting and appreciating morel mushrooms. The larger lesson of symbolic interactionism demonstrates that the entire social world is given significance by such interactive constructions of meaning.

Another area where Howard Becker made major contributions to sociology was his **labeling theory** of deviance and crime. Here, Becker challenged the idea that deviance and crime were simple objective realities and instead argued that selected social behaviors come under scrutiny of powerful authorities and get labeled as deviant or criminal. The behaviors of powerful groups that sometimes are more detrimental to society often escape such labels. Becker's focus was on the actions of authorities rather than the behavior of deviants and criminals as such. Going back to the example of marijuana use above, this behavior was not against the law in the early twentieth century. It became criminal only when authorities launched a disparaging media campaign that ultimately resulted in laws that stigmatized users as evildoers. Cocaine use today carries stiffer penalties for crack than for powder cocaine because the former is more prevalent among poor groups while the latter is a drug of the wealthy. Cigarette smoking in the United States today has become a rather disreputable practice, whereas only a few decades ago it was universally considered a glamorous and "cool" behavior.

Becker also considered the process of becoming deviant or criminal to be one of interaction with authorities. **Primary deviance/ crime** is the initial act of individuals who violate the norms established by authorities. Once an individual gets caught by police, or identified by other authorities as deviant, a process of **secondary deviance/crime** may set in where subsequent interactions of the labeled parties with courts, counselors, and peers leads them to internalize the label as part of their **identity**. The deviant and criminal process thus takes on the character of a **self-fulfilling prophecy** where authorities' actions eventually create concordance with the very labels they initially imposed on people. Becker is not simply saying that crime and deviance are learned behaviors—learning happens of course, but only in conjunction with the labeling processes that are infused with power, authority, and social control. In this instance, Becker is skillfully merging elements of symbolic interactionism with conflict theory (discussed later in this chapter).

Erving Goffman's Dramaturgical Sociology.   A very important figure who combined strands of symbolic interactionism with other modes of social theory was the eclectic anthropologist of everyday life Erving Goffman (1922–1982). Goffman was as well steeped in the classical sociologist Emile Durkheim's sociology of rituals (see further discussion of Durkheim in Chapter 3) as in Mead's early sociology of the self. Moreover, like Howard Becker, Goffman was quite aware of the role of social power and conflict in everyday interactions.

Goffman's sociology is called **dramaturgical sociology** because he saw society as analogous to a theatrical production. Just as there are scripts, roles, stages, and props in theater, so social interactions are plays of sorts. "All the world's a stage, and all the men and women merely players," lamented Shakespeare's character Jacques in the play *As You Like It*. For Goffman, social realities are often quite scripted, but there also is a great deal of deceit, pretense, uncertainty, and playfulness—in short, drama—that pervades social life.

There also are socially acceptable and unacceptable ways of conducting oneself in particular situations, just as theatrical performances are bounded by the rules of genres such as comedy and tragedy. Goffman (1974) called these different situations **frames**. A wedding, for example, demands a different set of roles, norms, and customs than a birthday party, and a birthday party carries different expectations when conducted for a baby than for a grandmother.

These frames of social behavior often are arranged geographically such that people must quickly switch roles in various regions of social experience. This **region behavior**, as Goffman called it, sometimes is divided into **frontstage and backstage behavior**. The formal theatrical selves of stage actors seldom are the same as their "real" selves backstage. The same principle applies to society, as for example in the case of restaurant employees who portray a courteous, hygienic, smiling self to their customers at tables in the "front-stage," only to drop the pretense in the "backstage" (kitchen), where they slander customers for their rudeness, smoke cigarettes, and finger the food.

For Goffman, the social self was a very manipulative, and often manipulated, being within various frames of social interaction. The guiding principle of selfhood was that people sought to maintain appearances of "competence" and "sound moral character" in social interactions. Through **impression management**, we seek to give others in given situations the idea that we know what we are doing and that we are respectable in our roles. Our actions, language, tastes, manners, and body language are vehicles for giving off these appropriate impressions to others. In the British comedy television series *Keeping Up Appearances*, the working-class character Hyacinth is seen in a constant effort to manage impressions of herself and her family in order to interact with upper-class people. Or, imagine a young man who, on his first dinner date with a young woman, dresses up and seeks to show he is in control of the situation by pretending to know all about exotic menu items and by ordering the waiter around. Similarly, members of street gangs may demonstrate their toughness and preparedness to fight through dress, derogatory language, and defiant or provocative gestures. People's claims of knowledge of music, art, perfumes, the stock market, cars, and other topics seek to establish reputations in everyday social interactions.

Social power also is played out at the level of interactions. People don't merely try to enhance their own positive impressions—they also seek to damage and diminish others' sense of self-worth in order to dominate them more effectively. Impression management is a two-edged sword. Goffman (1961, 1979, 1981) explored the subtle ways that gender advertisements subordinated women, how doctors stigmatized and ruined the self-esteem of mental patients, and the ways that everyday conversations were infused with social power. These **degradation rituals** establish and maintain social inequalities. From a Goffmanian perspective, shopkeepers' hawking surveillance of blacks in stores, bosses' expectations that secretaries arrive early to work to make the coffee, and heterosexuals' joking disparagement of other forms of sexuality likewise are concrete exercises of power in social interactions that produce large-scale social inequalities.

Goffman understood the fragility of the social world just as Garfinkel did. Looming in all social interactions is the potential for actors to experience failures, just as dramatic performances may be flops. In impression management, people sometimes engage in rituals that Goffman called **preventative practices**—actions that seek in advance to protect their character and competency from questioning. Students in a classroom setting may preface a question to their professor with "this may sound stupid, but. . . ." People routinely wash their hair before going to get it cut in order to maintain impressions of proper hygiene. In order not to seem heartless when breaking up with a lover, the initiating party tells the other, "I know this will hurt, and I do care for you, but. . . ." These utterances are all preventative practices that anticipate and attempt to avoid damage to selves.

Another ritualized set of **corrective practices** may be set in motion when social selves or entire situations are in fact damaged or break down. These practices are designed to remedy selves and situations. The expression "I'm sorry" is a common response of this type that people make when their self-impression has been damaged in some way. If we stumble on a crack in the sidewalk, we may try to keep our composure by looking back at the crack as though it was at fault, or by simply gliding into a graceful stride as though nothing really happened.

A classic corrective practice that Goffman (1967) analyzed was embarrassment as a social ritual. I had a particularly embarrassing incident that may help to illustrate Goffman's points. It was a Christmas dinner, with me and all my relatives seated around a big table full of food. Just as we all were about to begin eating, I became ill and vomited all over the table. The whole frame of dinner, in Goffman's terms, was ruptured to the point that no one knew quite what to do next. I naturally was deeply embarrassed by this personal lapse in social competence, but the important point is that so was everyone else. The embarrassment spread through the group as people felt uncomfortable with the uncertainty of the situation, and additionally became embarrassed *for me*. Eventually, someone cracked a joke about the matter, and once things were cleaned up and I was placed in bed, dinner again proceeded. What happened in Goffman's terms? The collective embarrassment was a corrective practice that arose in response to the shattered situational frame of dinner. It gave people a sort of ritual "time out" that denied for a time the reality of what had gone wrong, much as the joking that occurred as a related corrective practice sought to deny the seriousness of the problem. For Goffman, both embarrassment and humor are intimately tied to what people see as acceptable social realities. To be embarrassed, one must know what proper social behavior is, just as to get a joke one must know the social reality that the joke is making fun of.

Goffman's dramaturgical sociology offers great insights about the seldom-examined underbelly of social existence. His perspective is a creative blend of a variety of sociological perspectives, including the conflict perspective that I will cover next. First, some remarks on the strengths and limitations of symbolic interactionist thought are in order.

Symbolic Interactionism/Constructionism: Are the Trees Hiding the Forest?

The great strengths of symbolic interactionist/constructionist thought lie in its insights about social life as it is lived on a daily basis in social interactions. We learn how selves are formed and manipulated, how people come to think and act as they do in particular venues, and the importance of collectively constructed meanings that emerge from social interactions. These all are lasting contributions to sociology.

There is little question that sociology must be grounded in the micro-level realities of social existence. When we want to speak of racial inequality in America, it is not the statistics that really matter, but what happens to people in social situations. We should be able to understand an economic recession in terms of what people do and think in hard times, not merely as a structural problem within an economic system.

One potential problem with interactionist thought is that a focus on isolated, purely situational realities may not yield the big picture of the macro-level world—the forest may be lost for the trees. However important the meanings that jobless inner-city blacks attached to their experiences over the last twenty-five years may be to an understanding of this group's perception of social reality, an independent, macro-level, structural transformation of the economy happened and sent their jobs elsewhere. The problem developed over historical time. Social structures and history are the basic elements of the **sociological imagination** outlined by C. Wright Mills (1959). The unemployed of Detroit and Los Angeles are in similar structural positions whether they perceive it that way or not. Can we adequately get at these matters from an interactionist starting point? Many sociologists would argue that this approach would be awkward at best, and therefore it is necessary to analyze some social facts with different, macro-level theories.

Another issue is more one of convention among some practitioners of this theory than of logical shortcomings of interactionist theory as such. There has been a tendency among some interactionists to downplay or outright ignore the role of social power and its influence over social interactions and the cultural meanings that emerge within them. This silent conservatism is consistent with the rational choice and functionalist approaches discussed earlier. Other interactionists, including Becker and Goffman mentioned above, have been much more attentive to social power and social inequalities in their work, merging the interactionist perspective with a variety of the conflict theories that we now turn to.

CONFLICT THEORIES: ARENAS OF POWER AND INEQUALITY

On any given day in the United States, there are millions of children who go malnourished in their homes, as their parents' wages are insufficient to fill their cupboards with adequate food. Many other Americans on the same day roam city streets in search of shelter and food, part of the desperate homeless population. Factory workers toil away for wages that have steadily eroded for decades, as they await news that their workplace will be closed forever by a management that favors relocation of the plant to Mexico, where cheaper labor and fewer government regulations promise greater profits to the company. Wall Street investors cheer the impending move, and company stocks skyrocket. The nation's burgeoning prison population disproportionately is made up of poor people and minority group members who awaken fed and sheltered, but behind bars for crimes whose severity often pales in comparison to the unpunished financial atrocities committed by rich business and political leaders.

Meanwhile, elite citizens (a decidedly smaller group) awaken in suburban mansions that easily could house four families. Increasingly, these estates are located in "gated communities," literally guarded by a private militia from intrusion, or even sight, by outsiders. They gorge themselves on the most expensive foods available, all prepared in kitchens with equipment that rivals that found in fine restaurants. At daybreak, the kids are off to private school. After a workout and morning round of tennis at a private health club, some of these people may drive to the office in a vehicle that is worth more than the mortgage on average Americans' homes. The workplace may be a spectacular, glassed-in, mirrored structure, with fountains and gardens outside, and located on the "beltway" of the city where many other corporate headquarters dot the landscape with similarly ultra-modern, expensive buildings. Once inside, the day consists of meetings where the competitive feasibility of keeping the aforementioned factory workers' plant open is decided over a catered-in lunch costing $100 per head. At 2:00, there is a meeting of company lawyers to develop a strategy to avoid paying court-ordered fines and restitution for a plant disaster that killed forty women at a new Indonesian installation. The day rounds out at 3:30 with a trip into the city to watch a ball game and discuss some impending tax issues from a sky booth shared with the mayor and several city council members. After the game, it's dinner and drinks at one of the city's most exclusive restaurants. Then finally, it is home to a well-deserved hour in the Jacuzzi, and bed.

How is it possible for some people to enjoy such incredible abundance, while others suffer so horribly? These are the sorts of questions that **conflict theories** seek to answer. Moreover, conflict theories try to show *why* such differences exist, and how they are *perpetuated* over time. *The abiding thesis of conflict theories is that various forms of* **social power** *are key determinants of the structure of society; social inequalities in economic, political, and cultural spheres typically are the results of differential power of social groups.* For these theorists, **social stratification**—the structure of social power and inequality in societies—is a key concern. Conflict theorists study how complex types of power produce and maintain grouped differences between people's experiences of life. At their best, these theories analyze both **micro and macro levels** of social life—social interaction, culture, and social structure—giving just due to issues of social solidarity and social discord. Conflict theories may well be the most broadly integrative perspectives in the field, so it is hardly surprising that they occupy a prominent place in contemporary sociology. Before we begin a careful look at these theories, it may be useful to compare some of their basic assumptions with the theories that we just covered.

The Interplay of Conflict Theory with Other Perspectives

Conflict theorists share with rational choice theorists the assumption of human self-interestedness but argue that entire groups act in self-interest, often consciously against the interests of other groups. Social power thus is a central concern for conflict theorists, whereas this concept and reality remain rather peripheral to rational choice theorists.

The centrality of social power in conflict theories obviously pits them in opposition to the rather naïve notions of ultimate social harmony expressed in some versions of functional theory. We should not overstate the opposition between functional and conflict theories though, for there are some critical areas of general agreement. For example, conflict theorists largely accept the fact that social solidarity exists *within particular groups*, especially in those groups that need such cohesion in their struggles with other highly organized groups. Successful armies, after all, do stick together because it serves their interests to do so. Similarly, workers seek solidarity in their ranks as they confront management about wage deficiencies. Social solidarity itself is an organizational asset, rather than some pristine state of nature, as some functionalists held. Solidarity is a resource that groups seek to develop among their members, even as they try to fragment the internal cohesion of enemy groups.

Another area of general agreement concerns what Georg Simmel (1908), and later Lewis Coser (1956), termed the **functions of social conflict**. Conflict actually can help *create* social solidarity. For example, social conflict may provide an outlet for aggression that actually enhances social order. Without occasional, carefully planned and controlled releases of discontent, subordinate societal groups may be prone to engage in real conflicts that seek to change their unequal circumstances. Thus, strategic power-holders typically try to stage various forms of ritualized conflict that does not really change the power structure but satiates the grievances of subordinates. College students and college administrators often stand in such a relationship. For example, some college campuses in the 1970s sought to abolish the bawdy outdoor concerts that had come to be a spring-time commonplace on their grounds. In truth, administrators and townspeople were more upset about the symbolic messages that these festivals sent off than any substantial damage that they caused. Once abolished, however, students became really upset and began to organize to rectify the situation *and other issues* that previously had gone uncontested. In many cases, administrators then recognized their blunder–they had eliminated a crucial outlet for student unrest. Wise leaders then substituted more symbolically palatable outlets for student release of frustrations, this time in the form of alternative "rites of spring," many of which persist today. The basic metaphor at work here is that of a teakettle set to boil–there always is potential for a blow up, and without an effective steam valve to release that potential away from the kettle, it may happen. Of course, in the case of humans, the additional nuance is that the people who in fact are just releasing steam have to *believe* that their actions actually are real protest. Clearly, this prerequisite invokes yet another theoretical perspective–the social construction of reality by powerful groups.

Indeed, the greatest recent theoretical collaboration has concerned the merging of cultural elements of symbolic interactionist/constructionist thought with conflict theories. The social sciences in general, and sociology in particular, have witnessed what has come to be called a "cultural turn" over the past twenty years. While some classical conflict theories, particularly Max Weber's, already had paid close attention to cultural factors (collective meanings, consciousness, and rituals associated with particular cultural objects and events), a veritable flood of attention to these matters now exists. The construction and exchange of cultural meanings in everyday social interactions, far from being a benign act of individual creativity, is heavily infused with social power and inequality.

Powerful groups have an upper hand in shaping other people's definitions of what is going on–in constructing their realities. These powerful groups' definitions of reality profoundly impact less powerful groups, who frequently must interpret their lives with cultural meanings that are not in their best interests, or of their own making. One of the most important reasons why unequal social structural arrangements persist is that subordinate groups do not effectively challenge their circumstances. Why not? In many cases, people stay in their place because they do not realize—at the level of cultural meaning—that others in fact dominate them. The stability of unequal social structures is greatly facilitated by cultural definitions of situations as "just," "inevitable," "my own fault," and similarly pacifying interpretations of events that are promulgated by powerful groups.

Conflict theories occupy a prominent place in sociology, and are responsible for a good deal of the distinctiveness of the discipline. There are as many kinds of conflict theory as there are specific areas of social power and inequality—class, race/ethnicity, gender, sexuality, age, politics, media/culture, organizations and work, environment, crime, and so forth. A number of these types will be encountered in subsequent chapters. For now, it will be helpful to examine in greater detail two important variants of conflict theory that have their roots in the work of Karl Marx and Max Weber, respectively.

Karl Marx' Enduring Legacy

It is customary to start with Karl Marx (1818–1883) in discussions of conflict theory, even though a number of non-Marxian power theories would serve just as well as a takeoff point. Marx was a German social critic who lived most of his adult life in London where he was privy to the early social consequences of the industrial revolution. Marx' sociology was an analysis and critique of **capitalism**—the modern economic system based on the pursuit of individual profits and the utilization of wage labor in industrial production.

The convention of beginning discussions of conflict theory with Marx unfortunately tends instantly to turn too many students away from an appreciation of the broader insights of conflict theory. After all, why study Marx? Did not communism fail and capitalism triumph? Well, first of all, it probably is too early to ring the death knell of communism, since some such societies still exist (Cuba, for example), and even more societies have strong socialist tendencies (Sweden, France, Germany, Denmark, and a host of other nations). Also, the ability of capitalist societies to *cause* failure in communist societies through trade barriers and warfare hardly is an argument that capitalist economies inherently are "better," except in a pure power sense that is thoroughly consistent with Marx' own arguments.

All of this debate about what types of societies have survived really misses a more important point, anyway. Yes, Marx predicted the downfall of capitalism, but that was more of a propaganda strategy to mobilize workers to revolt than a scientific prediction. Few people realize, for example, that Marx' *Manifesto of the Communist Party* (1848), where many of his more colorful exhortations about capitalist downfall are located, actually was designed as a pamphlet for mass distribution to factory workers, not as a scholarly tome.

Marx' real genius lay in his successful diagnosis of the dominant structures of power and inequality in his own day. Even though industrial capitalism was only in its infancy in the early nineteenth century, virtually unfolding before Marx' eyes, he was able to perceive its essential social machinations. Meanwhile, other economists and philosophers such as Adam Smith had developed little insight about the social consequences of the emerging economy, save for rather lofty observations about "laws" of supply and demand. Capitalism does persist, and major portions of Marx' depiction of this system still can help us to make sense of the darker side of current affairs.

The Basic Marxian Argument.   Marx and his collaborator Friedrich Engels offered a good synopsis of some of their most important ideas in the first part of *The German Ideology* (1846). Central to Marx' thought was the idea that struggles for economic control, specifically ownership of the prevailing historical **means of material production** (industrial factories, in his day), were the most influential determinants of social life. These battles issued in **class struggles** between groups who stood in varying relationships to the means of production. In the industrial era, the most important class relationship was between owners of factories (capitalists or the **bourgeoisie**) and their wage laborers within the plants (the workers or the **proletariat**). The source of economic inequality in these class relations lies in the fact that capitalists are able to exploit workers by paying them less in wages than the workers contribute to the production of goods. **Exploitation** of wage labor is the source of capitalist profits. Wealthy capitalists further seek to increase profits by substituting machine technologies for human labor, thereby creating unemployment among workers, and driving less affluent capitalists into the ranks of workers and the unemployed. Eventually, an economic overproduction crisis occurs and there are not enough working consumers to buy the products being made. It is at this point that Marx felt workers would have the opportunity to overthrow the system, and substitute a communist one.

Marx sometimes is referred to as a practitioner of **economic determinism** because of the disproportionate role he allotted to these economic factors in shaping the rest of society. The economy was for Marx the **infrastructure**, or foundation of society. The ruling economic class (the bourgeoisie) controlled all other aspects of society, including politics (control of the state and military) and culture (control of the production of dominant ideas). Political and cultural elements thus were the **superstructure** of society—less critical, second-order forms of power and inequality built upon economic control. The state mainly was an apparatus of coercion that the bourgeoisie used to further their economic interests. The state upheld contracts, taxes, and criminal laws that supported the ruling class. The police, courts, and military likewise acted in ruling-class interests.

Culture and meaning were likewise manipulations of the bourgeoisie. Marx remarked that "the ruling ideas of any given age are the ideas of its ruling class." What he meant was that the bourgeoisie, because of its economic and political power, was able to influence the production and dissemination of ideas and beliefs by manipulating the institutions that specifically are charged with this task. Religion, for example, was the primary cultural institution of Marx' era. Religious ideas—forms of culture and mass consciousness—were shaped by ruling-class control over what got produced and spread to workers. Protestantism preached to workers the value of hard work, devaluation of material possessions, and spiritual salvation in an afterlife—all very convenient ideas, if one were a capitalist. Religion, Marx felt, was the "opiate of the people." That is, religious culture merely distracted workers from the real economic oppression that faced them in the form of the capitalist system. Religion, of course, is just one example of cultural control. Marx well understood the similar role of the mass media (newspapers) in his day. The entirety of such misleading cultural meanings he referred to as **ideology**. The net result of ideological production was that workers failed to recognize their true economic situation because they were beset with a **false consciousness**. Marx' political goal was to help workers realize and change their economic position by instilling in them a different sense of identity—**class-consciousness**.

We see in Marx the weaving together of economic, cultural, and political elements that are so characteristic of all social theories. His is a comprehensive theory of social organization rooted in economic struggles between social classes over the means of production. The role of social power appears in each arena. There are real actors behind the structures Marx speaks of (social classes), and their culturally conditioned motivations and thoughts receive reasonable, although not abiding, attention.

Marxian theory remains quite relevant for an understanding of economic and political trends in the contemporary world. His basic predictions that capital would concentrate in the hands of a few, that small businesses would be driven out by larger enterprises, that workers' wages would stagnate, and that cultural/media discourse would serve merely as a distraction from real debate about the distribution of economic resources have a ring of truth to them. One need only think of the monopolistic character of Bill Gates' Microsoft Corporation, the inability of traditional downtown businesses to compete with Wal-Mart, the wage stagnation of the U.S. working class since 1980, and the economic irrelevance of media-accentuated political issues such as the Bill Clinton–Monica Lewinsky scandal to find reasons for appreciation of Marx' early diagnoses.

Of course, much has changed in capitalist societies since the 1800s. Services and information assume larger roles alongside material production in the economy. Ownership and control of firms rests with stockholders and managers, rather than with individual capitalists. The state steps in to avert major economic crises by regulating banking and investments, providing some degree of welfare to the poor, and short-circuiting worker rebellions. The overall standard of living has risen in industrialized countries, if not in the poorer nations of the world. Thus, while capitalism continues to generate social inequalities, the contours of such structures have altered.

Some have argued that Marx' prediction of the downfall of capitalism essentially was correct, but its timing was off. Immanuel Wallerstein's books (1974–1989) on **world system theory**, for example, point to the *global* nature of economic exploitation of workers in the poor countries of the world, arguing that once this supply of cheap labor mobilizes resistance, a worldwide economic crisis and proletarian revolution is still possible. Advances in information technology surely would aid communications in such an event. The jury

If Karl Marx were alive today, what types of people and organizations would he see as the main power brokers who rule our lives? New information technologies such as personal computers and the Internet might force Marx to rethink his focus on industrial capitalists' control of the production of basic necessities of life in traditional factories. Control of services such as health care, monopolies over the distribution of goods in mega outlets like Wal-Mart, and manipulation of access to information may now be important arenas of social power. Bill Gates (left), the CEO of Microsoft Corporation, and others like him might be prime targets for Marxian critique today. Some analysts have extended Marx' thought by suggesting that in addition to the exploitation of workers, capitalists now must also exploit consumers. In order to bolster demand for products and services that are hardly necessities of life (as food, clothing, and shelter are), advertisements and other marketing techniques create global consumerism (see Chapter 5 for further discussion of this topic). The photo of a "greeter" at the grand opening of a German Wal-Mart store (right) suggests how extensive this global trend has become. (Left: © Judy Griesedieck/CORBIS. Right: © AFP/CORBIS.)

is still out on this prospect, but I will return to the issue of globalization in the final chapter of this book.

There is a troubling neatness to Marxian theory, with its tendency to relegate cultural and political matters to mere masquerades of ultimately economic factors. Then too, Marx' depiction of the economy itself as ultimately centered on production of material goods may obscure other areas of economic struggle. Marx' insights were constrained by the very early stages of capitalist development that he witnessed. Later conflict theorists have had to take account of these changes in their efforts to locate prevailing structures of power in modern societies. Undoubtedly, the first major revision of Marxian conflict theory, and one that has stuck with us, was accomplished by perhaps the greatest sociologist of all time, Max Weber.

Max Weber's Multidimensional Conflict Theory

Max Weber (1864–1918), like Karl Marx, was born and educated in Germany. Weber grew up well steeped in politics. Indeed, he was groomed for political office himself, as his parents' Berlin home was a meeting place for many high-ranking officials. Still, Weber largely shunned ambitions for political office in favor of intellectual pursuits and activism. He excelled in university training, and achieved notoriety in his own time as the leading intellectual and social critic in Germany, which at that time was the world center of university education. Weber's range of knowledge about historical and comparative societies was unmatched. Contemporary sociology still borrows heavily from Weber's insights about topics including capitalist economic organization; bureaucracy; states; politics and law; and religious, racial/ethnic, educational, and other cultural groups. There are few socially relevant topics that Weber's work does not shed light on, as the ambitious title of his most important work, *Economy and Society* (1922), suggests.

For all of this breadth, it is rather strange that Weber primarily is known outside of sociology (and sometimes within the field) for one journal article, later published as a book, *The Protestant Ethic and the Spirit of Capitalism* (1904–1905). Weber shares with Marx (in his *Manifesto of the Communist Party*) the dubious honor of having a rather obscure fragment of scholarship become the focal point of popular thought about his work. *The Protestant Ethic* essentially argues that religion played a formative role in the very development of the capitalist economy as a motivating factor for capitalists' economic actions. The Protestant work ethic tied vocational devotion, calculative efficiency, saving, and reinvestment in capitalists' enterprises to capitalists' hopes for salvation in an afterlife. This focus on religious ideals has led some people to believe that Weber basically was writing against Marx' "materialism," in other words, that Weber was saying that culture determined the material world, not vice versa. That is, Marx was a materialist and Weber an idealist. This view is very short-sighted insofar as it does not take account of the place of the Protestant ethic article amid a much larger body of writings that focus on the crucial role of economic and political developments in the formation and sustenance of capitalism. The difference between Weber and Marx is that Weber realized more than Marx how important and complex the interface of politics and culture with economic realities was, and hence went to great pains to elucidate such matters. In addition to Protestantism in the West, Weber wrote entire books on the differential effects of Hinduism, Buddhism, Confucianism, Islam, and Judaism on economic developments in their respective regions of influence. Weber's view of the economy as such also differed from Marx', even though Weber basically agreed about the preponderant role of economic forces in shaping societal inequalities.

One other popular misinterpretation of Weber has it that he was a "symbolic interactionist." This depiction of Weber is very misleading, and based only on brief allusions that Weber made to the idea of interpretive understanding (Ger. *verstehen*) of the cultural meanings that motivate human actions. Weber felt that social scientists should take account of cultural motivations (e.g., religious ethics, economic interests, or customs) of social actors in addition to analysis of larger structural factors. Weber mainly wanted to know the power and inequality ramifications of social actions, not the "inner life" of people for its own sake. Unlike Mead and Cooley, he developed no serious treatment of the social self, and he wrote little about the micro-level interactions and rituals that other symbolic interactionists later studied. While Weber's views are thoroughly consistent with later symbolic interactionist thought, it misses the major social stratification thrust of his work to suppose that he simply was a symbolic interactionist. His pathbreaking work on the three arenas of social conflict—economic, cultural, and political—is the trunk from which other branches of his contributions stem.

Multidimensional Stratification: Class, Status, and Party.   The main elements of Weber's stratification theory are set forth in a section of *Economy and Society* (1922) entitled "Class, Status, Party," where he discusses the economic (class), cultural (status), and political (party) dimensions of social power and inequality. Weber conceives social classes differently from Marx, and he sees cultural and political groups sometimes overlapping and reinforcing class interests (as Marx said), but other times existing as independent entities, pursuing their own interests. The three dimensions of social power are analytically distinct, but in real life they tend to blend in myriad ways that are worthy of our attention. Weber's analysis of **multidimensional stratification** is contrasted with Marx' views on the structure of inequalities in Figure 2.5.

Weber's **social classes** derive from economic positioning, of course, but he views the economy itself as a more complex institution than Marx, who again focused on control of the means of

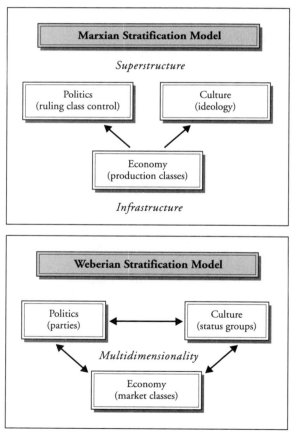

Figure 2.5   Marxian and Weberian Conflict Models of Social Stratification

production as the ultimate economic reality. Weber's classes are determined by **market position**. For Weber, the economy consists of control of various "markets," only one of which was Marx' production of material goods market. Weber argues that there are several types of economic markets, and each generates its own form of class struggle between antagonistic participants. Land markets give rise to landlord and tenant classes; credit markets pit creditors and debtors against one another; labor markets feature struggles between competing occupational groups; commodity markets issue in seller and consumer classes. To get a feel for the complexity that Weber had in mind, within a manufacturing company that is listed in a stock market, there are a number of distinct economic classes—brokers, investors, shareholders, plant managers and workers—each with different economic interests, embroiled in market competition.

These market-determined economic classes are not just different from Marx' "owners and workers"—their struggles also are *irreducible to* this particular form of market struggle. For example, loan sharks who gouge borrowers who are down on their luck with exorbitant interest rates are in this form of exploitation on their own, not in collusion with capitalists. Likewise, landlords who band together to raise all their tenants' rents uniformly are acting as economic groups who are separate from capitalists engaged in material production. Union construction workers who seek legal means to exclude nonunion workers from a job site don't readily fit Marxian categories, but they are trying to control a labor market. When all the oil companies get together and raise gas prices, even as there is an oversupply of oil, they are manipulating an economic market to the detriment of another class—consumers. In all of these examples, it is possible, of course, to imagine a more or less distant linkage to the goods production market and its worker/owner conflicts, but it is quite mistaken to say that all other markets simply and completely are reducible to the goods production market.

So, there are Weber's self-interested economic groups, more profuse than Marx' owners and workers. Two problems immediately arise. First, there is the question of how these various social classes maintain *solidarity* in their economic pursuits. After all, we know from rational choice theory that the "free-rider problem" exists for all such groups. Second, there is the problem of how winners in these various economic markets stave off external scrutiny of their crass material pursuits, so as not to engender resentment and possible challenges to their dominance. Dominant classes, in whatever market, ideally would like to have losers in such struggles come to see their unequal outcomes as "just deserts," and simultaneously come to see dominant classes as "justified" in taking the lion's share of the market. We need to know how dominant economic classes internally hold together, and how these same classes get the rest of society, including their immediate class adversaries, to accept their dominance as a natural occurrence.

Weber's answer to these questions declares that cultural and political forces play critical roles in maintaining the structures of economic domination. Consider first cultural groups, or what Weber called **status groups**. Status groups are defined by their degree of social "honor" (or dishonor), prestige, morality, and other measures of cultural superiority. Status groups are consumers of distinctive forms of culture. Examples of contemporary status groups might include the Daughters of the American Revolution; Harvard University graduates; Congregational Church members; exclusive health, golf, and other social club members; racial and ethnic groups; natural food consumers; devotees of a rap artist; or residents of an elite housing development. Cultural beliefs associated with status groups simultaneously can unite groups with common ideals, and pacify/subordinate other groups. Dominant economic classes maintain their power partly because they are highly *organized*–they think of themselves *as* a group, and act accordingly. Their organizational solidarity tends to extend beyond mere economic interests, to feelings and emotions that they "are" a group in a moral and cultural sense. They establish internal "codes of ethics" for members, develop a distinctive group lifestyle that may partly be based on common patterns of consumption and leisure activity, and otherwise believe and behave in ways that the group deems honorable. In other words, *dominant classes tend to become organized as status groups.*

The second reason why particular economic groups develop distinctive cultures is because this practice helps them to exercise their dominance without subordinates' recognition that power lies behind their success, and consequently without resistance. Subordinate classes, who typically have not been so successful at organizing their interests in a particular market, tend to accept their failures as justified because they accept the cultural superiority of their competitors. The same groups that successfully organize as privileged status groups often seek culturally to disable their subordinates by defining them either as a dishonorable status group, or merely as a set of "individuals" who failed in a fair competition. That is, dominant groups seek to impose their cultural worldviews on others, particularly those groups who stand in closest proximity in markets as competitors. Dominant groups use their influence over the mass media, education, political rhetoric, religion, art, music, and other institutional centers of culture to disseminate favorable images of themselves, and disparaging stereotypes of competitors. Thus, automobile manufacturers in the United States seek to characterize their workers as lazy, money-grabbing unionists, while physicians attempt to cast doubt on the credibility of alternative health care practitioners by calling them mystics, and landlords tell city officials that their buildings need not meet health and safety codes because their tenants are disreputable people who just like to live in filth. In some cases, a single group may be the object of economic oppression in many markets, and suffer cumulative cultural deprecation as a result of this fact. These negatively characterized status groups are lower **castes**, as in the case of the untouchable caste of India, and some would say of African Americans as a group until very recently, and lower-class African-American males to this day.

The final type of stratification is "political" inequality, which is embedded in power groups that Weber called **parties**. It is important to be mindful that Weber meant more than simply political parties in the sense of, say, the Democratic and Republican parties in the modern United States. He meant a much broader meaning of power groups that includes people who rule and are ruled in all types of organizations—from governments to schools to workplaces.

Parties "live in the house of power," so to speak. They occupy positions in organizations that are vested with the ability to influence others' situations, even against resistance. Power-holders of this sort can count on others in the organization to come to their support in demanding compliance to their orders.

The power that parties hold is not always exercised in the form of brute force, though. Force merely is "pure" power, and anyone with political power has the use of force as one way to get compliance from others. More often, the ability to use force combines with other economic and cultural incentives to achieve obedience. For example, compliance may be gained by using some form of (typically unequal) "exchange," as in the case of the economic exchange of money for work performed.

Obedience also may follow from the fact that subordinates "believe that they ought to obey," a situation that Weber termed **legitimate authority**. Legitimate rule has a cultural component insofar as beliefs stand at its base. Sometimes people obey authorities because their group always has followed the orders of another group (e.g., peasants who obey a king because they believe his membership in the lineage of a royal family legitimates his power). This power arrangement is **traditional authority**. In more recent times, people have come to obey authorities because they think that the "rules" of organizations are rational and just, often with some added belief that these rules are the result of democratic enactment. This modern type of authority that is so characteristic of bureaucratic organizations is **rational-legal authority**. Finally, Weber discussed obedience to extraordinary individual personalities, such as Mahatma Gandhi, Adolph Hitler, or Jesus Christ. Such **charismatic authority** tends of necessity to become transformed into one of the previous two types of authority, or end, because individuals eventually die. I shall return to a more detailed discussion of social power in Chapter 4.

While it is possible to separate political power from economic and status issues analytically, their interpenetration is frequent in empirical cases. A CEO of a corporation can enhance her or his own economic standing in ways that common workers cannot. If one controls the decision-making process in any organization—a critical political power mechanism—it is much easier to see one's economic interests served by the organization as a whole. Organizational leaders also are able to affect various cultural construction processes that define their positions to onlookers as prestigious—in other words, to transform themselves into privileged status groups with legitimate authority. Powerful political leaders, just as powerful economic classes, tend to buttress their political power with social status.

Educational Inequality: An Extension of Weber's Stratification Theory. Weber's ideas about classes and status groups have been a springboard to much contemporary discussion of the relationship between economic and cultural realms of life. French sociologist Pierre Bourdieu (1930–2002), for example, asked how economic classes perpetuate themselves over time. Drawing on Weber's prior work on the topic, Bourdieu and Passeron (1970) elaborated the concept of **social reproduction** to account for this phenomenon. Classes reproduce themselves—make themselves solidary and recognizable to one another, and exclude others from their ranks—by producing and then monopolizing esoteric cultural practices. For example, tastes in music, abstract art, architecture, literature, food and drink, sports, home décor, clothing, landscaping, and even pets vary by social class. Knowing the appropriate cultural tastes and corresponding behaviors in the presence of cultural objects and events is a matter of possessing what Bourdieu calls **cultural capital**. Just as economic capital is concentrated in particular classes, so cultural capital accumulates and is exchanged in restricted social circles (markets). Knowing that red wine goes with red meat is not a natural thing (I think it goes just fine with chicken) but a practice that is learned and positively reinforced as part of a class culture.

A key institution for the cultivation of cultural capital in modern societies is the educational system (along with the family). Obviously, the more years of schooling that one has, the more cultural capital one tends to acquire, but there is more. In education, children often get segregated into separate schools and/or programs within schools ("tracks," or the now fashionable term "ability groups"). These various schools and programs teach different forms of cultural capital by providing different curricular and extracurricular training for students. The British linguist Basil Bernstein (1971–1975) demonstrated that students even develop class-specific language patterns, or linguistic codes, in these contexts that enhance or constrict students' abilities to communicate effectively with a variety of types of groups. Upper- and middle-class children learn language that enables them to interact in a variety of settings, while their lower- and working-class counterparts learn language that only facilitates interaction within their local groups. Language—verbal and written—is a critical form of cultural capital in modern societies that poorer children need in order to escape the cultural stigma of their own class cultures. These language skills, or lack thereof, are among the most easily identifiable markers of membership in different social classes. Think of how often you place strangers on an implicit social scale on the basis of how they talk. Add to that the various other forms of cultural capital—dress, etiquette, knowledge, and so on—and you have a rather reliable ensemble of identifiers that frequently determines whom one chooses to interact with, and how the interactions flow.

Education is more than simply a commodity that some people "get more of" and others less. Weber himself realized that one of higher education's primary consequences was the "credentialing" of degree holders as the only "qualified" candidates for particular, rewarding jobs. This was the case, even though the content of such education frequently bore little relationship to subsequent job performance. People without degrees could do the job adequately, if not better, but they were barred from the hiring process by legal or informal organizational conventions that favored graduates. Credentials thus *create* occupational monopolies for degree holders, and exclude nondegree holders from the market for such jobs. Subsequent research (Brown 1995; Collins 1979; Labaree 1997) on the effects of education on jobs has verified Weber's insights, and shown the United States to be the nation with the most thoroughgoing credentialing system in the world.

Education also is an active force in *daunting* the aspirations of those students who fail in school due to their lack of appropriate cultural capital to excel in educational lessons that are framed in dominant group cultures. Education recreates inequality. The cultural deck is stacked against subordinate groups who must compete in schooling that uses the language, idioms, examples, and other "hidden curricula" of dominant groups. If one's family life has been such that one has never seen the opera or ballet, never heard Beethoven or Bach, or never been to Europe, then the lessons of theater, dance, music, and history that are couched in such cultural trappings inherently are difficult to pay attention to, let alone master. Some groups have traditions of spoken culture and communication, with much less emphasis on written language. Yet formal schooling almost entirely is predicated on performance on written examinations—in other words on performance that uses the cultural medium of ruling groups. While it may be difficult to imagine an alternative, oral system of evaluation (elements of one existed when U.S. education was reserved for a more homogenous population of elites), this written language convention is a serious disadvantage for already economically and politically subordinate groups.

Poor performance in education follows from these cultural idio-syncrasies for entire groups of students—class, gender, racial/ethnic, urban/rural, and other social divides—that are mirrored in educational culture. To the extent that students who are so destined to fail actually believe that the educational system offers a fair chance for them as "individual" contestants for culturally neutral educational goods, the consequences are devastating to disadvantaged students' ability to challenge the power-ridden process of social reproduction. Paul Willis' (1977) research on British schools, and Jay MacLeod's (1995) parallel studies of American counterparts, demonstrated that poorer children often come to *accept* their bad jobs and poverty in later life precisely *because* their interpretation of their "failure" in education follows the cultural ideology that "it was their own fault for not trying harder in school." Individualistic thinking of subordinate groups plays into the hands of dominant groups who, of course, likewise accept the fiction that their own "success" was a result of unadulterated individual genius. Education thus reproduces dominant groups *and* subordinate ones.

Conflict Theories: Too Much Pessimism, or Sober Realism?

Advocates of conflict theories believe that this perspective has distinct advantages over inherently conservative theories such as rational choice, functional, and some variants of symbolic interactionist theory. After all, the social world has always displayed social power and social inequality, so why not attempt to explain the facts at hand rather than ignore them or sweep them under the rug? Far from merely acknowledging that conflict always has existed, conflict theorists have delved deeply into the sources of social inequalities. This effort has been a major contribution not just to sociology, but also to social science in general. Conflict theories rightly occupy a central place in sociology today. One of the major assets of this theoretical perspective has been its ability, in some cases, to accommodate both macro and micro sociological approaches.

There are many varieties of conflict theory, and some of these types do not readily mesh with one another. Marxian and Weberian perspectives, noted above, represent one example of this tendency. It appears that while there is agreement about the basic existence of power and inequality in society, conflict theory still has much work ahead in reconciling the exact ways that these forces work, and which forms of inequality and power are most important for understanding social stratification. The ambiguous concept of social class, so different in Marx and Weber, has led some analysts to conclude that America indeed is a classless society (Kingston 2000). The relative significance and interplay among class, gender, and race/ethnicity are continuing matters of debate among conflict theorists.

Perhaps a more serious charge is that conflict theory simply overstates the role of power and inequality in society—it underplays the significance of social solidarity and social order that functionalist theories note, and the role of individual choice that rational choice theories highlight. Many conflict theories fail to explain how society holds together to the extent that it does, which is considerable. The thing to be explained may be social order more than discord. To be fair though, it should be noted that other conflict theories do reserve an important place for social solidarity and order—it is just that they see solidarity as a resource that groups use in conflicts, and they view social order as a stable, accepted power structure (as legitimate authority). Likewise, some conflict theories do allot a limited place for individual choices within the parameters of rather strong constraints of social power and inequality.

CONCLUSION

Sociological theories, again, can be viewed as paradigms—models that one compares to actual worldly events and circumstances. These models each reveal particular aspects of observable facts. Some theories appear more consistent with such facts than others, and thus have come to be influential lenses through which sociologists view the world. The four broad types of theory discussed in this chapter were rational choice, functionalist, symbolic interactionist/social constructionist, and conflict theories. Easily the most prominent types of social theory today are symbolic interactionist/social constructionist and conflict theories, but there are important dialogues between these two types and the others I have discussed.

There are many variants within each of these types, only a few of which were discussed here. New paradigms may emerge in the future of social thought, but these four orientations surely have been, and continue to be, important models of sociological reasoning up to this date.

The most fruitful approach to thinking sociologically is to see the interplay between social theories and the concepts embedded in them, and carry this recognition to the maze of social facts at hand. As one of my more astute teachers once remarked to me, "A little theory goes a long way." The theories outlined in this chapter will help you to frame the concepts and examples that are covered in subsequent chapters.

SUGGESTIONS FOR FURTHER STUDY

Will Wright. 2001. *The Wild West: The Mythical Cowboy and Social Theory*. Thousand Oaks, CA: Pine Forge Press.
This intriguing book takes a look at social theories from a unique starting point—the image of the West and the cowboy in American culture. This history reveals an unexpected array of theoretical perspectives.

Kristin Luker. 1996. *Dubious Conceptions: The Politics of Teen Pregnancy*. Cambridge, MA: Harvard University Press.
Luker's study of the politics of this socially constructed problem is exemplary sociology that creatively combines a variety of theoretical perspectives to lend greater understanding to the issue.

Erving Goffman. 1959. *The Presentation of Self in Everyday Life*. Chicago: University of Chicago Press.
This very readable and timeless classic is one of Goffman's most famous books. Social interactions won't be quite the same for you after reading this one.

Gary Alan Fine. 1996. *Kitchens: The Culture of Restaurant Work*. Chicago: University of Chicago Press.
If you have ever worked or eaten in a restaurant, this book is a must read for you. Fine uses symbolic interactionist principles to reveal the underbelly of these organizations.

Candace Clark. 1997. *Misery and Company: Sympathy in Everyday Life*. Chicago: University of Chicago Press.
Your emotions are as much sociological as psychological phenomena. Clark uses symbolic interactionism to better understand the role of emotions—here, grief and sympathy—in social life.

Jay MacLeod. 1995. *Ain't No Makin' It: Aspirations and Attainment in a Low-Income Neighborhood*. Boulder, CO: Westview.
In this disturbing extension of Pierre Bourdieu's reproduction theory, MacLeod uses the voices of real teens to explain why it doesn't much matter if they try or not in school—they still lose in the end.

Robert Heiner. 2002. *Social Problems: An Introduction to Critical Constructionism*. Oxford: Oxford University Press.
In this provocative book, Heiner combines interactionist and conflict perspectives to better understand a variety of pressing social issues, including the family, crime, and the environment.

Roger and Me. 1987. 91 min. Directed by Michael Moore.
The Big One. 1997. 90 min. Directed by Michael Moore.
Roger and Me is one of the best documentary films ever made. Moore combines humor and bit-ing social criticism in describing the devastating social consequences of capitalists' decisions to close unionized auto factories in Flint, Michigan, in order to make cars cheaper overseas. *The Big One* is a sequel that looks at the human price of corporate downsizing and the plight of ser-vice workers in America.

CorpWatch. Online: www.corpwatch.org.
Economic Policy Institute. Online: www.epinet.org.
You may be shocked by the decidedly different picture of what is going on in America provided in these two websites. Good alternatives to the standard fare of network media and the hum-drum commentaries of politicians.

CHAPTER 3

Culture, Structure, and Interaction

Unraveling the Fibers of Social Life

"It's society's fault—our culture—that makes people act like that," we sometimes hear in reference to any of a variety of societal issues. Some words have deeper meanings than casual references reveal. What exactly do people mean when they refer to "society" and "culture," and what relationships do these terms have to peoples' actions? In this chapter, you will learn to speak of culture, society (or social structure), and social interactions with greater precision and understanding. Sociologists discuss social life using three levels of analysis—their immediate actions in groups (social interaction), the meanings that they attach to their experiences (culture), and their place in society by virtue of long-term patterns of behavior (social structure). Social interactions, culture, and social structure also have complex interrelationships that will require especially careful study.

INTRODUCTION

Sociologists are interested in explaining the behavior of humans in relation to one another. We call these social behaviors **social interactions**, meaning that individuals' actions are influenced by the actions of other individuals and groups. Very broadly, these social interactions are shaped by two factors: the beliefs, knowledge, meanings, and tastes that form our **culture**, and the patterns of behavior that we have become accustomed to—what sociologists term **social structure**. These social forces of culture and social structure are active at the deepest levels of our consciousness.

An example of these processes can be drawn from the simple matter of eating. When people decide what to eat for supper, their actions frequently are guided by what others with whom they regularly interact are eating (a social structure), and by related mental judgments about the appropriateness of a given food for a particular occasion (a culture). If everyone you know is barbecuing meat out-doors on Labor Day, you feel constrained by their common actions to do the same thing, rather than cooking vegetable soup indoors, for instance. Moreover, we may tend to adopt our friends' beliefs that charred meat actually is the right thing to prepare for Labor Day, and we question why anyone would do otherwise. Vegetarians, of course, develop different cultures of food in their circles, but the important point is that we take an active role in maintaining a men-tal culture of what constitutes proper eating.

To take a similar but more consequential example, many people grow up in neighborhoods where beliefs about the moral inferior-ity of minority groups in their midst abound, and where their peers routinely act with distrust and derision toward these groups. Under these circumstances, many people adopt the beliefs and actions of their friends. Not surprisingly, minority groups often are kept structurally different (e.g., in terms of education level, jobs, and political offices) from dominant groups by such cultural beliefs and actions.

The dual influences of patterned actions, or **social structures**, and group beliefs about the worlds they inhabit, or **culture**, are pow-erful determinants of our own thoughts and actions, however much we individually may try to resist them. More often than not, these forces unconsciously guide our social being as a sort of second na-ture. The task of sociology is to bring these realities to the surface, and to gain analytical precision regarding their causes and conse-quences. Beneath the simple notion that groups exert "peer pres-sure" lies a great deal of complexity that needs to be unpacked. We may begin by exploring the concepts of social structure and culture as determinants of social interactions.

DISTINGUISHING SOCIAL STRUCTURE, CULTURE, AND SOCIAL INTERACTION

For sociologists, the terms "society," "culture," and "social inter-action" refer to different, albeit related aspects of social life. By "society," we mean the "social structure," or patterned actions of human existence. By contrast, "culture" refers to the mental beliefs, symbols, and meanings that groups share and use to interpret their existence. "Social interactions" are behaviors that directly or indi-rectly involve others. Figure 3.1 illustrates these distinctions.

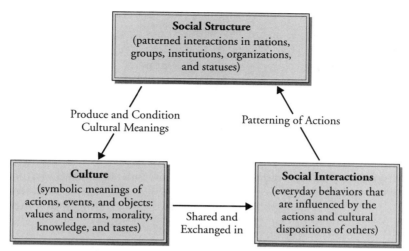

Figure 3.1   Social Structure, Culture, and Social Interactions

The concept of **social structure** really is an abbreviation, or abstraction, that seeks to summarize the relatively similar actions and situations of a given set of individuals. It may be useful to think of social structure as "the way that social life is set up," meaning that patterned activities create benefits and constraints (e.g., financial and other rewards and assistance, punishment, and ostracism) for individuals who inhabit them, and thus encourage behavioral regularities. There are numerous levels at which we may conceive social life as structured activity. Whole **nations**, such as India, Tanzania, France, or Brazil, are social structures insofar as their members regularly act differently because they are embedded in different economic, political, and social circumstances. **Groups** within societies, such as racial/ethnic, social class, gender, sexual orientation, religious, age, and occupational groups also are social structures. Activities in societies tend to be divided along a number of major lines that serve societal needs, for example, within the economy, politics, education, family, and religion. These general areas are social structures that sociologists refer to as societal **institutions**. Within each institutional arena, there are specific **organizations**, such as Microsoft Corporation, the National Organization for Women, Greenpeace, the Republican party, and the Ku Klux Klan, that are somewhat smaller segments of social structure. Finally, within or-

ganizations, there are various departments and within them there are
statuses that people occupy, such as purchasing agent, secretary, and
committee chair, that likewise may be viewed as patterned actions.
Clearly, there are many areas of overlap between societal, group, institutional, organizational, and positional structures, but it is useful
to think of these levels as rather elementary forms of social structure.
People who inhabit similar social structures tend to produce distinctive cultures.

Sociologists give **culture** a specific, technical definition that differs from everyday usage of the term. A "culture" is not the same
thing as a "society," although the two concepts are related. Culture
refers to the symbolic meanings of experiences that people exchange
within social structures. Culture is a collective interpretation of social existence that gets expressed in language, thought, and human
artifacts. Notice that while national and racial/ethnic cultures are included in this definition, it actually is much broader than just these
two examples—the idea is that *all* social structures develop and maintain distinctive cultures. Thus, we may speak of the organizational
culture of Nike Corporation, the occupational cultures of beauticians versus plumbers, youth cultures, urban/rural cultures, the varying cultures of universities, and so forth. For every slice of social
structure, we would expect to find corresponding cultural dispositions. It is useful to think of culture as a "repertoire" of beliefs,
values, norms, and other symbolic meanings that people who are
embedded in various social structures can "pull from" as needed in
concrete social interactions. On St. Patrick's Day, for instance, people of Irish descent can "play" their ethnic culture, whereas this culture remains inactive most of the year. Similarly, on job interviews,
people frequently try to appease interviewers by putting forth particular cultural preferences (e.g., tastes in music, dedication to sports
teams, or familiarity with places they have traveled to) that they feel
their prospective bosses will appreciate.

Finally, by **social interaction**, we mean the actual behaviors of individuals in relation to one another. In social interactions, people
take account of the actions of others (including imagination of
probable actions), and the cultural values and meanings that others
ascribe to behaviors, events, and objects. Culture is shared and exchanged in social interactions. Social action thus differs from actions
that are purely individual undertakings. Even acting "alone" may be

a profoundly social matter when thoughts about others inform the action. The vast majority of human activity, from dreaming to dying, is social interaction. The intensity of social forces present in such cases varies from high to low. Snacking alone generally is a less intense social experience than sharing pizza with friends, where the allotment of slices tends to be regulated by social norms. When social interactions become patterned in the latter manner, we may speak of the sum total of such regularized interactions as "social structures."

SOCIAL STRUCTURAL DETERMINISM, CULTURAL AUTONOMY, AND HUMAN AGENCY

Do people think and act as they do because of their place in society, or is their place in society a result of their thoughts and actions? In other words, what is the causal connection between social structure and culture? The fact that there is a relationship between our cultural and social structural makeup is undeniable, but there is much debate about the direction of causality. We shall see that there is considerable merit in both of these positions, which suggests that culture and social structure are intertwined in complicated ways.

Structural determinism is the view that our cultural outlooks and actions are direct results of the societies, groups, and organizations that we belong to. Karl Marx, for example, believed that people's economic class position determined their cultural consciousness, and that ruling classes (capitalists, in his view) tended to impose these cultural beliefs on subordinate groups (wage laborers, for Marx). From this standpoint, the economic power structures of societies are mirrored in their cultural and action systems—thus, political and media presentations of issues economically are conservative because the production and dissemination of this culture directly is controlled ("owned," in the Marxian argument) in the interests of the ruling classes, in other words, to maintain the unequal status quo. The same general principle applies to a variety of other conflict perspectives on society and culture, in less conspiracy-based terms, for example, where social power groups of all sorts (not just classes) develop distinctive cultural repertoires and practices that suit their economic and political interests. Men and women, blacks and whites, adolescents and adults, and teachers and students each think, interpret, and act in life in ways that match their structurally defined interests.

Other thinkers focus on social solidarity, rather than conflict, in making similar, structural determinist arguments regarding culture. Emile Durkheim, for example, launched an enduring school of thought that sees "cultural representations" of social structures serving unifying purposes for societies, groups, and organizations. Essentially, he argued that if we all believe the same things, and ascribe the same meanings to events, it helps to cement us together as cohesive social structures. Here, as with Marx, structure drives culture. The difference is that Durkheim sees culture as something that bonds equals together, whereas Marx and other conflict theorists see culture as something that groups use to subordinate and/or compete with other groups.

Critics of structural determinist views of culture have argued that neither Marxian economic control of culture, nor Durkheimian functional solidarity-building models are sufficient for a full understanding of culture. A number of social researchers call for an appreciation of the independence, or **autonomy of culture**, from social structural determinants. Often associated with this view is the idea that **human agency**, or social action, significantly eludes the grip of social structures. In this model, not only can cultural development and human intervention sometimes have their own internal dynamics that are separate from dominant economic, political, and other social structural moorings, but also culture and action can powerfully *shape* other social structures.

Max Weber's classic study *The Protestant Ethic and the Spirit of Capitalism* (1904–1905) made this sort of argument in saying that the onslaught of economic capitalism in Western Europe was made possible not merely by favorable structural circumstances (technical innovations in economic production, the development of states and legal systems, the spread of political rights, etc.), but also by the advent of a corresponding cultural disposition that was rooted in early capitalists' Protestant (especially Calvinist) religious beliefs. The **Protestant work ethic** spelled out that one should work hard to advance one's business interests (vocation), but that the fruits of these labors should be reinvested in the enterprise, rather than spent on sinful, worldly luxuries. These religiously grounded practices were the motivational sources for the accumulation of profits that defines capitalism as a structural system. This cultural motive was lacking in other parts of the world, most notably in China under Confucianism, even when favorable structural inducements to capitalist development existed.

Weber's argument about Protestantism and capitalism has spurred a great deal of debate, but there can be little question that he was right about the underlying principle—economies are not simply self-contained, law-like, systems of the sort that conservative economists seem to imagine. Cultural forces and social power exert large influences over widespread areas of economic activity, ranging from the social meanings of economic goods and markets, to advertising and consumerism, to the cultural significance of money. The cutting edges of modern economic analysis clearly are honed with sociological insights.

A number of contemporary social theories seek to resolve the duality of structure and culture/agency (and the related opposition of macro and micro sociological modes of inquiry) by examining how the two interpenetrate one another. Anthony Giddens' (1984) **structuration theory**, for example, argues that society is essentially a work in progress with social structures suggesting but not fully determining the direction of culture and agency, while the same structures are constituted and maintained by cultural beliefs and human actions. Pierre Bourdieu's social reproduction theory (discussed later in this chapter) likewise sees a mutual dependency between structure, culture, and agency.

In order better to see the dynamics of structural determinist, cultural autonomy, and human agency arguments, we next will look at an argument that the cultural phenomenon of religious belief is determined by social structure. Then, we will examine a cultural autonomy and human agency argument with regard to money and economic exchange.

Beyond Good and Evil: Religion as an Emblem of Society

One of the most influential early statements of the deterministic relationship of social structure over culture was the great French sociologist Emile Durkheim's early twentieth-century analysis of the social meaning of religion. Durkheim's arguments about the meaning of religion were published in his famous work *The Elementary Forms of the Religious Life* (1915). His insights were extended to analyses of the social meaning of many other types of culture, and thus deserve close attention.

In Durkheim's day, data about the "bizarre" beliefs of "primitive" (really, just non-Western, Third World peoples) was flowing back to Europe in the accounts of Christian missionaries, colonial administrators, and sundry global travelers. These societies engaged in various forms of ancestral worship, nature religions, witchcraft and shamanism, and totemism (identification with sacred animals), to name but a few common themes. Since these belief systems had seemingly little in common with Western religions (many lacked an all-powerful deity or a belief in an afterlife, for example), most European scholars were content simply to dismiss them as irrational, magical ravings of ignorant peoples. The main appreciation of these societies only came in the form of a voyeurism that flowered in the artifact exhibits of Western European museums (and which sadly continues to the present in a variety of Western forums, such as The Discovery Channel on television).

Durkheim, however, saw something worth exploring. He wanted to show that these various belief systems indeed were religions, just as any other. His strategy was to find the "elementary forms" of religion, that is, to discover what all religions had as a common denominator. It was immediately apparent that there were no particular beliefs that would serve as such a universal content (deities, afterlife, incest, and other taboos were far too variable). Different groups revered widely disparate phenomena—ancestors, mountains, animals, objects, events, foods, buildings, blood, and so on. Amid this incredible variety of beliefs, the only commonality was a purely formal practice—all religions conceptually distinguished in one manner or another the **sacred** (awesome, powerful, respected, and feared phenomena that required special, ritualized treatment) from the **profane** (ordinary phenomena that needed no special attention). This dichotomous sacred–profane classification of groups' experiences of their worlds thus was a universal way of knowing or cosmology, and of orchestrating human actions.

The question remained, "Why do human groups bother to believe in sacred things in the first place?" One answer to this question, common in theological and philosophical camps to this day, was that these beliefs answered basic existential questions that people face, such as the meanings of death and suffering. Durkheim chose not to go this route for good reason—some religions simply don't worry much about the meaning of death, and people's experience of suffering itself often depends on essentially social definitions of misfortune that are intimately bound up with what they regard as sacred. In other words, there is too much social variability in the concepts of death and suffering, and that is exactly what needs explanation.

So, again, why do groups establish religions? Here is Durkheim's stunning conclusion: Social groups create sacred, symbolic images of *themselves* as social entities precisely in order to bind themselves together as groups. Religion (and culture more broadly) creates **social solidarity**. Important social functions, rights, and responsibilities tend to be heavily represented in religious ideas. The sacred is what Durkheim called a **collective representation** of society and its constituent parts. The metaphor "the sacred is society" runs deep. Groups, like sacral phenomena, are both part of individuals and greater than any one person. They are powerful, awesome, respected, and feared. Some aspects of social life, such as weddings, trials, harvests, elections, wars, and trade, are critical (sacred) to society and so require individuals' solemn commitment to their groups, whereas other mundane (profane) realms such as collecting daily firewood or taking out the garbage are accompanied by little religious fanfare.

Sacred **symbols and rituals**, perennial elements of religious life, serve several social functions. Symbols provide palpable external foci of attention that divert individuals' self-interests to larger social imperatives in economic and political life. Collective participation in periodic social rituals reminds individuals of their social places, and generates emotional, as opposed to purely utilitarian, commitment to the group. The rhythmic frenzy of the war dance, and its display of group symbols, gets warriors "psyched up," or more accurately "socialized," in a manner that will sustain their group loyalty in battle, even when circumstances rationally would dictate that they cover their own self-interests. The symbolization of sociological outsiders and elements of their cultures as embodiments of evil further cements groups together in self-righteous persecution and killing of others who are viewed as subhuman creatures who deserve such treatment.

Food consumption and associated dietary taboos are frequent topics of sacred representation. Ritual consumption of a sacred animal (or, alternatively, the enemy or its animal) provides powerful bodily symbolism of group solidarity (or domination). The social symbolism of the breaking of bread and communion is common in many religions. The collective emotions involved in the ritual of Thanksgiving turkey consumption, prepared as a whole rather than in the mundane, individualistic settings of leftover turkey sandwich eating, is an analogous affair. From these examples, we might well presume that Durkheim would have revised the popular phrase "You are what you eat" to "*We* are what *we* eat."

So far, it may appear that Durkheim saw religious culture merely as a representation of undifferentiated, whole societies. Actually, there is more, for he wanted to show that the intricate structures of societies (including groups and organizations within them) are reproduced in the system of ideas and beliefs. Religious systems will be as complex, differentiated, and hierarchical as the social structures that they represent. Simple, egalitarian societies with few differences between members indeed will have simple, overarching religions that represent the whole group (e.g., a single totem animal), but complex societies with multiple levels of social inequality will have more elaborate, distinction-making belief systems (e.g., multiple, unequally empowered gods and saints, separate temples, male and female deities and shrines). Matrilineal societies that trace ancestries through female descendants will have female deities; age-differentiated societies will have separate rituals for young and old persons; feudal societies will develop variants of the dominant religion among aristocrats and peasants; and class, race, and ethnically divided societies will evince separate churches, beliefs, and ritual practices in stratified sectors of their populations. One might easily extrapolate from Durkheim a prediction that the Protestant/ Catholic religious divide in Northern Ireland only will end once real, structural inequalities in political and economic spheres are leveled. At that point, religious differences would lose their social salience or purpose, much as the social significance of Protestantism, Catholicism, and Judaism in America has receded over the course of the twentieth century, as the ethnic groups that originally were members of these religious bodies became more similar in economic and political terms.

Durkheim's insights were radical enough as they applied to religious beliefs, but the real import of his argument stretches much further than just to religion. What if *all* deeply held beliefs, values, norms, and practices—all *culture*—carries this same sort of linkage to important elements of the collectivities that we belong to? The ramifications of such an idea truly are far-reaching—and positively frightening to our individualistic sentiments. Still, the task before us is to enter this brave new social world that Durkheim opened.

In modern societies, there can be little doubt that the nation-state (e.g., the U.S. federal government) has become a pervasive influence over people's lives—it is an important element of social structure. Are there secular (nonreligious, in the church sense of the term) cultural symbols and rituals that bind individuals in loyalty to the nation-state? Well, consider our sacred texts (the Constitution), chants (the National Anthem), rituals (elections, inaugurations, impeachment trials), animal symbolism (bald eagle, donkey, elephant), gods and myths (George Washington and the cherry tree), temples (the White House), burial grounds (Arlington cemetery), and war dances (media-driven patriotism after the World Trade Center attacks and during the Second Gulf War). Of course, other nation-states develop different counterparts, as the case of the former Soviet Union shows with respect to Marx, The Communist Manifesto, Red Square, and the like. It is telling of the structural importance of the state in modern societies that it probably is a greater transgression of the American faith not to join voting rituals than to fail to attend church or synagogue.

Of special significance is the flag, that omnipresent emblem of unity amid diversity (the stars and stripes) and of victory over enemies (e.g., the famous and inspirational raising of the flag over Iwo Jima during World War II). Nothing seems to generate Americans' frenzied, emotional solidarity with their state (or their hatred of others) quite like the flag. Many people actually experience physical reactions (chills run up their spines, tears well up in their eyes, lumps lodge in their throats) when the flag is raised and the national anthem is played at major ritual events, such as the Super Bowl. Some people even vicariously can partake in these convulsions in utter privacy via televised events (all the more so, when media icons, such as Ted Koppel, act as narrators and high priests). Michael Welch's book *Flag Burning: Moral Panic and the Criminalization of Protest* (2000) shows that desecration of the flag—or perception of the same, as in the case of recent moral outrage about practically nonexistent flag burning–can raise our most virulent anger and persecution of non-believers. Americans practically ran out of flags just after the September 11, 2001, terrorist attacks, although plenty of "Made in China" lapel flags materialized to resolve the shortage. Recent controversies over the flying of the Confederate flag over public buildings in the American South point to the multiple layers of significance these symbols have, in this case symbolizing historical resentment of northern political influence over the federal government, and ongoing racial antagonism in the present.

There are countless other types of secular culture that display familiar symbolic and ritual features. In musical culture, for example, lovers proclaim "their song" as a sign of solidarity; devotees of bands become "groupies," the original Woodstock concert comes to represent an age group distinct from younger rap enthusiasts. Males and females, and straights, gays, and lesbians, similarly adopt socially significant differences in musical tastes. The social proof of the pudding in each case is the difficulty non-members have in "appreciating" (i.e., deriving collective emotional energy from) cultures of other groups. The reason why old hippies don't like rap music as much as younger people do is because the former are not part of the various social structures that gave rise to rap appreciation.

The larger calling of Durkheim's sociology of religion, again, is to extend the analysis to all forms of culture and their correlates in social organization. If he was right, differences in culinary tastes and associated food taboos–from dog eating to not eating sacred cow meat–should follow delicate social contours. Reading habits, ranging from romance novels to the *Wall Street Journal*, ought to represent distinct groups. Architectural styles, from Gothic to Modern, would be expected to reflect the historical types of social organization that produced them. It is a newly intriguing world indeed that this perspective opens for us, and one that challenges the platitudes of our everyday sensibilities.

Beyond Cold Hard Cash: The Sociology of Money

While structural determinists hold that society shapes culture and action, cultural autonomy and human agency theorists say just the opposite. Money, the very basis of modern economic exchange, is a perfect example of a culturally mediated economic phenomenon.

Many people think that money is an abstract medium of exchange that is set in utter opposition to the natural rhythms of social life–that money is dehumanizing. Money, in this view, corrupts our thoughts, as people become "money hungry." But is that really all that can be said about money? In this section, we shall see that money is a deeply social symbol both in its origins and its current uses.

We may begin by observing that currency is based on social trust. Beliefs that banks, businesses, consumers, workers, and others will in fact honor paper notes as though they actually were worth something stands at the foundation of monetary systems. Economic collapse frequently is associated with loss of faith in these networks of trust. Remember what it says on the backs of dollar bills–"In God We Trust." We are urged not to question the obviously insignificant worth of the paper, and the fact that the government no longer backs it up with a national reserve of precious metals, but rather to trust God.

Historically, it is not surprising to learn that it was very difficult to establish common currencies that could be used for trustworthy transactions across territories that were inhabited by different groups who held divergent cultural beliefs. The world was a very diverse place, prior to the introduction of capitalism and before the globalization of Western culture. Trade in kind (e.g., cattle for grain) was common in such circumstances, but it severely restricted the flow of credit that was necessary to launch expansive economic systems such as capitalism. Proselytizing world religions, such as Christianity, played a large role in establishing common ethics ("do unto others as you would have them do unto you," "treat thy neighbor as thyself") that established trust across groups, while the birth of nation-states provided military and legal sanctions against those who tried to abuse credit.

The historical standardization of currencies has been a profoundly social endeavor. But what about today? Is such standardized money not a depersonalizing invention that predicates money over people? Not so, says sociologist Viviana Zelizer in a fascinating study entitled *The Social Meaning of Money* (1994). Money, Zelizer argues, has many cultural meanings that depend on people's social structural circumstances. People symbolically infuse currencies with themselves, and the social structures that they inhabit, as they earmark money for social purposes.

Consider the difference between money that one earns as wages or salary and money that is received as a gift. Wages are exchanges of services for cash (a social power relationship) that can be disposed of as one pleases, without much thought about where the money came from. Gift money, by contrast, may be a special attempt to establish or maintain **social solidarity**, as in the cases of courtship, wedding, and anniversary gifts. Recipients of gifts (money or goods) may feel constrained to use them in certain ways. Some gift money may be earmarked for special uses, such as savings for college, or for purchase of something special. A lover's gift should not be exchanged for cash. Inheritance money often is strongly imbued with this sense of propriety about the disposal of income in a way that honors the gift-giver. It would be unconscionable for most people to spend their grandmother's inheritance money on prostitutes, for example. In all of these examples, the money itself is a carrier of symbolic social meanings.

Donations to organizations, such as the National Association for the Advancement of Colored People (NAACP), the Sierra Club, the National Organization for Women (NOW), or one's local church or synagogue, are gifts that seek to establish individuals' identities along racial, political, gender, and religious lines. Giving such money affirms who we are, in sociological terms. In each case, the money given also carries expectations that the organization will spend it in ways that are in keeping with the donor's identity.

The above examples show money creating social solidarity. Other forms of money serve a reverse function in symbolically breaking social ties. Divorce settlement money and alimony payments are prime examples of this type of money. Divorce settlement cash, apart from establishing equity to the partners, symbolically says that the relationship is over. Alimony payments may add further complexity to divorces in saying that the spousal relationship is over, but not the relationship to children. Graduation gifts also may signal that graduates have passed to a new level of financial self-sufficiency from their parents, and now are officially "on their own." This is an example of a **rite of passage** that marks the transition from one status to the social demands of a new one. Wedding gifts and the confiscation of possessions prior to imprisonment are further examples of monetary exchanges that symbolically facilitate transitions from single to married and from citizen to prisoner.

Other money has distinctive **social power** meanings associated with it. Poor people's money, particularly funds or tokens received from the government or charitable organizations as poor relief, often carries cultural stipulations about the appropriate use of the funds. Donors frequently assume the financial irresponsibility of the poor, and so attach limitations that the money only be used for necessities of life, as defined by the donors. Food stamps in the U.S. welfare system are a manifestation of this earmarking of money. The poor are symbolically labeled and stigmatized as "children," who don't have sense enough to curb their passions for evil or ignorant expenditures.

Within households, children's money itself is tabbed with limitations on its use, as in the case of allowances and trust funds. Household money is stamped along gender dimensions, as well. Women's money traditionally was, and in many cases still is, considered different from men's money in terms of how it may be spent. Historically, women's out-of-household earnings were designated as "pin money" that they could spend on specific "womanly" things. Employers of women justified low wages for females on their presumption that the money would be used only for frivolous items and services.

Loaned money, or credit, is treated differently from earned money, and loan recipients are distinguished along social lines of age, gender, race, and ethnicity. Banks have been notorious for their discrimination against women and minorities who seek housing, automobile, and other loans. It is common in many loans to require that the recipient carry insurance on the house or car as a guarantee of payment in case of loss. Government loans also carry social markings. While farmers, businesses, and nonprofit organizations can go bankrupt on government loans, student loans remain the sole type of credit that is barred from the provisions of bankruptcy law (although students can apply for multiple credit cards, pay off the student loan, and go bankrupt on the credit card companies).

Money, then, is used to create and uphold basic societal units of solidarity and hierarchical power. Just as the federal government's budget includes special provisions for farmers' money, children's money, old people's money, poor people's money, and corporations' money, so too ordinary people invest large amounts of social meaning in the money than flows between them. Monetary systems are structural components of economies that are heavily influenced by cultural factors.

UNDERSTANDING CULTURE AND SOCIAL POWER

Cultural differences are not always so benign as typical travelogue coverage of "odd" cultural beliefs and practices would have us believe. **Power and inequality** are intimately tied to cultural differences. Take the example of fashion. Among groups of young American women, blacks, Asians, Hispanics, and whites have significantly different tastes in clothing, jewelry, makeup, and perfumes, even though there obviously are some shared preferences among these groups. Many clothing stores are geared toward provision of racially/ethnically distinctive styles.

As Pierre Bourdieu (1979) has noted, there are similar differences in tastes for sports across **social classes**. Working-class people are much more likely to enjoy NASCAR stock car racing, bowling, or professional wrestling than upper-class individuals, who are more apt to take in polo, tennis, or steeplechase. Again, the obvious reason for this difference—that it costs more money to play or watch some sports than others—is only a partial explanation. Even where it does cost an equal amount to play or watch sports (e.g., attending a NASCAR race versus attending a tennis match), the two groups value and choose different sports. We could refine NASCAR tastes even further by observing that within the working class whites are more avid fans than blacks, Hispanics, and Asians.

While some of these differences undoubtedly are due to simple wealth disparities between the groups, there remain salient cultural variations even where wealth is held constant. So why do these differences exist? If we answer that group "heritage" socializes people to different tastes, we merely are stating the obvious—the real question is why socialization processes differ in the first place. Socialization explanations often promise more than they deliver.

In these cases, and many similar ones, there is something going on that extends beyond mere money or tradition. In sports, upper-class people don't merely "like" polo better than professional wrestling—they also believe that their tastes (and, by association, themselves) are more "refined," and in essence "better" than others. Prissy, upper-class white girls don't just see revealing, leopard skin–patterned clothes as "different," but also as "gaudy" expressions

*In sporting culture, some sports such as baseball (bottom) clearly are shared across so-
cial groups as the "American pastime." Other types of sports are characteristic of particular groups, even if not all members of the group practice the same exact set of sports.
The nuances of rowing or crew (top right) are little known except to more affluent Americans who may learn the sport in elite schools. By contrast, professional stock car racing
has a far more modest fan base. Many upper-middle- and upper-class Americans barely
knew who Dale Earnhardt (top left) was, let alone mourned his tragic death as did his
faithful followers in the working class. The American South was the hotbed of early development of stock car racing, but now NASCAR promotion of the sport has made it
a national phenomenon. (Top Left: © Duomo/CORBIS. Top Right: © Reuters New-
Media Inc./CORBIS. Bottom: © Bettmann/CORBIS.)*

of inferior humanity. These cultural judgments would not be so per-
nicious if each group simply viewed the other group with disgust
and left it at that. There is more, though. Sometimes, the very
groups who occupy subordinate social structural positions (e.g.,
class, race/ethnicity, or occupation) come to view their own cultural
inventories (e.g., language and idioms, dress, food, and home décor),
and themselves, as inferior to other groups. There is a fine line between cultural envy and loss of self-esteem. Historically in the
United States, some blacks have wanted to "be" white in order to
escape oppression, poor people most generally have envied the
lifestyles of the rich, and rural people have admired the cultural sophistication of urbanites. Of course, whites, the rich, and urbanites
have done their level best to affirm such notions of their cultural
and moral superiority. In each case, the vaunting of others' cultures
has degraded the value of subordinate groups' own cultural traditions, and with that their sense of worth.

Just as there can be no concept of "hot" without a corresponding
one of "cold," cultural superiority necessarily implies inferiority.
Groups engage in cultural practices and develop beliefs in *relations*
of superiority/inferiority to other groups' cultures. Sociologists once
used the rather misleading anthropological term **ethnocentrism** to
refer to this process of defining one's own culture as superior to that
of other groups, but that term only gets at part of the picture de-
scribed above (i.e., we need to account for subordinates' feelings of
inferiority that develop alongside dominant groups' claims of cultural supremacy). For a better understanding of these complex
processes, we may turn to the important work of a contemporary sociologist on culture and power.

Cashing in on Culture: The Flow of Cultural, Social, and Economic Capital

French sociologist Pierre Bourdieu wanted to explain how and why
powerful groups tend to stay powerful, generation after generation.
In his book *Distinction* (1979) and elsewhere, Bourdieu developed
the concept of **cultural capital** as a useful way of discussing the intricate relations between culture and social power. Cultural capital
includes social variations in tastes in literature, music, fashion, gardening, sport, architecture, interior design, art, and many other domains. Groups possess different cultural inventories across all of

these categories. Bourdieu suggests that groups develop distinctive cultural inventories, and feelings of moral superiority or inferiority, primarily in the institutional spheres of the family and education, where cultural differences between groups are "mis-recognized," and made to seem "natural" differences. Schools and families obscure the fact that they *produce* cultural differences between groups. For Bourdieu, cultural differences have profound economic and political inequalities at their source, but there is an even more complex matter at hand here.

Social differences in culture actually play a decisive role in maintaining over time social structural advantages in economic and political arenas. Powerful groups have different cultural capital, which they exchange in everyday social interactions in order to establish beneficial social and political ties to other people, or **social capital**. Social capital, in turn, can be transformed into economic benefits, or **economic capital**. As powerful economic groups raise their offspring in schools and at home, the cycle begins again in a process known as **social reproduction**. Figure 3.2 portrays these ongoing processes.

Our distinctive mental dispositions coalesce in what Bourdieu refers to as a **habitus**, a cultural point of reference that categorizes our experiences of social networks and social structures or **fields**, as Bourdieu calls them. Habitus and field are matched, so that it is difficult for people of a given habitus to effectively interact in foreign fields.

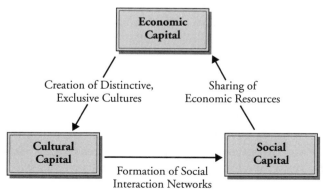

Figure 3.2 Cultural, Social, and Economic Capital in Social Reproduction

Simple language differences (e.g., vocabulary and accent) between groups play a large role in this process, as does competence in systems of complex cultural meanings, such as ethnic and collegiate cultures. If, by virtue of attending an Ivy League college, I gain sufficient cultural capital that I can revel in Goethe's writings, Romanesque architecture, and all sorts of esoteric topics, it will be easier for me to strike up conversations with other powerful people who similarly were trained, and to count them within my network of friends as part of my social capital. Conversely, if I cannot "walk the walk and talk the talk," I likely will be excluded from their social circles. Over time, interactions within networks of powerful people will provide economic capital in the form of job-related information and recommendations, contracts for services, investment opportunities, and even beneficial marriages that keep economic capital flowing in restricted circles of elites.

Cultural capital can be more a matter of feigned knowledge than real, and still effectively create social and economic ties. David Halle, in his book *Inside Culture* (1993), studied social class tastes in interior décor and discovered that while there were large differences in class tastes, there were also similarities in class interpretation of the meanings of cultural objects. The upper class, for example, had far more abstract art displayed in their homes than the working class, but when asked what was represented in particular examples of such art, the overwhelming majority of members of both classes said that they saw "landscapes" in the paintings. Thus, the upper class demonstrated little real sophistication in school-taught aesthetic appreciation that Bourdieu implies in his work. Nevertheless, the upper class uses their supposed knowledge of abstract art, and of a variety of other class-differentiated tastes, in everyday interactions to accomplish the social capital and economic capital ends that Bourdieu identified. In an episode in the old television show *M*A*S*H*, the working-class character Radar O'Reilly is taught by the more sophisticated Hawkeye Pierce how to impress an upper-class woman by faking his knowledge of classical music. Radar pensively utters to the woman, "Ahhh . . . Bach," in a heavy German accent, when Bach's music is played. Of course, Radar ultimately messes up on a number of other tests of his cultural capital repertoire, belying his working-class origins. In many other cases, though, individuals' exercise of class and other group cultures may be imperfect in fluency, yet effective in practice.

Bourdieu's scheme vividly demonstrates ongoing relations among culture (cultural capital), social interaction (social capital), and social structure (economic capital) that are building blocks of any comprehensive social theory. Moreover, he shows how sublime this fluidity of types of "capital" is in everyday life. The processes are so little recognized that we seldom reflect on the matter, and instead tend to view our positions, beliefs, and practices as part of some natural, hierarchical order of things. Taken to its logical conclusion—that *all* cultural judgments are acts of what Bourdieu calls "symbolic violence" against other groups—this perspective is at once deeply disturbing to our moral fibers and full of intellectual intrigue.

Roads Between High Culture and Popular Culture

Sociological understanding of culture is more inclusive than traditional humanities notions that view culture merely as distinguished art, literature, music, and theater, that is, as **high culture**. While Shakespeare's sonnets and Renoir's paintings certainly are included in this sociological definition (we would link them to the historical structures in which they emerged), we also are concerned with all manner of **popular culture**, ranging from styles of body piercing jewelry to the evolution of Barbie dolls, to the changing social meaning of hip-hop music from its historical antecedents to urban black resistance cultures, and on to suburban and rural white audiences. We indeed are entering a remarkably diverse field of analysis.

The transition of cultural forms from exclusive, high culture to mass or popular culture, and vice versa, is an interesting phenomenon. In the United States, for example, Shakespeare's drama emerged in the nineteenth century as a form of popular culture in the bawdy barroom atmosphere of the Old West (as the film *Tombstone*, starring Kurt Russell and Val Kilmer, depicted), and only later became monopolized as high cultural fare in the exclusive urban theater scene of elites. In Italy, however, opera is a form of popular culture that thousands of Italians from all walks of life crowd stadiums to watch as spectacle, whereas the transplanted American version is quite exclusive. Jazz and blues appreciation and tastes for various ethnic foods in the United States typically have followed trajectories from indigenous popular cultures of racial and ethnic groups to cosmopolitan, high culture of urban elites, and then sometimes on to mass cultural

Today, polo is a sport that generally is associated with privileged groups who have access to horses, riding clubs, and knowledge of the game. It is a form of high culture. Interestingly, though, British colonists appropriated the game from its historical roots in India, where it was popular among peasant horsemen. The British took this popular culture and transformed it to an exclusive activity of the wealthy in their own society. (© Bettmann/CORBIS)

distribution. Cajun cuisine, for example, emerged in the backwaters of the Mississippi Delta, was imported to five-star restaurants across the country, and now (in hardly recognizable form) can be found in everything from fast food chicken wings to potato chips.

Fred Davis (1992) observed that changes in clothing tastes offer other prime examples of the interchange of high and popular cultural forms. The Abercrombie and Fitch line of products, once available only in exclusive, urban boutiques, now is becoming a staple in shopping malls across the United States, and even appears as a T-shirt logo. This movement surely marks a loss of cultural prestige value of the clothing, as availability becomes easy. Other brands, such as Polo/Ralph Lauren, Calvin Klein, and Tommy Hilfiger, have displayed similar movement. New forms of high culture are developed that fill the prestige vacuum left behind by the popularization of these cultural artifacts. Who knows which of these fashions will be resurrected in the future as a "retro" look in clothing, as bell-bottom jeans are today in the United States?

On the reverse route, popular clothing also has risen to the status of high fashion. Blue jeans, of course, originally were working-class attire that were adopted by upper-middle-class college students in the 1960s as a form of symbolic abandonment of their parents' class position, and of students' sympathy with underdogs. More recently, the trademark uniform of the construction industry, the Carhartt brand of drab tan outerwear, has similarly become upper-middle-class student fashion wear that is available in shorts, underwear, and other items in a variety of colors, and even plaid patterns. "Carhartts" went from mundane to cool in a very short period of time.

Needless to say, the high-popular culture continuum suggests that different cultural practices may be linked to social power as modes of social exclusion and domination. Beyond the simple fact that high culture may be expensive to partake in, groups also are stratified by their differing knowledge of what cultural appetites supposedly constitute good tastes. Even subordinate groups may develop varieties of cultural capital that seek to imitate elite culture, as the next example shows.

Interpreting Pink Flamingos: Everyday Expressions of Social Positions

When I was a child, my parents often took me to visit my great-aunt Jen, who lived in a small, inauspicious home in a Midwestern rural town. Aunt Jen never had much wealth. She was a widow of a working-class man with whom she had survived the Great Depression and much other economic hardship. Her house was cluttered with treasures of years past—family pictures, china plates, embroidered pillows, old books and magazines, a spoon collection, and what not. She didn't have much, but what she did have she was proud of.

When the weather was nice, I played outside in her yard—or, I should say that I tried to play, because the yard also was cluttered. It was amazing, for nearly everywhere you turned there were various lawn ornaments. There were birdbaths, cast concrete likenesses of ducks, squirrels, rabbits, and deer. Strange, mirrored metallic balls stood on pedestals. There was a statue of the Virgin Mary sheltered in a little shrine made out of an old bathtub that was sunk upright in the ground (my great-aunt was very Catholic). It must have been impossible to mow the yard, and I suspect that no birds dared traverse this bizarre flowering of folk culture to take advantage of the birdbaths. The highlight of the whole extravaganza, though, was the flock of plastic, pink flamingos that were staked in the ground. Aunt Jen took particular pride in these ornaments, as she periodically moved the flock to different front yard locations.

It might be tempting to suppose that this woman just had strange tastes, but the reality of the matter probably runs deeper than that. After all, she did not invent the pink flamingos, nor was she the only one who practiced this type of landscaping. Indeed, there were other homes in her area that displayed similar, if not identical, gaudy ornaments. Moreover, I am sure that she must have received her fair share of compliments about her arrangement from fellow connoisseurs of this genre of décor. While I naturally didn't realize it as a child, it now seems to me likely that the pink flamingos were cultural expressions of a specific amalgam of social class, region, age, gender, and perhaps other social structural positions of this woman, that is, she shared this culture with similar others. Strangely enough, it is also possible that the flamingos were in her eyes an emulation of groups that she did not belong to. The state of Florida, where Americans would encounter flamingos, had emerged as an affluent vacation and retirement destination by this time. While Aunt Jen had never traveled, and would only have known about Florida through magazines, the plastic flamingos may have offered some symbolic participation in the exotic leisure life of such people. I believe that at that time the flamingos had multiple layers of cultural and social significance.

Certainly, not every person in Aunt Jen's social situation culturally "spoke" of who they were in the exact same way (through flamingos), but people of similar structural position nevertheless tend to develop a distinctive, bounded, "repertoire" of cultural tastes from which they select particular expressions. In other words, if you were to look at the whole set of cultural tastes (food, music, magazines, etc.) of older, female, rural, working-class people during this period, you would find very palpable differences from, say, young, male, urban, upper-class people. I would even venture to guess that you would find fewer pink flamingos adorning the yards of the latter group.

A Virgin Mary shrine is framed by pink flamingo ornaments (left), and a tiny trailer home is adorned with similar ornaments (right). Even the most mundane cultural objects may have deeply embedded meanings for the groups who display them. Can you imagine seeing these particular cultural expressions in the yards of wealthy suburban housing developments? Probably you cannot, but why not? Social groups create distinctive cultural repertoires to remind them that they are members of the same group, and to mark boundaries between themselves and other groups. (Left: © Philip Gould/ CORBIS. Right: © Dave G. Houser/CORBIS.)

We need not restrict ourselves to the history of pink flamingos to see the general utility of these ideas. It is a revealing exercise to travel through different types of neighborhoods—wealthy suburbs, working-class row houses, and poverty-stricken ghettos—with a mindful eye to differences in landscaping and dwellings that are outward expressions of profound social and economic differences. Take a ride. The subtle, "natural" layout of suburban homes, with their rock gardens, driftwood, trimmed bushes, and ornamental trees, and their matching earth-tone house colors, sometimes contrasts with the loud, forthright display of home colors, decorations, and household possessions (cars, boats, swing sets, etc.) in working-class neighborhoods, or the simple absence of distinguishing markers in the rental properties of the poorest neighborhoods. Perhaps the subtlety of wealthier neighborhoods says culturally, "We *are* rich and noble; we don't have to *show it*," whereas working-class people are more prone to public display of their possessions, as if to say, "See, we're making it." Today, in the same rural area where my aunt lived, many farmers have acquired television satellite dishes (not just the little ones, but also the NASA-size monstrosities!) that they commonly plant right in their front yards for all to see, rather than in a more discrete, equally functional location. Our manners of consumption appear to vary by social group. It is not difficult to overlay other social filters, such as race and ethnicity, to reveal further modes of cultural expression. For example, furniture stores in urban, ethnic Italian neighborhoods often carry ornate, gold-leafed pieces that would seem out-of-place in stores frequented by members of other racial and ethnic groups. Grocery stores and restaurants obviously vary along similar lines.

So, why do these different groups produce and live distinctive cultural meanings? It would be shallow, and also bigoted, to explain this fact by saying that these groups "just are that way," as though it were some genetic predisposition. The simple fact that groups change their cultures over time, and that some elements of poor people's culture get adopted by rich people (music is a prime example) shows the futility of such thought. In any case, there is no intrinsically greater value or morality in earth-tone versus pink homes, in Volvos versus pickup trucks, or in Beethoven versus rappers NWA (Niggas with Attitude) or Nelly. Likewise, the argument that "it's all money" is very superficial because there is significant variation in culture even within economic categories of people (e.g., differences by race, ethnicity, occupation, and age). A more penetrating explanation of cultural differences must recognize that these expressions are complex phenomena that remind individuals of who they are as social beings, and proclaim to others that they are active parts of larger groups that demand peculiar behaviors among their members.

"Lions and Tigers and Bears—Oh My!" The Cultural and Political Construction of Social Problems

Crime, drugs, school violence, terrorists, teen pregnancy, welfare, drunk driving, and cults—the very words evoke strong, fearful emotions in most Americans that our society has gone awry. Like Dorothy in *The Wizard of Oz*, these images of demons in the social forest seem so real at first glance that we seldom question their authenticity. And why should we not be alarmed, given the constant media and political reminders that we hear about these "issues" being the most pressing ones facing the country? The nightly television news features a steady, monotonous litany of stories about street crime and court sentencing, even while we learn from reliable FBI and census sources that overall crime rates are not rising, but falling slightly. We are led by other media sources to believe that priests are pedophiles, that the child next door is a terrorist in disguise, and that postal workers are walking time bombs. Few of these imaginary dangers have factual evidence to support the levels of fear that they arouse.

We learn from politicians and the media that welfare is a social problem because so many people are abusing the system. The 1990s witnessed politicians garnering votes by playing on popular hatred of the poor with calls for "an end to welfare as we know it," and "welfare to work" programs. The imagery was that of poor, primarily black, inner-city–dwelling "welfare mamas" and renegade black men who would rather collect government pay checks "generation after generation" than do an honest day's work for pay. The facts about poverty and welfare recipients fly in the face of this sort of mythology:

- The majority of the poor are white, many from rural areas.
- Children are the single largest category of poor people.
- Poor families on average are about the same size as other families.
- The majority of the adult poor do work, many full time, and still are poor.
- Many disabled and mentally ill poor people are unable to work.
- Only 1 in 100 of the poor remain poor every year over a ten-year period.
- At some point in their lives, 1 in 4 Americans fall into poverty.
- The United States has the least generous welfare system of all industrialized countries.

The "social problem" of welfare recipients is largely code language for racial/ethnic hatred, particularly of blacks. Historically, government assistance was seen as an entitlement, not a problem, in the post–World War II era. As late as the 1960s, under the Johnson administration, the nation launched a "War on Poverty" that recognized that the poor were poor for reasons beyond their control. It has only been in the late twentieth century, as more blacks were extended benefits that were previously held back, that the mass media, politicians, and racial majority groups reversed public policy to a "War on the Poor," as Herbert Gans (1995) termed it.

Meanwhile, issues such as the widening income gap between rich and poor (including 1 in 5 children living in poverty); the deleterious effects of free trade agreements with Mexico (NAFTA); corporate global sweatshops; monopolistic businesses (Microsoft and many others); inadequate health care for large segments of the population; mass marketing of toxic chemicals to consumers (e.g., Dow Chemical's now banned Dursban nerve agent pesticide); the worst mass transit system of all industrialized countries; and the deterioration of sewers, bridges, highways, and school infrastructure receive scant, if any, mention. The syndicated press fares little better than television in identifying truly high-priority public issues that threaten our society. How is it that Americans worry more about things that don't even affect them, than about basic and ominous problems?

More precisely, we should ask how particular "social problems" become objects of national scrutiny and fear, while other troubling issues remain unknown and are not addressed. Social problems in America frequently are "bad people" problems, in other words, deviant and criminal problems, so we further should ask how certain people become deviants and criminals, while others escape these fates. These questions about social problems and deviant people open an ideal forum for sociological perspectives on society and culture. The **social and cultural construction of social problems** perspective addresses these concerns in a manner that combines insights of symbolic interactionist and conflict theories (Heiner 2002).

There are several basic propositions that sociologists working within this research genre advance in analyzing the development of social problems. First, selection of a purported societal condition as "problematic" depends on successful *cultural definition* of the situation as one that deserves attention and has a solution. Second, since powerful, well-organized groups are more likely to affect the media and political organizations that play the largest roles in culturally defining situations as problematic, those issues that best suit the interests of such power groups are most likely to emerge as social problems. Finally, the interests of power groups usually are limited in some respects by the independent (autonomous) interests of media and political cultural producers themselves in consumer and voter markets.

The selection of social problems is informed by the interactions of a variety of parties. Neither power groups, nor media and political figures can muster public support for just any designated problem. Rather, social problems tend to play on existing public sentiments and prior histories of problematic issues and people. In the United States, crime, alcohol, sexuality, and youths have legacies associated with them that stretch back at least to the nineteenth century (Beisel 1997). These issues nearly always are available, with new twists here and there, as "plausible" problems in the public consciousness. Joseph Gusfield's (1963, 1981) studies demonstrate that alcohol use was originally raised as a social problem by WASP (White Anglo-Saxon Protestant) women's temperance societies in the nineteenth century as a way to address marital infidelity among husbands who frequented saloons and to stigmatize the lifestyles of immigrant groups, such as the Irish. In the 1920s, the prohibition movement incorporated much of the antiethnic cultural imagery of the earlier movements in its successful campaign to ban alcohol. The anti–drunk driving movement of the late twentieth century and the ongoing identification of college students as "binge drinkers" were easy targets due to the prior, constructed history of alcohol as a legitimate social problem.

Other social problems may have objectively damaging societal implications that go unnoticed until they get fashioned from scratch by well-organized interest groups. The environmental movement is a good example of such a phenomenon. Environmental concerns had little history prior to the 1970s, when the movement took hold. Typically, these efforts to forge entirely new issues have faced opposition from threatened power-holders and reluctant mass media managers and politicians who have questioned the market and vote-getting potential for such issues. Under these circumstances, grass roots efforts to shape popular thought about the seriousness of conditions sometimes have proven successful in capturing audiences, and eventually gaining media attention. The introduction of the cultural icon of "toxic waste" in the 1970s, for example, was an extremely successful strategy for environmentalists.

The perceived "solvability" of issues is another important determinant of their status as social problems, and of the simplicity with which the nature of so many social problems is presented. If "cults" are manufactured as the problem, then there are a number of obvious educational and legal measures that can be taken to stem their supposed growth. The same can be said about supposed epidemics of drug abuse, such as the recent uproar over the drug Ecstasy—police and other authorities can easily target the user population as youths who tend to congregate in certain locations, bust them, and give tough sentencing that shows that the problem is being handled. Meanwhile other drug abuse that is firmly entrenched in societal centers of power and difficult to change, such as the powder cocaine industry, fails to gain recognition. From a strategic standpoint, politicians and bureaucrats who are supposed to be in charge of the national welfare have much to gain in terms of public legitimacy by addressing issues that are at once perceived as problems by the public, and that seem to have palpable solutions. Conversely, authorities have much to lose by acknowledging problems that they cannot rectify. This sheds some light on the triviality of many social problems that make headlines in the newspapers. If crime is not really on the rise, there is little to be lost by launching a crime war. If schools already are safe, a campaign to make schools safe is bound to succeed. Public audiences rather like to think that their government works, and that problems have easy solutions, so their susceptibility to such ploys is high. Additionally, the American market for trashy news that serves a greater entertainment than information function is large (Kerbal 1999). The market for complex presentation of distressing social problems simply does not fit America's current cultural definition of news intake as an admixture of leisurely, fun activity and freak show entertainment.

There is a further, compelling argument to be made that privileged societal groups benefit from the public's fascination with these juicy, ultimately inconsequential, issues. When popular consciousness is busied with the outcome of the Elian Gonzalez deportation case, the O. J. Simpson trial, and the ongoing circus of talk show topics, other issues that might challenge existing societal power centers are not raised for serious consideration. Network television news is notorious for its focus on titillating subject matter to the neglect of larger social issues. Whether by the elite's own initiatives, or by market and voting considerations of media and politicians, or both, many social problems assuredly divert popular resistance to social inequalities to emotionally charged sideshows.

The symbolic drama of these morality plays, with their good and evil players, is quite evident in the construction of many social problems. Predictably, the evildoers usually depicted in these problems are members of relatively powerless societal groups who, in the American tradition, misleadingly are portrayed as bad individuals. Sociologists engaged in **labeling theory** have long known that an adequate explanation of deviance needs to take account of the historical and political processes whereby definitions of deviant behavior, such as "marijuana user," "welfare mama," and "militia member" get created. In other words, sociologists turn the analytical tables toward authorities that define entire categories of group behavior as problematic. Many of these problems, and the people implicated with them, do not really have sound empirical evidence to back them up as objectively troublesome issues, nor do they constitute grave dangers to the nation (Glassner 1999). At best, they tend to be exaggerations, and at worst they are malicious lies that make miserable the lives of entire groups of people.

CULTURAL PRODUCTION, DISTRIBUTION, AND INTERPRETATION

Have you ever wondered exactly how some cultural objects and/or the people who produce them ever attained their significance in societies? For example, nearly everyone is familiar with those fuzzy little toy creatures called "Beanie Babies," but how did these items become objects of such phenomenal consumer passion? We might ask similar questions about other elements of our culture. Whether we liked the film or not, most people are familiar with *Titanic* and its surrounding cult of devotees. What made this film a blockbuster hit, while other worthy films have languished in obscurity?

Clearly, people make culture, but why do certain individuals play a greater role than others? Consider singer Elvis Presley and psychologist Sigmund Freud. Why did these individuals make it in music and the intellectual world, respectively? Were there not other talented people who did equally good work, yet remained undiscovered? A more troubling notion for some people concerns the cultural development of Christianity. Why, among all the prophets of biblical times, did Jesus Christ emerge as the "superstar"? What role did his disciples play in moving Christianity from a small cult to a mass religion? Perhaps there were similarities between Jesus Christ, Gautama Buddha, and Confucius in terms of the cultural development of their beliefs by schools of thought that followed them?

Sociology offers unusual insights that may answer these and similar questions. First, though, it may be worthwhile to consider shortcomings in some commonsense explanations of these cultural innovations. The most obvious, if misguided, idea is that maverick, individual geniuses produce cultural forms. In fact, this notion of personal creativity is exactly what popular accounts of cultural entrepreneurship point to. This businesslike model of rugged individualists who strike out on their own, breaking with all tradition to display their objective talent to audiences that passively and unambiguously pass judgment on "good" and "bad" cultural products, is deeply flawed. The reason, quite simply, is that this model fails to take into account the multiple social relationships that inform the cultural production process.

Successful cultural creators, such as singer Mariah Carey or director Stanley Kubrick, seldom are the utterly isolated individuals that the imagery of "starving artists, toiling away in the seclusion of their run-down apartments" brings to mind. In fact, continuing social isolation of artists is a very strong predictor of *failure* in terms of recognition of their cultural products. Even among the few noteworthy examples of isolated individual producers who posthumously get "discovered," the discovery process itself generally is social in nature. While it is true in some cases that people may work alone on cultural production, their work ultimately must pass muster through a complex variety of social sieves. Within these pipelines of cultural production we find heavily socialized creative processes that are embedded in school-taught or other forms of institutionalized training. Large organizations such as AOL/Time Warner administer activities in hundreds of cultural outlets in film, home video, cable and regular television, publishing, music, sports, and other endeavors. Those products that "make it" do so by virtue of intimate connections with other social actors who are in positions either to advance or snuff out the popularity of cultural forms. Those individuals who succeed in getting their work out invariably follow the contours of very well trodden career paths. We need a conceptual model that illuminates these dynamics of **cultural production**.

A Basic Model of Cultural Production Processes

As Wendy Griswold (1994) and David Croteau and William Hoynes (2000) have shown, a good model of cultural production needs to take account of organizational processes that whittle down the vast number of cultural producers to the few who in fact become cultural icons. It also will need to give just due to the influences that consumers of culture have on producers. Some key elements of such a model of **cultural production, cultural distribution**, and **audience interpretation** are depicted in Figure 3.3.

To begin, imagine the total supply of individual producers of a given type of cultural object, say all aspiring fashion designers. In most cases, there is an oversupply of requisite competence among individual producers, such that the entire pool cannot advance to positions of influence within organizational centers of cultural production as producers. In the case of fashion designers, not all the highly competent producers can go on as designers for Tommy

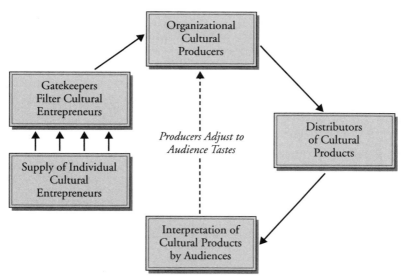

Figure 3.3   Cultural Production, Distribution, and Interpretation

Hilfiger or similar organizations. The question then becomes, "How do some producers move on, while others get left behind?"

Intermediary **gatekeepers**, such as schools that credential competence (e.g., Parsons School of Design, or Fashion Institute of Technology), talent agents, and personal references, act as "filters" that reduce the eligible pool to a limited number of people who can be absorbed in the cultural industry under question. While some members of the pool may be cut because of utter incompetence, the assumption here is that large numbers of perfectly qualified people don't make it. These filtering processes thus are somewhat arbitrary, insofar as they are based on luck and social connections of successful producers, rather than the incompetence of all of those individuals who get passed by.

Once individual cultural producers enter larger organizations, their creativity often is tempered by the demands of organizational **production of culture**, such as market competition. Adjustments to cultural styles of fellow workers, and of the industry as a whole, are common. Cultural organizations such as Tommy Hilfiger, themselves are embedded in complex **cultural distribution** relationships with other organizations. Tommy Hilfiger jeans must gain entry to various industry fashion shows where the products may be publicized to chain stores such as The Gap that ultimately order and sell the pants to consumers. Separate advertising agencies may be contracted to build a suitable cultural image for the jeans vis-à-vis competitors, based on their understanding and targeting of specific consumer audiences.

The entrepreneurial model of culture also suggests an oversimplified audience of culture consumers. In this model, people seem either to be passive receptors of cultural forms and meanings that are imposed from above by powerful, supply-side producers, or alternatively to be isolated demand-side "experts" who consciously weigh the merit of various cultural objects that are put before them and thereby drive cultural markets. In reality, **audience interpretation** of culture is far more complex than this scenario suggests, as are the interactions between audiences and producers.

The meanings that cultural products have for audiences may be ambiguous and variable. Audiences may alter the intended uses and meanings of cultural objects, and producers may pick up on these trends in order to fine-tune product marketing. Within the jeans industry, a good example of this process was the development of "pre-washed" and "distressed" jeans. Consumers altered the meaning of the original products and came to value worn and aged jeans. Manufacturers responded by appropriating this audience transformation of products in jeans that already looked worn when consumers bought them. The authenticity of country music artists is established in a similar dialogue between producers and audiences (Peterson 1997). Even the development of flavored potato chips (sour cream, cheese, bacon, etc.) was an analogous process of producer adaptation to consumers' cultural creativity in combining the chips with other foods.

Change in the meaning of products sometimes unfolds over long stretches of time. Mouthwashes, of all things, exhibit this tendency. In England, prior to the invention of tooth brushing, people naturally had atrocious breath. An enterprising person developed a special sauce with a strong odor that, when swished around in the mouth, covered up people's bad breath—Worcestershire sauce. Only later, through audience innovations in the use of the sauce, did this now famous condiment take on value as a steak sauce. So whatever happened to people's breath? Well, tooth brushing solved much of the problem, and what remained was addressed with a new mouthwash called Listerine. This antigerm agent itself originally was developed for a different purpose—as a soak for athletes' foot fungal infections. Only after it failed to work in that area did it emerge with a new meaning.

Finally, it is important to note that there is a great deal of conservatism built into the organizational dynamics of culture production. **Organizational innovation** in culture production usually takes place in close relation to competitors. At any given historical period in the fashion industry the varieties of casual slacks available at shopping mall clothing stores (from straight leg to bell-bottom, from hip-huggers to grunge) are quite limited. There tends to be a great deal of similarity among available jeans. When the "baggie look" is "in," everyone produces baggies, with minor variations among producers to mark their product. To take another example from the publishing industry, it is much easier for an author to publish a work that is only marginally different from existing works in the field, than to make a complete break with tradition (as this book does, I hope!). There are risks involved not just for the author who wishes to write an utterly innovative piece, but also for the publisher who must weigh the market prospects of such work among audiences. For this reason, *limited* creativity tends to happen within the genre boundaries of writing. Authors seldom stray into virtually unknown territory. The same thing might be said of many other fields of cultural production. The network television animated show *The Simpsons* featured a certain level of lewdness that a later series, *King of the Hill*, copied in large measure. *South Park* appeared in a different venue, cable television, and extended this genre in some respects, but not to levels that audiences would find unrecognizable. In the music industry, beginning in the early 1990s, a series of female vocalists gained national recognition by offering different versions of a popular, high-pitched, whiny, teenage "waif" sound in their lyrics (e.g., Nina Persson of the Cardigans, Jewel, and the Spice Girls). More recent beneficiaries of this organizational tradition include singers Britney Spears and Christina Aguilera, who have successfully competed in this cultural market. Organizational processes severely constrain cultural creativity in each of the above cases.

At this point, it may be helpful to explore a couple of case studies of these various cultural production, distribution, and interpretation forces. The first example will be drawn from the music industry, while the second one is derived from human uses of animals.

Making Chili Peppers: Organizational Processes in the Rise of a Band

If you are an audiophile (music lover), you probably have in your collection of recordings a number of artists who are virtual unknowns on the national music scene, or who were "one-hit wonders" who quickly receded to "has been" status. There may be artists within your holdings who made several albums that remained of only local interest in a given city or region. As a rock and blues fan, I have in my collection quite a few of these types that I suspect most people never have heard of—McKendree Spring, Bill Quateman, The Siegel Schwall Band—see what I mean! I also have one tape entitled *The Red Hot Chili Peppers*, made by a new band of the same name in 1983. This selection sat idle for many years, as I listened to it only once and didn't really like it much. It turns out that not many other people were enthralled by this album when it came out either, but as some readers already may know, RHCP eventually rose to great fame with later releases, and even this first tape sounds better to me now, by virtue of that fact. Their case is instructive whether one likes their music or not.

In many ways, RHCP was an unlikely success story, and one that is instructive about the sociology of cultural production. Again, the first album just wasn't very well received, and their third work, *The Uplift Mojo Party Plan*, likewise initially flopped. Several band members had debilitating drug problems (the original lead guitarist died of a heroin overdose), and turnover of band members was a chronic problem. Still, there were a number of notable material and strategic advantages that kept the band afloat, and some prototypical **cultural production** mechanisms that eventually catapulted RHCP to fame.

Originally, the band was called Anthym, and they had reasonably strong connections to the music and film worlds of Los Angeles and Hollywood. The first band members were friends at Los Angeles' Fairfax High School. Bass player Michael Balzary ("Flea") was born in Australia, the son of jazz musician Walter Urban. Balzary played in the Fairfax Philharmonic Orchestra, and he counted actor River Phoenix among his closest friends. Two Jewish youths, Jack Irons (drums) and Hillel Slovakand (lead guitar) formed the remainder of the original trio. Slovakand was born in Israel, and he modeled his music and life after his idol and cultural model Jimi Hendrix (right down to his death by heroin overdose). A fourth member, Anthony Kiedis (vocals), was a "groupie" who followed the band around various Los Angeles club engagements and joined the band to form RHCP. Kiedis' father is a wealthy actor named Blackie Dammett, who earned the nickname "Head Honcho" for his role in promoting the band and running its website. All in all, RHCP had some very impressive **organizational resources** at its disposal from the outset.

Even with these ties, the band needed to maneuver its way through a variety of common **gatekeeper organization** "filters" that separate and advance some music, and exclude other forms. With only two original songs in their repertoire in early 1983, RHCP was able to negotiate two initial "breaks"—opening for an established band (Run-DMC) at a local music festival, and sponsorship by a talent scout named Mark "Rooster" Richardson for appearances at some reputable Los Angeles clubs, including the prestigious Kit Kat Klub.

The Red Hot Chili Peppers band members include "Flea" (left) and Anthony Kiedis (right). From a sociological perspective, this band's members easily could have ended up in routine careers outside of stardom. The sociological puzzle is to explain why some cultural producers succeed, while others fade into obscurity. Social and organizational processes create opportunities and constraints that play a key role here. Explore the social histories of your own favorite cultural producers to see what social circumstances and forces created them. (© Reuters NewMedia Inc./CORBIS)

These club appearances gained RHCP sufficient legitimacy in the Los Angeles music circuit to move them one step forward on the organizational path to success—they were given their first record contract with EMI America to produce seven albums. The EMI label, and the professional promotional staff of that organization, would try to help RHCP get further concert appearances around the country, solicit disc jockeys and program managers to provide airtime for their songs on radio stations, and sponsor cameo appearances in films and other cultural media. With the contract, however, came additional organizational constraints on RHCP's creativity. Their first producer, Andy Gill, was partly responsible for a change in RHCP's musical style that led to the miserably disappointing first album. Two new producers followed in rapid succession, one who dropped the band because of their inconsistent performance and drug problems. By 1987, RHCP remained a marginal club band, despite intense promotional efforts, including a European tour. There was little reason to believe they ever would do much better.

Things began to change in 1988. That year, RHCP lost its lead guitarist to heroin overdose and added an eighteen-year-old graduate of the Musician's Institute of Technology, John Frusciante, as his replacement. One thing that RHCP always had going for it was nudity—and lots of it. Kiedis brought the band some publicity, for better or worse, when he was charged and convicted of sexually harassing a woman backstage (he exposed himself). The band had always displayed plenty of skin, usually playing bare-chested, and sometimes revealing more. There was much sexually provocative material in their lyrics and onstage gestures. This sexuality probably reached its height in the 1988 release *The Abbey Road E.P.*, the cover of which portrayed the band crossing in a row that infamous street that appeared on the Beatles' original cover, except that the RHCP members were pictured nude, save for long white socks which covered their penises. Alas, the album was a success. Of course, many other bands included sexuality in their personas, so it is doubtful that sex alone could have done much more than keep a precariously rocking RHCP ship temporarily afloat in troubled times.

The real rise to notoriety of RHCP took place around 1990. They built their own reputation by forging ties to other centers of organizational reputability across the entertainment industry. Their successes in these efforts likely fed off one another in a spiraling rise to stardom that brought larger and larger audiences to listen to and develop their own interpretive "appreciation" of RHCP albums new and old.

In 1989, RHCP released *Mother's Milk*, which followed up on the success of *The Abbey Road E.P.* in terms of its style. Several connections to other cultural industries subsequently emerged. A band member was invited to sing the national anthem at a Detroit Pistons basketball game. Promoters arranged for cuts from their albums to appear in a number of 1990 films, including *Pretty Woman, Back to the Future, Point Break*, and *My Own Private Idaho*.

Suddenly, the RHCP members were stars, even in the music industry. They left EMI for a $10 million contract with Warner Brothers. Appearances with other stars, such as Nirvana and Pearl Jam in 1991, further cemented their image as legitimate box office attractions. Their song "Give It Away," off the *BloodSugarSexMajik* album, won a Grammy Award the same year. In another cultural medium, their music video won an MTV award in 1992. The band again temporarily had to replace its lead guitarist, but RHCP now was sufficiently established that it easily weathered such mishaps, going on to star in the Lollapalooza concert and to play with a host of celebrities at Woodstock (the second one, where RHCP dressed as lightbulbs in an act that became part of cult lore about the band).

RHCP crossed an important threshold by 1995, with the release of *One Hot Minute*. No longer a band that was *seeking* organizational and cultural legitimacy, RHCP now occupied a position in the cultural hierarchy that controlled access to the cultural mainstream, and potentially could spread its own success and power. The band offered its services to Alanis Morisette's budding career by playing in her song "You Oughta Know" in 1995, and was solicited for the soundtrack to the hit film *Twister* in 1996. Vocalist Kiedis even was able to strike up relations with the world religious/political community by spiritualizing with the exiled Tibetan Dalai Lama in India for a period of time, and reciprocating the favor with the band's appearance in a Free Tibet concert.

A considerable lull in productivity followed RHCP's mid-1990s success, until the release of a new album in 1999. The second time through organizational filters and audience interpretation of songs is easier than the first, as RHCP well knows. RHCP no longer faced doubting disc jockeys who would not play their songs, music store purchasing agents who bypassed their releases, and people in audiences, like myself, who passed quick judgment on their efforts. *Californication* (1999) was eagerly anticipated by the music industry and audiences as part of what finally could be construed as an ongoing legacy of the band. In April 2000, RHCP was at the pinnacle of a most tenuous climb to cultural reputability—on the cover of *Rolling Stone* magazine. Success bred further success as the July 2002 release *By the Way* streaked to number one on the charts in sixteen countries. Now, even RHCP's early failures are being rereleased and reinterpreted as part of an "inevitable" rise to stardom.

Pets or Meat? The Interpretation of Cultural Products

Michael Moore's brilliant film *Roger and Me* (1987) has a segment in which an unemployed woman in poverty-stricken Flint, Michigan, is selling rabbits from her home in order to make ends meet. She offered the bunnies either as "pets" or as "meat" (gutted, skinned, and ready to cook). The dual **cultural meaning** of these rabbits that the woman recognized for marketing purposes is instructive. There is a whole sociological subfield dedicated to the study of pets and society. Many animals, as well as other cultural objects ranging from novels to sports, assume different meanings in varying social contexts. These meanings are set in a variety of group, organizational, and societal structures that they at once reflect and sustain. Consider, for example, the case of dogs, "man's (and presumably woman's, as well) best friend."

In the United States today, the dominant, although not exclusive, cultural meaning of dogs is that of companions or pets. Many people regard their dogs as regular members of their families, sending them (and themselves) to training schools, holding funeral and visitation services for dead dogs that then are buried in pet cemeteries, and seeking pet bereavement counselors to help them cope with their losses. We give dogs names, and provide them with food and shelter that sometime approach human levels of comfort. Entire economic markets are built on the provision of dog toys, clothing, specialty foods, and the like. Dog product conventions and sanctioned dog shows are huge draws all across America. Many dogs actually have more money spent on them for preventive medical care than do average human beings in the poorer strata of the nation. Some dogs even achieve media celebrity status, as the cases of "Lassie" on television and "Spuds MacKenzie" in beer advertising suggest. For most Americans, dogs are utterly useless except in this companionship role, and they are very expensive to keep. The notion of having a "dog's life" surely refers to these pets.

Not all Americans view their dogs solely or even primarily as pets, of course. Some dogs have other ostensible purposes for their owners. The protection function of dogs is another cultural meaning that people ascribe to these animals, where they are used as home and business guards, and in police work. Seeing Eye dogs for blind people serve an obvious, beneficial purpose. A sizable number of dogs are used in hunting, although ironically the game that such dogs assist in killing is not always consumed. Dogs are raced in gambling ventures, although again the utilitarian value of such practices for the public good is dubious.

The companion versus utilitarian cultural meanings of dogs, and breed preference, vary remarkably across U.S. social groups. A direct linkage exists between people's social structural positions and their cultural beliefs about the appropriate place of dogs in relation to humans, and about what types of dogs within the species are most desirable. American men and women, for example, differ considerably in their tastes for dogs. Many males tend to avoid association with toy breeds, such as Pomeranians, Pekingese, and Lhasa Apsos, that many females cherish for their petite size. Males favor more often what they regard as "real" dogs, that is, larger hunting and working dogs such as the Golden Retriever, German Shepherd, and Mastiff, that mirror their images of masculinity (sometimes regardless of the actual sex—male or female—of the dog in question).

Economic structure also plays a part in cultural tastes for dogs, where poorer groups in the United States tend to value dogs more for their uses as hunters or protectors than richer people. Because of poor people's frequent use of dogs as guards, individuals from this background often carry a culture of fear and distrust with respect to other people's dogs that is less pronounced among upper-middle-class professional and managerial workers and their families who have "pet" dogs. Moreover, the upper-middle class is more likely to own "purebred" dogs of all sorts, as opposed to mixed-breed "mutts." These purebred animals are invariably more expensive to buy, sometimes running in excess of $1,000 for prized bloodlines, than dogs that are born of the normal promiscuity that marks the species, and that often are free for the taking.

For the upper-middle class, such purebred dogs often assume a meaning that stretches beyond mere companionship or marginal utility, to the status value of dogs that are rare and expensive. That is, they use their purebred dogs as cultural ways of saying "I am better than you" to poorer people who must own mutts (or "equal to you," in the case of interactions with other purebred owners of the same class). It is a mark of distinction for such groups to be able to spend unwarranted sums of money on essentially useless animals, much as $150,000 automobiles hardly can be justified for mere transportation purposes (Veblen 1899). Here, dogs are a form of **cultural capital** that, unlike the economic capital that gets exchanged in markets, is "capital" in the form of cultural knowledge, tastes, and meanings that get exchanged in social interactions. Of course, this rarity of purebred dogs is simply the result of an organizational process of exclusive breeding among registered kennels, and not a fact of nature. As in many other economic markets, scarcity of supply in the dog market is manipulated by self-interested sellers who get more money for "rare" dogs, and by buyers who get the prestige value of owning a rare dog. Innumerable dog shows and field trials stamp individual dogs as better than others, while the American Kennel Club certifies the lineage of such dogs.

We see then, in the American case, tremendous variability in the **audience interpretation** of dogs by different groups. Far from being a random distribution of tastes, these differences are tightly intertwined with elements of U.S. social structure. These cultural differences become even more vivid as we scan even wider social structural terrain, to the differences between nations. One such case is Korea.

Much has been made of the profound differences between dogs in some sectors of the Korean population and in the West, including the United States. While some Korean dogs indeed are kept as pets (especially the Jinko breed), others are considered legitimate meat for human consumption. The lines between these two meanings can be quite fuzzy (no pun intended) in Korea, much to the misfortune of some pet dogs. "Rarity" of dogs, in the Korean case, can mean something quite different from in the American one!

There are a number of organizational and other social processes that inform Korean dog-eating practices. While the practice of commercial dog production is illegal in Korea, the underground market for dog meat as a cultural good is too large to allow suppression of the industry. Dogs are farm-raised in large complexes where crowded pens restrict their movement, and thus keep their meat tender, much as veal and other meats in the United States are intentionally constrained during breeding. The dogs never leave these filthy pens until they are readied for market. That process involves blowtorching the live dogs en masse in a pen until they are dead and their juices are seared within their charred bodies. The dogs then are transported to open-air markets, where they are stacked like fish, with their eyes bulging and their teeth bared in a final grimace. Not all Koreans eat dogs though, any more than all Americans eat beef liver or oysters. In fact, another social structure intersects in the demand for dog meat—gender. Some Korean men prize dog meat because they believe that it enhances their virility.

As Elspeth Probyn (2000) brilliantly illustrates, we are what we eat, and we eat what we are—food establishes our identities and vice versa. Korean dog eaters simply do not culturally define dogs as pets, nor do they see them as particularly close to humans in the chain of animals. Few Americans eat dog meat, or horsemeat, for the opposite reason. Americans have constructed beliefs that dogs and horses are rather "close" to humans. After all, what American can imagine eating the old television stars Lassie the dog, Flipper the dolphin, Bambi the deer, or Mr. Ed the horse? As cultural anthropologist Marshall Sahlins (1976) perceptively noted, "Edibility inversely is related to humanity." We tend to eat things that we see as being unlike ourselves, and to avoid things that we imagine are nearer to humans. Of course, this principle is but one of many that governs the sociology of food. People also develop dietary aversions and other fears of animals that seem "strange" to us from the standpoint of our own, culturally based system for classifying creatures. Mary Douglas (1966) contends that such animals are "monsters" that don't fit our limited cognitive schemes. The Book of Leviticus in the Old Testament of the Bible is an interesting compendium of ancient Israelites' thoughts on such matters, given their understanding of biological categories. Snakes, for example, were animals that looked like lizards, but had no legs, and thus were an "abomination" that could not be eaten. Other animals and insects are minutely examined in Leviticus for conformity with the prevailing system of belief about "proper" animal traits. So, perhaps we have here yet another tool to aid us in the understanding of cultural differences, namely that things that don't conform to our existing system of cultural meanings are labeled dangerous, disgusting, evil phenomena.

CONCLUSION

The goal of this chapter has been to show how basic sociological concepts can be used to examine phenomena that range from everyday events to large-scale political and economic realities. With these tools in hand, it should be possible to extend from the examples I have provided to matters that are closest to your life.

Conceptually, it is possible to distinguish social interactions, cultural beliefs and meanings, and social structural patterns. Lived experience, of course, is a jumble of these categories of existence. In the middle of a lecture neither the professor nor the students usually give pause to dissect their performance, its cultural assumptions, or the various social structural realities that they at once are enacting, and that provide the templates for their actions. They "just do it," as the famous Nike advertisements say. Sociologists themselves spend most of their lives caught up in the very forces that they study, but they are able to step back from the tide of life experience in their work.

The reason why sociological separation and analysis of these elements of social life are worthwhile is that they allow us to cut through the illusion that society simply "is the way it is," to get at explanations for why things are as they are. These diagnostics are preconditions for informed efforts toward social change—for "making a difference," as the adage goes—and for preserving what is desirable about the social worlds we have concocted. Societies and their component cultural and structural organs are extremely complex phenomena that deserve serious, sophisticated study by anyone who wishes to assume responsible citizenship or leadership within them.

SUGGESTIONS FOR FURTHER STUDY

Wendy Griswold. 1994. *Cultures and Societies in a Changing World.* Thousand Oaks, CA: Pine Forge Press.

Michelle Lamont and Marcel Fournier (eds.). 1992. *Cultivating Differences: Symbolic Boundaries and the Making of Inequality.* Chicago: University of Chicago Press.

These two books are a good beginning point for an understanding of culture, social structure, and social interaction. Griswold's excellent little book gives a stimulating overview of the culture–social structure relationship. Lamont and Fournier's volume offers a diverse array of articles on the role of culture in creating and sustaining social inequalities.

David Croteau and William Hoynes. 2000. *Media/Society: Industries, Images, and Audiences.* Thousand Oaks, CA: Pine Forge Press.

C. Lee Harrington and Denise Bielby (eds.). 2001. *Popular Culture: Production and Consumption.* Oxford: Blackwell.

The production of culture perspective can be further explored in Croteau and Hoynes' text and in the many topical articles—on *Hustler* magazine, hip-hop and alternative music, football, Batman, and Dolly Parton, to name a few—in the Harrington and Bielby reader.

Bruce Carruthers and Sarah Babb. 2000. *Economy/Society: Markets, Meanings, and Social Structure.* Thousand Oaks, CA: Pine Forge Press.
If you get tired of hearing business-minded people speak the usual platitudes of management education, take a look at this very accessible and enlightening sociological critique of economic thought. It is not just money (discussed in this chapter) that is deeply sociological in nature, but all economic phenomena.

Michael Welch. 2000. *Flag Burning: Moral Panic and the Criminalization of Protest.* Hawthorne, NY: Aldine de Gruyter.

Karen Cerulo. 1995. *Identity Designs: The Sights and Sounds of a Nation.* Piscataway, NJ: Rutgers University Press.
One wonders if Welch could have published his book after the September 11, 2001, attacks on the World Trade Center and the Pentagon. Both of these studies shed new light on the meaning and significance of modern sacred symbols and rituals in ways that are consistent with Durkheim's sociology of religion.

David Halle. 1993. *Inside Culture: Art and Class in the American Home.* Chicago: University of Chicago Press.
Pink flamingos (discussed in this chapter) are not the only household objects with cultural and social significance. Halle's classic study looks at cultural capital in the form of class-based differences in home décor.

Barry Glassner. 1999. *The Culture of Fear: Why Americans Are Afraid of the Wrong Things.* New York: Basic Books.
This one is a real romp through the social and political construction of so-called social problems in the United States. You'll be surprised to learn among other things that tainted Halloween candy never did exist as a serious threat to children.

Deena Weinstein. 2000. *Heavy Metal: The Music and Its Culture.* Cambridge, MA: Perseus.

Richard Peterson. 1997. *Creating Country Music: Fabricating Authenticity.* Chicago: University of Chicago Press.
Yes, I really am suggesting that heavy metal and country have something in common. You may learn more by reading about something that you don't like than you think. These two books reveal the hidden social meanings that emerge among producers and audiences of two disparate musical genres.

Denise Bielby. 1995. *Soap Fans: Pursuing Pleasure and Making Meaning in Everyday Life.* Philadelphia: Temple University Press.
Have you ever wondered why some people are so into pursuits that you find no interest in? Bielby provides sociological answers to this question—in this case by examining the culture of soap opera fans.

Elspeth Probyn. 2000. *Carnal Appetites: Food/Sex/Identities.* London: Routledge.
The social significance of food extends beyond pets as meat (mentioned in this chapter). Sociologically, you are what you eat, and you eat what you are. Probyn's book explores the sociology of food, which is an important area within the sociology of culture.

The Making of Citizen Kane. 1996. 108 min. Directed by Michael Epstein and Thomas Lennon.
This film details the production of the classic film *Citizen Kane*, which was influenced by political controversy between actor/writer/director/producer Orson Welles and newspaper magnate William Randolph Hearst.

CHAPTER 4

Power and Authority

In Social Movements, States, and Organizations

"Mean People Suck," declares a contemporary bumper sticker with utter simplicity. People can readily sense that they have been influenced by power in some cases, but they may not understand exactly how it happened. Other times, people may not even realize that power shapes their lives. Sociologists know that power is a more complex matter than people generally take it for. There are a number of interrelated principles that will enable you to decipher the hidden significance of social power in everyday life:

- Social power is based in groups rather than individuals.
- Social power creates social inequalities or social stratification.
- There are political, economic, and cultural dimensions to social power.
- Cultural beliefs may mask social power as legitimate authority and mute resistance to it.
- How social power is exercised has further social consequences.
- Social movements are organized attempts to change or maintain social power.

In this chapter, I will use examples drawn from social movements, organizations, the workplace, and government to illustrate how these essential mechanisms of social power operate.

THE SOCIOLOGICAL PERSPECTIVE ON POWER

"Power," as the organizational sociologist Rosabeth Moss Kantor (1979) aptly put it, "is America's last dirty word." We now can freely speak of sexuality as a natural, complex, interesting topic, but to talk of power in a similar vein still is to be branded either as a radical malcontent or a psychopathic demagogue. In her work as a business consultant, Kantor learned how uneducated many business leaders and management educators were about the power phenomena that were part and parcel of their organizations. Management education has tended to treat power in organizations as an aberration—something to be purged at all costs, in order to make more effective, cooperative, goal-seeking enterprises. This attitude toward power is rather naïve, of course, whether it is in the business world or other areas of social life. Like it or not, social power is an enduring reality of human existence. Blindness to power and its machinations may reflect a sort of innocence, but just as surely those who ignore the nuances of power relations unknowingly will suffer their consequences. Power, as Robert Bierstedt (1950) eloquently argued, is not always transparent. It may hide in nooks and crannies that we never imagined as power-infested places, events, and modes of thought. Much like the air that we breath, power is always there, but seldom manifest, for power works most effectively when those who are subject to it do not recognize its existence.

This chapter explores some more and less obvious aspects of social power. As you will see, power is never absolute, nor does it pertain simply to powerful "individuals." Essentially a social entity, power is bound up with manifold group processes in political, economic, and cultural life. It is crucial to untangle these forces and see basic elements of collective struggles if we are to understand more fully the social inequalities that are a consequence of unequal social power.

For illustrative purposes, I will focus on examples of social power in organizations and workplaces, in social movements, and in government or states. My intention in this focus is not to obscure the importance of power in other areas of society—bear in mind that the elementary processes that I describe apply to all regions of social life, such as gender, racial/ethnic, class, age, and sexual orientation inequalities. In fact, as Charles Tilly (1998) explains, inequalities between groups such as these tend to be created and maintained by the exploitation, opportunity hoarding, and emulation of practices that occur *within* the larger contexts of organizations and work, social movements, and government.

The Power Prism and Its Refractions: An Analytical Tool

To hold **social power**, Max Weber (1922) asserted, means to have the ability to influence others even against their will. In considering

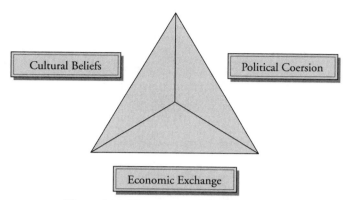

Figure 4.1 Three Faces of the Power Prism

the sources of such influence it may be useful to think of social power phenomena as Randall Collins (1975) does, in terms of three interrelated dimensions—the political, economic, and cultural aspects of power. Figure 4.1 depicts these power dimensions as a "prism," which perhaps is an appropriate metaphor, since the three faces of power indeed tend to reflect upon one another.

The most obvious kind of power is simple **political coercion**, where the use or threat of force, violence, and other elements of harm compel actors to submit to the will of other actors. Politics here means more than the military wings of governments. It includes all political coercion in a variety of other social organizations, ranging from workplaces, to schools, hospitals, construction sites, and other loci of social life.

A second major type of power relation occurs in situations where one individual or group influences other actors by offering some tangible good or service in exchange for compliance. This is an **economic exchange** basis of power. Wages for work are a common example. The power relevance of such arrangements is most acute when economic exchanges are unequal (exploitation), as we shall see. Economic exchange clearly is a taming of the brute violence of political coercion because unequal exchanges may be unrecognized as exploitation by subordinates.

Even more obscured from subordinates' recognition is power that manifests itself in the minds of subordinates. Many lower-tier workers in organizations actually believe somewhere in the deep recesses of their consciousness that they "ought" to be paid less than their bosses, and that they have no right to decision making in the workplace. Beliefs that compel people who are ruled to accept or take for granted their subordinate positions create what sociologists refer to as **cultural legitimacy** or **legitimate authority**. These beliefs are a critical determinant of the nature of power relations. Cultural beliefs that spell out and justify power structures sometimes are imposed on subordinates by authorities that control dominant idea-making institutions, such as the mass media.

Violence, exchange, and beliefs come into play in a wide range of everyday experiences of social power. Sometimes one or another of these types of power relations is the primary mode of influence governing a particular social situation. Depending on which types of power prevail—political, economic, and/or cultural—there are a variety of consequences in wider regions of societies. Figure 4.2 portrays these consequences as refractions (of light, to continue the metaphor) from the power prism. Power arrangements produce an array of effects on parties immediately or even distantly involved in power situations. Ensuing discussions will focus on a variety of these effects, but here a brief word about each will help set the stage.

The most immediate effect of the use of power is on subordinates' reactions and interpretations of the meaning of a power situation. People who are ruled by brute force tend to muster resistance to such power wherever possible. Economic rewards generate less resistance, and cultural beliefs in the righteousness of power structures

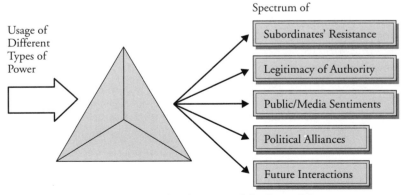

Figure 4.2   Social Refractions of the Power Prism

almost by definition snuff out resistance. The **legitimacy**, or acceptability, of power-holders' actions toward their subordinates is most strongly maintained where economic rewards and/or the use or threat of force are augmented with such cultural beliefs. The interpretation or definition of the propriety of power relations matters not only to the parties immediately involved, but also to a variety of external actors. Chief among these groups in modern societies are politicians and the mass media, who can have decisive influence over the way that wider audiences understand power relations (e.g., as justice, or as abuse of power). Other external parties who may more or less carefully observe power struggles are those groups who represent potential or actual allies of one or another party directly involved in a situation. Here, too, the legitimacy of the conduct of contestants in power relations may draw such allies into the fray. Allies also are likely to look for evidence of the eventual outcomes of struggles, and enroll or withdraw their support according to calculations of self-interest.

Finally, as Charles Tilly (1978) reminds us, it is important to understand power relations as temporal events that unfold as histories. Contestants in social power struggles are thinking humans with memories of past events. Thus, the actions of adversaries at one point in the career of a power relation (e.g., illegitimate force that ruptures trust in peaceful negotiations between parties) profoundly can shape future interactions. Power relations, in short, are a **political process** that unfolds and changes over time.

The three facets of power—political force, economic exchanges, and cultural beliefs—influence much of our existence as social beings. Even where we are not directly involved in power relations, the refractory effect on our lives is often significant. We now turn to some closer considerations of the nuances of social power.

SOCIAL POWER AND SOCIAL MOVEMENTS

"So you want to start a revolution, well you know, we all want to change the world," begins the old Beatles song about political unrest. Nearly everyone can imagine something that they would like to see changed, but there usually are others who want it to stay the same. As we already have seen, inequalities often are maintained by a variety of legitimating power structures that tend to dissuade subordinates from even making demands on authorities. In order to better understand social power, it will be helpful simultaneously to consider social movements, which essentially are power in action.

Given the many ways that unequal power structures are upheld, we might reasonably ask how power structures ever change. **Social movements** are conscious, relatively organized, collective efforts to bring about or resist social change (Diani and Della Porta 1997). Changing social power structures indeed is difficult, but successful movements for change do happen, typically against the forces of opposing **counter-movements** that are set in motion by those who wish to maintain existing power structures. The basic principles of organized power in action, or social movements, can shed light on both large-scale change (e.g., revolutions) and more circumscribed changes in organizations (e.g., a strike). The study of social movements is a robust area of sociology that combines insights from organizational, political, and cultural research to help us understand the processes and outcomes of social conflicts.

As I proceed, it may be helpful to imagine the one power-related inequality that you most would like to see changed through a social movement, and then consider how as leader of the movement you would propose to deal with the many issues involved. Perhaps you would like to see changes in gender, racial/ethnic, age, or sexual orientation inequalities? Current political issues such as campaign finance reform, health care provision, environmental abuse, world trade, abortion, and public school reform also would be fair game. Whatever the case might be, you would be wise to address some basic conceptual issues regarding the prospects for change. A key determinant of who wins out in these struggles is the **resource mobilization** abilities of contestants. How well can a movement bring a variety of assets to bear on their causes? I will group these resources into material and organizational/cultural types.

Material Resources.   First of all, who is with you? Bodies are material resources of sorts. This observation means several things: (1) the number of people who actually are affected by the issue at hand, (2) the degree to which these individuals perceive a grievance against authorities, and (3) the probability that those persons who are affected and perceive a common problem in fact will take some sort of corrective action. The last point is the critical one, of course, for there are plenty of circumstances where the first two points are satisfied, but people fail to mobilize and act. Assuming that your cause has a numerical majority over potential opposing parties, you may be in good shape. Majorities often are needed to defeat minorities (in the simple numerical sense of that term) who command more substantial material resources of other sorts, and/or who are better organized. Even when majorities lack other material resources, they sometimes can make demands on authorities through the sheer threat of force that numbers command. Mass demonstrations, riots, boycotts, and strikes all rely on the potential or actual power of majorities.

Money, of course, is a material resource, but it is not merely having a lot of money of one's own that is important. Rather, it is having access to others' money (e.g., through income, gifts, and credit) that normally is critical. Social relationships of dependence and trust are fundamental to social power. Also, one must think it terms of an ongoing financial process, where one usually has to generate more and more funds to keep pace with the increasing cash flow of the opposition. Why is money important? This one is rather obvious, in that such finances may allow a movement to purchase what it needs in terms of communications, transportation, and other technologies, to buy safe and adequate housing and related amenities, and to pay staff.

Have you thought about weapons to support your cause? As with money, it is not necessarily the actual possession of guns, bombs, and the like, but having the ability to call on others' military resources (e.g., the police, mercenaries, or terrorists) to assist you. There are a number of military considerations in social movements. For one thing, if you lack money, military force may be an alternative means of procuring needed material resources. Even if you do have money, the opposition may attempt to block your access to monetary exchanges through military embargoes on trade.

There also are considerations about the military capabilities of opponents. If the other side has the means for violence, you may want it too, just to level that playing field. However, if the warfare capabilities of your opponents simply are overwhelming, you may not want to risk regular warfare. It may be more sensible for you to allow the opposition publicly to brutalize a few of your members in mock confrontations that produce public sympathy for your cause against a ruthless oppressor.

Alternatively, you may wish to use limited force, such as guerilla warfare or terrorist attacks, that avoids the disastrous consequences of direct confrontation. Colonists during the American Revolution, for instance, often refused to engage the British army in conventional marching battle lines, preferring guerilla warfare when faced with the overwhelming power of the British. **Terrorism** seeks to weaken a militarily superior opponent by challenging its apparent ability to maintain law and order—the objective is to weaken the will of authorities, and to loosen public support for authorities by raising doubts among the populace that leaders have the ability to protect public interests. Of course, terrorism runs the risk of backfiring, as perhaps in the case of the World Trade Center and Pentagon attacks of 2001, when public sentiment came to see terrorism itself as the problem and pledged further allegiance to authorities that were perceived to be addressing the issue.

Material support for a social movement clearly is very important. The success or failure of a movement often depends on making provisions for supporters, financial assets, technologies, equipment, weapons, and physical plant. Minor deficiencies in one or another resource often are surmountable, but disadvantages across a broad spectrum of material needs usually are fatal to a social movement.

Organizational and Cultural Resources.   Having sufficient numbers of supporters, money, and resources and the ability to manage force do not always guarantee victory, because the organizational ability and cultural solidarity to marshal these advantages against a worthy opponent can be the decisive factor. It is one thing to have the wherewithal to win, but it can be quite another matter to keep your group focused and committed, to have a good plan of action, and to make the right decisions when something unexpected happens. Successful movements need to be organizationally astute in the double sense of keeping their members together and knowing how to deal with the opposition.

Frequently, the opposition itself is a highly organized force. For these reasons, many social movements themselves tend to evolve from informal associations of individuals who know one another well to take on the traits of a highly organized **bureaucracy** with a businesslike permanent staff, hierarchy of formal and impersonal rules and procedures of operation, and rational planning. I will discuss the notion of bureaucratic organization in more detail later. This bureaucratization of movements is a very familiar process among longer-lived **social movement organizations** such as the National Organization for Women (NOW), Greenpeace, the National Organization for the Reform of Marijuana Laws (NORML), and the National Association for the Advancement of Colored People (NAACP).

Once a movement has a viable grassroots base of followers, **leadership** that can organize and emotionally charge members and devise ongoing strategies and tactics becomes critical. In some cases, a charismatic leader (e.g., Martin Luther King in the U.S. civil rights movement) can help mobilize a following, but even such extraordinary personalities typically find it necessary to enroll a staff of organizers, advisors, and specialists to manage the movement's affairs. Professional managers who have prior experience serving other causes may be recruited to handle a wide variety of administrative tasks. Where violence is an issue, social movements may call on specialists in various areas of violent and nonviolent protest—militia, terrorists, and trainers in nonviolent resistance. Since accumulation and dissemination of information are a pivotal resource, movements may find it beneficial to recruit researchers, writers, speakers, media managers, spies, counterintelligence agents, messengers, and interpreters. University students routinely are a vital source of activists, partly because they are freer from the constraints of paid employment that can be a liability for other would-be activists. With all of these positions, it is no wonder that many social movements acquire administrative headquarters, adopt administrative rules, and assume other traits of bureaucracies.

Cultural resources are critical in creating a movement's identity and character (Fantasia 1988). Powerful symbols such as flags, uniforms, martyrs, songs, and gestures are cultural resources that seek to unify members of social movements and win over onlookers. Cultural workers from other realms of society are often recruited to movements. Intellectuals from universities and the wider society often help the movement to formulate the "cultural discourse" (the ideological storyline, or propaganda, that defines the movement and its objectives as moral and righteous, and targets the opposition as evil oppressors). Cultural leaders such as artists, actors, and clergy often are sought out to lend the movement popular appeal.

A final, essential organizational resource is the ability of a social movement to forge **political alliances** with external parties and organizations. This requirement tends to become more urgent as the movement gains steam and encounters opposition from countermovements that represent coalitions of powerful interests. Frequently, it becomes necessary for a movement to gain the support of new groups who share their opposition to an enemy, but who have their own separate goals in terms of social change. This amalgamation of dissimilar members makes alliance building a challenging and risky venture for social movements. The danger is that the growth of a movement can lead to an ironic loss of focus, proliferation of factions, and ultimate solidarity failure. If one faction comes to believe that its efforts and goals can be achieved by the work of other factions, a version of the **free-rider problem** can emerge. People then may give minimal effort and still try to reap the collective benefits other members of the movement are producing. A further problem is that if one movement goal is reached before the others, there is no incentive for the satiated parties to continue their support of the movement. Knowing this eventuality, a general crisis of trust can sweep through the movement. The material resources gained through diversification of movements have to be weighed against such risks. A common cultural solution to this dilemma is to frame movements in terms of a singular, abstract, symbolic goal that overarches members' sentiments ("freedom," "equality," "justice"), rather than in terms of concrete, measurable, and achievable goals that can give rise to divisiveness.

Whatever social movement you have been thinking about in this discussion, it should be apparent that attempts to change power structures can meet with stiff opposition, and that realistic hopes for change demand serious thought and action. Far from being isolated outbursts of individual fanaticism, social movements are part of the very fabric of society and so are characterized by forethought, organization, and dialogue with the actions of opponents. Social movements, like all power phenomena, embody elements of political coercion, economic resources, and cultural beliefs and symbolism. It may be helpful at this time to examine a case in point.

Reading Power into Political Protests

The year 1968 was an election year in the United States. In the summer preceding the November elections, all hell broke loose on numerous social and geographical fronts. In Chicago, for example, thousands of primarily young Americans gathered in Grant Park, outside the Hilton Hotel on Michigan Avenue–along part of the city's "magnificent mile" of stores and skyscrapers–in what soon would become a violent confrontation with police. Inside the hotel, the Democratic National Convention was underway, with delegates from various states lobbying for presidential candidates such as Robert F. Kennedy and Eugene McCarthy.

Clad in the countercultural regalia of the day, the young people outside the Hilton were organizing a series of nonviolent protests, partly about their opposition to the escalating war in Vietnam, but also concerning a host of civil rights issues that focused on social inequalities. The protesters were a **political alliance** of a number of groups that composed the 1960s student and civil rights movements. Some of the protesters were student members of the national organization Students for a Democratic Society (SDS), others were nonstudent affiliates of organizations such as the "Yippies," who sought to distinguish themselves from the fun-loving "hippies," while still others were members of organizations such as the Weather Underground, which advocated more violent measures to redress societal ills. Supporters of the National Organization for Women, the National Association for the Advancement of Colored People (NAACP), the Black Panther party, and many other organizations that focused on underprivileged groups were present. There were others who joined the crowd as sympathetic individuals, curious onlookers, and people simply looking for a new variety of fun and thrills.

All national eyes were on Chicago, since the media were providing their usual full coverage of the convention. The real focus of attention though, was on the potential for conflict as the mayor of Chicago, Richard J. Daley, had vowed to deal harshly with any dissidents who dared smear the city's image. Daley prided himself on effectively running "machine politics" in Chicago, "the city that worked." He was not about to let a gathering of what he viewed as hooligans tarnish the reputation of his city before national camera crews.

True to his word, Daley unleashed the highly prepared Chicago police force on the assembled protesters in a bloody bludgeoning that shocked the nation. The nightsticks and tear gas of the police,

not to mention the unused guns, were overpowering. Lacking in such military power and poorly organized for engaging in physical violence with the police, the bewildered protesters quickly were dispersed or hauled off to jail. Inside the Hilton, national network reporters at the convention took breaks to watch on local television the unbelievable event that was happening outside.

Mayor Daley unambiguously had won the purely physical "battle," but in the months and years that followed he paid a price in terms of national criticism of what generally became regarded as an illegitimate abuse of his power. **Media and public sentiments** about the movement changed. Similarly, in an event that followed at Kent State University in Ohio, the decisions of authorities were called into question as nervous National Guard troops shot and killed four protesters and injured others. Both cases came to symbolize growing discontent for U.S. leaders' strategies for dealing with nonviolent protesters, and that dissatisfaction spilled over into some degree of popular support for the protesters' goals.

Much of the sympathy for the student movement shattered in 1970. A single event—a huge explosion that leveled a brownstone apartment building in Manhattan's Greenwich Village—turned the tables. Bill Ayers' *Fugitive Days* (2001) details the circumstances of this tragedy from an insider's perspective. Ayers was a 1960s radical who helped set off a bomb in the Pentagon, among other acts of terrorism. When investigators of the Manhattan explosion determined that the blast originated in a "bomb factory" in the apartment of sev-

---

Protesters at the 1968 Democratic National Convention in Chicago confront National Guard troops (top). Recent global protests over the economic, political, environmental, and gender-related consequences of free trade agreements and other global financial policies have similar dynamics. More than 150,000 protesters from 700 different organizations came to Genoa, Italy, for the G-8 Summit (political and economic leaders of eight powerful states) in summer 2001 (bottom). They confronted 20,000 heavily armed troops who kept the protest walled off from the convention center where the leaders were meeting. Media coverage of the event, including the killing of one protester, aired worldwide, making each side wary of how their actions would be perceived by the world. The mayor of Genoa marched in symbolic unity with the protesters, while thousands of Genoese citizens vacated their besieged city for vacation spots until the summit was over. See Chapter 5 for more on G-8. (Top: © Bettmann/CORBIS. Bottom: © Reuters NewMedia Inc./CORBIS.)

eral leaders of the radical Weather Underground of which Ayers was a member, the mass media flocked to cover the story and, as Todd Gitlin (1980) observed, the "whole world was watching" the movement. The widely read *Life* magazine ran a series of full-page photos of the ruins that resulted from an accidental explosion of various homemade bombs that were being prepared for terrorist activities. One dead female dissident (Ayers' girlfriend) could only be identified from medical records of body parts. Several occupants escaped the blast and remained in hiding as fugitives named to the FBI's "most wanted" list. Meanwhile, biographical searches revealed that most of the group's leadership came from wealthy families. The young woman who was identified by body parts was the daughter of a small town Midwestern millionaire, and granddaughter of the founder of the Boy Scouts of America. Ayers' father was a wealthy corporate executive. Americans were stunned to learn that such affluent young people had turned to violence in pursuit of their goals. Accordingly, the tide of support for the student movement receded as media-besieged Americans became convinced that the movement as a whole was misguided, or prone to unreasonable violence. The already fragile alliance of whites and blacks, and men and women within the movement began to splinter into separate movements thereafter.

Even though I personally was only a high school freshman at the time, I well remember these and similar events. Part of the reason for this recollection is that the young woman who was identified by body fragments actually was from my tiny hometown. I remember walking home from school the day that the news broke, passing the mansion where she grew up, and seeing television trucks and camera people surrounding the place looking for a scoop on this tragedy. I was awestruck by the idea that distant events and struggles had connections with my local world, and I suspect that my interest in social power in later life was primed by this experience.

It would be very naïve to suppose that the 1960s were unique as an era of contested social power. Prior and subsequent world history are replete with instances that display analytically similar dynamics. In late 1999, for example, around 50,000 people turned out in Seattle to protest and shut down a conference of the World Trade Organization (WTO). The mainly young protesters held a variety of grievances, including environmental, labor, and human rights abuses that they felt the WTO fostered with its "free trade" policies around the world. Seattle police harshly reacted to the entire gathering with tear gas, rubber bullets, beatings, and arrests when a minority of protesters broke store windows. The media, of course, aired the events worldwide. Many Seattle residents viewed the matter as an embarrassment to their city and blamed police and city officials for not anticipating the trouble. The Seattle police chief resigned days after the outburst, the city canceled its Y2K (2000) New Year's celebration, and planners of future WTO conference sites now must reckon with the historical violence associated with the Seattle event. Subsequent protests over the same issues have occurred in Washington, D.C., and Los Angeles and around the globe in Genoa, Prague, Quebec City, London, Barcelona, Bogota, and elsewhere right up to the present.

One need not directly experience grand-scale confrontations to appreciate the pervasive role that social power plays in life. It is possible to extract the basic elements of large-scale, historic power events and see these elements at work even in the most mundane situations of everyday life. Take, for example, the events of the 1960s student movement discussed above. The case rather clearly suggests social power at work. The use of violence, or force, undoubtedly is a power issue. Still, there are other ways to influence people, such as buying their compliance in some type of exchange relationship or by shaping their beliefs in such a way as to make them feel that subordination to others' desires is justified. The police likely obeyed Mayor Daley partly because they were paid to do so. They may also have been trained to believe that such obedience to authority is the correct and moral thing to do. And, of course, there would have been repercussions in terms of punishment by the courts if they failed to obey orders. Violence, exchange, and moral solidarity are very common mechanisms associated with social power.

The outcome of the Chicago confrontation—that the students were beaten and dispersed—suggests that winners and losers in power struggles are significantly determined by their relative ability to organize, pool resources, and act. The actions, supporting or opposing, of parties outside the main arena of dispute also are critical to power relations. Power has tentacles that often reach in obscure ways to hidden actors, such as the media in the case discussed above. Power thus is social in character. Mayor Daley successfully got others to carry out his will. The protesters lacked adequate connections among the array of organizations that were present at the rally to develop united and effective resistance to the force that Daley wielded.

The same strategies that inform large-scale social movements apply to all kinds of everyday power relations. Black organizers of the civil rights movement in the U.S. South forged alliances across multiple organizations (Morris 1984). An individual worker at a Wal-Mart store who wants to seek a change in the workplace (wages, benefits, hours, etc.) must consider if coworkers will go along with the demand, how managers will react, what external parties (e.g., unions, courts, media) can be depended on to support the initiative, and so forth. A student who wishes to challenge a professor's grading must assess similar potential power alliances, that is, with other students in the class, wider student organizations, other faculty, administrators, and the school newspaper. If we can come to understand the essential machinations of power, there are few limits to the scope of application of these insights.

Another point about power struggles is that the character of power relations is shaped by the type of conflict that people are engaged in. Violent and nonviolent contests have different dynamics. The process of conflict in Chicago changed from nonviolence to violence, and thereby sent ripple effects through external parties allied in one way or another to the event—the mass media, the public, students on college campuses, and national politicians. Conflicts also vary in terms of the type of issue that is contested. The Chicago affair largely concerned **political issues**—civil rights and decision making about the Vietnam War. Other power struggles may focus more on **economic issues** (e.g., labor strikes, product boycotts, landlord–tenant disputes, food embargoes) or center on **cultural, moral, and symbolic issues** (e.g., religious wars, racial/ethnic conflict, abortion debates, charges of media bias, and book banning). These three arenas of controversy may issue in three corresponding forms of inequality—economic, political, and cultural. Most power relations embody in varying degrees and at different points in time all three dimensions. Within any of these areas of conflict, some issues are more easily resolved than others. Simple wage demands can be directly addressed by workers and management, perhaps even with the assistance of an impartial, third-party mediator. Larger, symbolic issues such as abortion cannot so easily be resolved in this manner.

The police and protesters at Chicago knew that the issues were far too complex to be resolved on the scene, so their actions were not tempered by hopes of an immediate resolution. Persistent power struggles usually are **interaction processes** between parties, where social actors must interpret the meanings of unfolding events, calculate as best as possible the future actions of other groups, and remember past interactions.

One final point is truly critical. The power that one group wields over others very often goes unchallenged, or even unrecognized, by subordinate groups. Many of the issues that the student movement of the 1960s addressed were inequalities that had gone relatively uncontested by the groups affected for decades, or even centuries—for example, gender and racial inequalities, foreign military intervention in poor countries, and corporate power. So too, college students long had looked askance at wider social inequalities, preferring instead to advance their own interests in other power structures—the university and the labor markets that college degrees opened for students. Subordinates' and disaffected others' acceptance of the **legitimacy** of existing power relations as justifiable arrangements always has played a key role in the stability of unequal social arrangements, or social structures. Part of what changed in the 1960s (really even before then), of course, was that a variety of groups came to challenge—first in their minds, and then in their actions—existing power structures.

POWER, STATES, AND LEGITIMACY

Assessment of the sources and consequences of social power constellations clearly is central to sociological analysis. It would seem simple enough to ascertain the essence of social power if we were to take our lead from popular sentiments about the matter: "You either have it or you don't," "It's all about money," "Power corrupts absolutely," "Individuals are on 'power trips,'" and so on. Unfortunately, these platitudes about power are rather shallow in many respects—at best half-truths, and at worst simply misleading about the matter at hand. We need greater precision in discussing such an important aspect of our lives.

The idea of **social power** offered by the great German sociologist Max Weber (1922) stands as a useful point of departure in thinking about the topic. Weber saw power as the chances that one party within a social relationship will be in a position to carry out its will despite others' resistance, regardless of the basis on which this probability rests. Beyond the rather obvious idea that power involves influence over others, we may derive two critical points from this view of power: (1) power is more social than individual and (2) power need not overtly be used in order to be effective. Another of Weber's classic definitions is that of **the state** as "an organization that has a monopoly over the legitimate use of violence within a given territory." In other words, governments are fundamentally military entities that use political coercion or force (police, prisons, warfare with other states, etc.) with the consent of the people who are ruled. If we combine these insights about power and states, we see that there is some ambiguity involved—power is embedded in organizations that don't always use force, but need to be able to do so with the blessing of the people when needed. In this section, I first shall show how governmental power is profoundly social, then move on to examine some of the paradoxical ways in which power as force is used to maintain the allegiance of citizens.

Spreading Social Power in Authoritarian Regimes

When people think of power, influential individuals usually come to mind. National political leaders are good examples. Adolf Hitler surely was a powerful individual, for in Nazi Germany he led a regime that devastated countless cities in World War II, enforced martial law on conquered territories, and instituted a policy of genocide for over 6 million European Jews. Other dictators of that era included Joseph Stalin in Russia and Benito Mussolini in Italy, both of whom extracted a terrible toll on their countries and others through the use of brutal force. World history is dotted with many such individuals, including in more recent times the murderous rule of Pol Pot's Khmer Rouge regime in Cambodia, Mu'ammar Gadhafi's iron-fisted control of Libya, and Saddam Hussein's persecution of Kurdish people in Iraq. Even more nominally democratic and kind governments evince powerful individuals, as John F. Kennedy's and Ronald Reagan's rule in the United States vividly demonstrated. So, who could doubt that all of these individuals possessed tremendous power over others?

It also is easy to imagine powerful individuals in economic terms. After all, "money is power," at least according to conventional wisdom. Who could question that individual entrepreneurs around the turn of the twentieth century, such as Andrew Carnegie in the steel industry, John D. Rockefeller in the oil market, and Pierre DuPont in chemical and munitions manufactures, held virtual monopolies over major sectors of economic production? And today, doesn't Bill Gates–the founder of Microsoft Corporation–similarly dominate the computer and software industries?

Cultural icons also supposedly hold unlimited individual power, if we accept popular thought about the matter. When basketball star Michael Jordan talks, don't people listen? Reverend Jesse Jackson surely commands great power over audiences by virtue of his individual style. If Roger Ebert, the film critic, says that a movie is bad and people believe it, is this not his individual power of persuasion at work? When Pope John Paul II of the Catholic Church decries human rights violations in Latin America and it results in some tempering of abuses, this outcome certainly must be evidence of personal power, derived at best from the higher authority of the Christian God? Power over ideas generally is assumed to stem purely from such individual sources, just as power over military force and power over economic resources are thought to belong to great individuals.

However compelling these images of individual power may be, sociologists advise us to temper such notions with recognition of the profound social processes that even the most powerful individuals must confront and manage. Individuals do exist and sometimes they possess great power, but their power usually manifests itself in patterned interactions with others who either assist, resist, or passively stand back as directives are implemented. "Having" power means having the ability to call on reliable, supportive connections with other power-holding people in order to realize one's own objectives, even when others resist. "Using" such relations of power implies yet another social relationship, that is, with those who are ruled. People who speak of "power games" intuitively are correct, insofar as the game is not solitaire.

Let us return to the case of Adolf Hitler to examine the general contours of power relations in a concrete case. Certainly Hitler, like many other leaders, possessed a certain degree of "charisma," or purely personal leadership style, that facilitated his rise to power. But that was not *all* that he had going for him. Just think of all the charismatic people whom you know who *do not* achieve their goals. Why not? The difference, Ralf Dahrendorf (1967) noted, is that along the way to his political victory Hitler managed to forge a number of alliances with groups that supported various aspects of his political platform. First, he had to secure a grassroots following, and his personal character doubtless was helpful in that regard. But the upstart Nazi party also cleverly won the support of various industrialists and labor groups by portraying political adversaries as impotent fools who had in World War I disgraced Germany with military defeat, and who had accepted debilitating concessions to the Allies in the form of the Versailles Treaty that followed.

Once elected, Hitler's visions of empire expansion still had to rely on a trustworthy staff of military generals, engineers, intelligence agents, and the like to give advice and carry out commands. Most of these people themselves depended on others within their respective bureaus to get things done. All along the line of command, power was dependent on a flow of accurate *information* from parties that one depended on. Indeed, there were numerous strategic blunders in the Nazi war effort that essentially involved bad information, that is, failed communications in power networks. Knowledge is power, as the old adage goes, and one needs trustworthy, competent people to acquire reliable knowledge.

In general then, Nazi Germany resembled other modern governments as a vast bureaucracy that far outstretched the control capacities of even an individual such as Hitler, who wanted to run the whole show alone. Hitler had to spread and delegate his power to others, thus making it social, **institutionalized power**.

Even outside Germany, Hitler depended heavily on **political alliances** with other institutionalized powers. To the east, there was Stalin's Russia—a formidable nation that initially formed a pact with Germany not to intervene when Hitler's tanks stormed Poland. To the south, there was Mussolini's Italy, which formed an alliance with Germany that provided strategic geographical advantages in Hitler's conquest of North Africa. In some cases, Hitler won outright support from other power-holders, while in other instances simple acquiescence was sufficient to meet his needs. In Spain, Hitler was able to win grudging support from Franco, but unable to secure his trust—intentional provision of bad information by Spanish sources severely damaged the German campaign.

Finally, there is the issue of power relations between Hitler and his subordinates—his staff, the German people, and even Jews in concentration camps. Not all his staff or all German citizens equally accepted his commands, and the general attitude toward Hitler's rule changed over time. While it may be true that many Germans at the time of Hitler's rise to power were socially susceptible to acceptance of a hero figure or charismatic leader (the country was in economic turmoil following World War I), the reasons for obedience or resistance varied between social groups, and changed as the years passed.

For many people, of course, fear was the determining factor for obedience. As much power as Hitler wielded, including his power in networks and alliances, the actual use of violence and coercion was limited below its potential. **Political coercion** obviously was used to near full extent on Jewish populations, but even here Barrington Moore (1966) observed that some Jews actually became loyal to the Nazis in policing other Jews in the camps. Most Germans retained a sense of freedom in their lives, and a belief in the legitimacy of their government, however wrong they were in this belief. Some groups saw concrete benefits of **economic exchange**, or at least promise of such gains, in their support of Hitler's regime. Jobs, government contracts for production of goods and services, education, hospitals, and even military service could be construed as sufficiently rewarding to go along with the program. Still others longed for a strong Germany in a moral sense—solidarity with the idea of the nation, or "Fatherland," was a compelling reason for compliance in their cases. Their allegiance was based in beliefs about the **cultural legitimacy** of the regime. Three elements—force, rewards, and beliefs—again are common compliance mechanisms in power relations of all sorts. These motives naturally combined in complex ways in the consciousness of various social actors. The larger point though, is that Hitler's power over people was dependent on his ability to get others to support his wishes, both within his immediate administration, and in wider social contexts.

Theaters of War: The Social Construction of State Legitimacy

We normally think of warfare as a most serious power game, which of course it is. However, it would be short-sighted to imagine that wars are only about achieving the stated objectives of military generals and politicians. There always are ample opportunities for states to engage their enemies in war. So the question is, when, under what circumstances, and to what ends do states in fact undertake warfare? Sometimes states simply must attack their enemies in order to secure needed resources, or to defend themselves. But often the cause of war may involve challenges to the integrity of participants—minor transgressions that trigger deep, emotional reactions in a people can be as large a factor in causing wars as economic or large-scale military actions. So too, internal politics—citizen unrest, political scandals, economic depression, lingering feelings of inefficacy from prior military defeats—can be a powerful motive for leaders to initiate hostilities abroad. Power, then, has a significant theatrical, demonstrative component, where authorities need to show their competence and right to lead—their **legitimacy**—to their followers on a regular basis. Warfare is in some instances a large-scale manifestation of this tendency. War involves social drama, in Goffman's terminology.

Warfare as Social Drama.   Barry Levinson's 1997 film *Wag the Dog,* with Robert DeNiro, Dustin Hoffman, and Anne Heche, carried an interesting storyline regarding the relationship between power, warfare, and government legitimacy. The film begins with the U.S. president caught in a difficult predicament that threatens his reelection campaign—the election is in two weeks, and the president has just been accused of having illicit sexual relations in the Oval Office of the White House with a young girl visiting on a tour (intriguingly, the film actually predated the Bill Clinton–Monica Lewinsky scandal that absorbed the nation in 1998–1999). In order to deal with the situation, the president's staff hires a consultant, "Mr. Fix-it" (DeNiro), who quickly moves to create a media diversion that will channel public attention away from the incident. Much to the disbelief of the president's chief advisor on the matter (Heche), Mr. Fix-it arbitrarily decides that a fabricated "war" with innocent Albania will effectively galvanize public sentiments to national security issues, and blot out the sex scandal long enough to win the election. Mr. Fix-it enlists a notorious Hollywood producer (Hoffman) to the project, along with a songwriter (Willie Nelson), and together they mastermind a complex media blitz that includes fake footage of war damage, staged press conferences and news releases, a manufactured terrorist "attack," and even a supposed hostage situation. The effort is beset with numerous complications, including counterattacks from the presidential challenger, but ultimately the ruse works—the president is reelected amid national concern and patriotism surrounding the "Albanian situation."

Somewhere in the film, DeNiro makes allusions to recent real wars, such as the Gulf War and the Grenada invasion, which he says were also fabrications. (The infamous guided bomb seen through the cross-hairs of a pilot's sights going down a chimney of an Iraqi building prior to detonation, he sarcastically notes, was filmed in Falls Church, Virginia, outside Washington, D.C.) So, what are we to make of these accusations? Is it possible that wars are not real?

It obviously would be a mistake to think that wars simply don't happen, that they merely are fictions or video events. After all, people died in the Gulf War, it cost lots of money, and any reasonable effort to establish the veracity of these things quickly would prove that there was a war. Still, *Wag the Dog* does suggest some important facets of power as it is manifested in violence—that people who are ruled expect their leaders to demonstrate competence in dealing with internal and external affairs, and that leaders are quite willing to oblige these demands with dramatic shows of bravura. Indeed, we usually are willing to accept some measure of incompetence—even malfeasance and disgusting acts—from leaders if we believe that they can handle the big picture, that is, if they seem able to run the country and save us from our worst fears of economic collapse or conquest by even more ruthless leaders. We respect and comply with strong leaders—or at least those who periodically can show strength—in a trusting way. Our demands for such leadership tend to increase in times of internal strife, when we call for evidence of potency, and respond with loyalty, order, and solidarity to convincing episodes of dramatic will and personal flair.

The critical matter is that people *believe* that a given demonstration of power is necessary and effective, regardless of the actual urgency of an external threat. This point is why the farce worked in *Wag the Dog*, but more broadly and importantly, it is why a variety of real, though militarily unnecessary demonstrations of power tend to happen. Nothing unites a group and fires up feelings of moral solidarity like forming a "hate club" that claims to have justly punished evildoers. It was in this manner that Hitler's persecution of Jews as the internal "problem" with Germany and his attack on old national enemies such as Russia, Poland, and France served to generate feelings of nationalism that diverted attention from the country's real economic problems, and blinded citizens to the insanity of Hitler's programs.

U.S. Military History as Social Drama. The United States has not been immune to similar events. For example, Senator Joseph McCarthy's "Red Scare" in the United States, during the Cold War against communism, fueled patriotism by hunting down supposed communist sympathizers within U.S. borders. Many influential people and ordinary citizens suffered the wrath of this largely imaginary purge. Hollywood film producers and actors were key targets of the campaign, which rendered media opposition to the debacle a risky proposition to say the least.

In warfare, too, the United States has a long history of symbolic uses of military force. The 1950s Korean War was part of the Cold War and further cemented Americans' beliefs that the communist Chinese empire was spreading. Ultimately, in terms of its stated objectives, the United States lost the war in Korea, and subsequently languished before the eyes of millions of American television viewers in the similar events of the Vietnam War. Still, both the Korean and Vietnam conflicts served useful symbolic purposes for a time (until the student protests in the late 1960s and early 1970s) in uniting many Americans in support of their leaders, and in opposition to supposedly evil outside forces.

Just a few years after the end of the Vietnam War (at least of direct U.S. involvement in the conflict), the question of U.S. military preparedness and will to win came under heavy public scrutiny. After all, the United States had just lost two wars in rapid succession. Then, a dramatic, symbolic turning point happened. Iranian leader Ayatollah Ruhallah Khomeini had been holding Americans hostage at the U.S. Embassy in Tehran for months. Millions of Americans had been tying yellow ribbons around trees the whole agonizing time in public support of the imperiled hostages. Suddenly, by way of mass media broadcasts, a stunned American public learned that President Jimmy Carter had ordered a daring rescue operation that would infiltrate to the heart of Tehran, using an elite group of reconnaissance troops who landed in the outlying desert in helicopters. These troops were to have swiftly entered Tehran, freed the hostages, and whisked them away to the awaiting helicopters. Unfortunately, a sand storm in the desert at the outset of the operation caused the helicopters to crash and burn as they landed—killing most of the rescuers, and leaving survivors as easily captured prisoners of the Iranian military. The new hostages were paraded on Iranian television, which also aired in the United States. The botched rescue seemed all the more inexcusable since Israel recently had pulled off a magnificent, highly publicized rescue of their citizens who had been held by terrorists at Entebbe airport in Egypt. The question loomed, "Was America losing its military will?"

President Carter lost terribly in his 1980 reelection bid, as Ronald Reagan began the first of two terms in office. Defense spending soared during the Reagan administration, and he quickly set about building a "get tough" image with regard to communists and terrorists worldwide. However, the public façade of military activity in the 1980s markedly differed from the practices of prior years. "No more Vietnams," became the political buzz line, as U.S. leaders carefully avoided direct engagement in protracted military conflicts and sought to censor media coverage of the military events that did happen. As much as Reagan hated Fidel Castro, he would not risk a military confrontation with Cuba. Clandestine efforts masked the difficulties of warfare in troubled areas, as the Iran-Contra affair that at once freed Carter's Iranian hostages and gave arms to Reagan's favored Sandanista rebels in Nicaragua demonstrated. Meanwhile, carefully choreographed "in and out quickly" invasions of countries that were obscure to most Americans, such as Grenada and Somalia, sought to prove U.S. resolve both to the world and to its own citizens.

Still, there was something unmistakably lacking in all of these supposed victories, for Americans had not truly recovered a sense that their leaders and military could flex their muscle against a worthy opponent. True, the Russian empire had fallen apart, and the Berlin Wall had crumbled, but it hardly seemed as though the United States had defeated anybody. The Russians had lost their own "Vietnams" in Afghanistan and Poland. In truth, the Russians simply had overextended their empire, much as the Romans did centuries before—Russia merely had been shrunk down by costly rebellions and wars in its far-flung territorial empire. The Cold War was over, but the best Americans could say was that the arms race ran the Russians broke (which again, was only a partial truth that obscured the fact that the arms race had cost U.S. citizens dearly, as well). China and Cuba still existed, much as before, repressive governments abounded worldwide, and the United States was suffering massive job loss and wage decline as a result of Reagan's "trickle-down" economic policies that favored the rich. In short, there were no victory parades because no war had been fought let alone won, and the world—near and far—seemed no better off for the whole set of charades.

George Bush, the former director of the Central Intelligence Agency (CIA), took over where Reagan left off as president. He finished the messy Somalia invasion, and bathed in the afterglow of the fall of the Berlin Wall. His economic policies were mirror images of Reagan's strategies. By most accounts, Bush's presidency was very uneventful, save for two things: a financial heist and a war with Iraq. Just as he was nearing the busy period of his reelection campaign, a truly monstrous financial scandal surfaced in the media. It was the so-called Savings and Loan (S&L) Crisis, which involved a large group of unscrupulous savings and loan association bankers who used their institutions' money to invest in a large variety of risky, sometimes monumentally silly, get-rich-quick ventures that ultimately failed, thereby bankrupting numerous savings and loan organizations. The country faced an economic crisis if something were not done to bail them out. In other words, the collusion of the investors made very risky actions essentially risk-free, because they knew that the government would have no choice but to reimburse them if they failed. It was at the time the largest financial heist in world history (the Enron and WorldCom scams later exceeded it), and it cost American taxpayers billions of dollars.

Many high-profile corporate and government officials were involved in the S&L scandal, although few ever were brought to trial, let alone severely punished. Perhaps not surprisingly, Bush's own son had just been implicated in the deal (he was not indicted, though), when a seemingly urgent threat to national security emerged in the Middle East. It was the prelude to the First Gulf War. Americans learned through the media that tyrannical Iraqi leader Saddam Hussein "suddenly" had amassed an army on Iraq's border with Kuwait, and was poised for a "surprise" invasion of the tiny country that housed many major U.S.-based corporate oil-producing facilities. Practically overnight, Saddam changed in American public consciousness from an unknown figure to the epitome of human evil. Here was the stage for a real, honest-to-goodness "war" that at once would divert attention from an internal legitimacy problem of huge proportions (S&L) and satiate Americans' longing for a resounding military victory abroad. The costly military buildup and month-long First Gulf War that followed was one of the greatest, most carefully scripted, solidarity-building events of late-twentieth-century American history. The French sociologist Jean Baudrillard (1995) went so far as to say that the First Gulf War did not take place, meaning that our experience of it was a highly orchestrated media event.

Actually, the Iraqi invasion was anything but a surprise. The United States had embargoed supplies of food and other necessities to Iraq long prior to the invasion—that was part of what the Iraqi leadership was angry about. Moreover, Iraqi leaders were infuriated that Kuwait-based oil companies were pumping out underground Kuwaiti oil fields that stretched into Iraq at a greater rate than the ones that were purely in Kuwait's domain. Iraqi troops (mainly civilians with little or no military training) had virtually stood at the border while Hussein pleaded for some kind of compromise that he could respectfully present to his distraught people. No deal came from the Bush administration. The U.S. Embassy already had been evacuated in the weeks prior to the "surprise attack" (an obscure, late-night televised report by noted news anchor Peter Jennings demonstrated this fact—Jennings mysteriously disappeared from subsequent reporting of the war).

American casualties at the hands of Iraqi forces were in fact slight, despite the ominous vision the media and politicians painted of the potency of the Iraqi military, its elite "Red Guard" battalion, "Scud" missiles, and chemical weapons. There never was much direct engagement with well-trained, heavily armed ground forces. Hussein had placed civilians in forward positions, and the United States never pursued the Red Guard or an invasion of Baghdad, even when the opportunity presented itself—that all happened in the Second Gulf War. The First Gulf War largely was an air show that featured bombardment of Iraqi forces and Baghdad with missiles and bombs. The televised events, which aired round-the-clock on the emerging FOX network, showed spectacular, precise destruction of Iraqi tar-

State legitimacy concerns hit home in the United States after the September 11, 2001, attacks on the World Trade Center in New York and the Pentagon in Washington, D.C. These targets had deep symbolic and dramatic significance, in addition to the horrible loss of life that occurred. The terrorists did not just pick random buildings as targets. The World Trade Center was the symbolic center of global capitalism, while the Pentagon represented U.S. military power. While the tangible damage to the economy and military were substantial, the symbolic harm done was even more threatening as America and the world stood in shock that the country could be so vulnerable to such an attack. Identification of an enemy and an adequate response to the damages done were needed to restore legitimacy and faith in the abilities of the United States. Osama Bin Laden emerged as the individual incarnation of all terrorist evil, and a virtual manhunt ensued in the form of the war on Afghanistan's Taliban regime that aided Bin Laden, and later the bombing of caves where Bin Laden was suspected to be hiding. From there, the focus turned to a final reckoning with Iraq and Sadaam Hussein. American flag sales soared in the United States, and prior matters of internal political and economic dissent went dormant. Uplifted and unified by the seeming success of the war effort, Americans' confidence in their government's abilities largely was restored as the president's approval ratings rose to unprecedented levels. (© Reuters NewMedia Inc./CORBIS)

gets, but little bloodshed on either side. Discussions of the technical superiority of never-before-tried U.S. weapons often upstaged the people and strategies involved in the affair. Just like the Clinton administration's bombing of Yugoslavia that followed some years later, the Gulf War was no Vietnam, either in destructive scope or in media presentation of the violence that did happen.

Most U.S. onlookers were uplifted by the Gulf War experience, even though no discernible improvement in their stakes in the world followed from it. There were some lingering resentments that the military again had not "finished the job" (invaded Baghdad, killed Hussein, etc.), but by and large the war "worked." Bush was not re-elected, but that fact had more to do with his lackluster personality, his false promise not to raise taxes, and the failure of his party to raise new issues in his campaign against vibrant, young Bill Clinton in 1992.

The point of this discussion of warfare and power has been that the exercise of power can have strong symbolic and ritualistic elements. In this case, we saw how violence and cultural control can be combined in very provocative ways. At this juncture, I am going to switch the focus of attention from large-scale governmental power to something that perhaps is more close to home—manifestations of power in organizations and workplaces.

POWER IN ORGANIZATIONS

It is not necessary to limit our understanding of the workings of power to "governments," in the usual sense of that term. Business organizations of all kinds are, among other things, administrative power structures. College fraternities and sororities display power phenomena. Pizza parlors, professional sporting organizations, museums, environmental advocacy organizations, tattoo shops, professions, television networks, and churches each develop distinctive power relations among the people who inhabit them. Power is integral to the administration of virtually all groups, and the differences in power arrangements within and across such groups provide important lessons about power as such. The Catholic Church has a more complex, hierarchical power structure than most congregational churches. Elementary, secondary, and higher educational institutions vary in terms of how power is distributed among faculty, administrators, and students. Decision-making power at Ben &

Jerry's ice cream company is more shared than it is in many other businesses. In the professions, lawyers are a more tightly knit group than barbers or beauticians. Harvard University graduates receive more respect or prestige than graduates of average state universities.

We would be well advised to begin any study of organizational power by looking for the three basic modes of social power relations—force, rewards, and solidarity beliefs—that gain subordinates' compliance through coercive political alliances, exchange of valued commodities or services, and legitimizing of authorities, respectively. While these three forms of power often intermingle in practice, there are distinctive types of group relations and organizational settings that tend to emphasize one or another strategy over the others. The use of coercive force, usually in alliance with other parties, is characteristic of a broad spectrum of social organizations. States, as we saw before, are prime examples of coercive institutions. It is difficult to imagine a viable state that lacks the ability to wield power over its citizens, protect itself from intruders, or exert influence over other states. Virtually all states have police, courts, and prisons—organizations that themselves tend to rely on force to control their members. Economic exchange is the dominant mode of control in a wide variety of workplaces, where wages for services are the operative power mechanism. Other organizations such as churches, synagogues, charities, and museums may rely more on voluntary compliance of members, based on their cultural beliefs in the inherent value of faithful organizational service.

The type of **organizational recruitment** to groups—be it force, rewards, or cultural commitment—tends to correspond with the climate of control within the group. If violence is used to recruit new members to a society or organization, then the same strategy typically is used to control them and keep them in the group. Workers who are drawn to a job only by the pay promised to them might leave the organization unless the compensation keeps pace with the wages that are available elsewhere. Members of cultural organizations remain loyal only so long as the values espoused by the organization remain consonant with their own values.

Many organizations, of course, display some combination of the three basic forms of power relations. Schools are good cases in point. Education can be a field of coercion, depending on one's social circumstances. In schools, teachers resort to more coercive controls of students who are forced by law to attend (i.e., compulsory public schooling in elementary and secondary education) than in circumstances such as college education, where students enroll by choice. Students at whatever level of the educational system will show less resistance to schooling (see it less as force) when they perceive some future return for their compliance with teachers' mandates (e.g., where they believe it is a fair exchange for future employment chances). Wealthier children can "see" education as a reward system better than poorer children, who see schools more as prisons, because rich kids' parents and peers offer better evidence of the benefits of schooling than poor kids' social worlds offer. Undergraduate education today generally carries an economic exchange mentality in its student–faculty power relations, where vocationalism (education as a means to jobs) is pervasive. In other areas of education, such as graduate and professional schools, the incentive of occupational payoffs more tends to blend with yet another form of control–cultural or moral solidarity beliefs. In medical, legal, and many other kinds of advanced education, students become "committed" to the values and norms of the profession in a way that extends beyond mere monetary interests. Students' commitment to education in these contexts is viewed as an "end-in-itself," as a worthy pursuit that is justified quite independently of coercion and economic rewards.

We spend the majority of our lives inhabiting organizational power structures. As members of class, gender, racial/ethnic, and age groups, organizations are the major mediators of our economic livelihood, political power, and cultural esteem. One of the most important venues of organizational power is the workplace, which deserves careful consideration at this point.

Power and Control in Workplaces

It is an interesting exercise to contemplate how you have been controlled, or how you have controlled others, in workplaces, school settings, churches, social clubs, and the like. That is, what are the dominant strategies that have been used to establish and maintain the power structures of such organizations? What, if any, forms of resistance have subordinates developed to contest power? How do different types of organizations differ in terms of their power structures, and what do you suppose the sources of such variations are? These sorts of questions about one's everyday life can help bring home the pervasive nature of social power. If you don't like your job (or even if you do), it probably means in part that the power structure of the workplace does not meet (or does meet) your desires.

As an illustration of the various power strategies that organizations may use in different situations to control their workers, let us imagine an enterprise that produces shoes—call it Brown's Shoe Co., where I am Mr. Brown, the owner. Imagine yourself as one of my workers. My primary goal as owner is to make the best shoes possible (for advantages in market competition) for the lowest labor cost. In other words, my goal is profitability. There are several ways to increase my profits (gouging consumers, better technologies, driving out competition, etc.), but here I will focus on just one power relation—interactions between owner and workers. We already know that there are three basic ways that I can seek to influence workers to serve my interests (to exercise power). I can (1) try to force workers to serve me, (2) offer rewards for workers' compliance, and/or (3) attempt to convince workers that serving me is the right thing to do. Each method has its peculiar set of advantages and disadvantages, depending on the situation that my company faces. Consider the power dynamics of each strategy, remembering that I may choose to employ the three devices in some combination.

The Limits of Coercive Power.   Assuming that I have the capability to force employees to work, it is a singularly cheap form of labor relations. For example, by standing in a tower with a machine gun, I could simply kill workers who failed to perform up to snuff. Maybe I could even shoot a few workers for no reason at all, just to remind them of the reign of terror! Provided that there were a ready supply of new workers that I could procure through capture or some other means, this tactic might make good sense in terms of the profit motive that drives the organization. Workers essentially would be slaves, and it might even be provident to forgo feeding them, work them to death, and get replacements. While there are plenty of examples of this type of abuse in the history of slavery, it is more common for even the most hideous oppressors to afford their subjects some measure of subsistence. In the case at hand, I might be lucky enough that workers would face disastrous outcomes if they were to leave my work place (e.g., unemployment, starvation, or mistreatment by even more sinister rulers). Then, it might be smart for me to present my arrangements with workers as a sort of "protection" from external dangers, as often was the case in feudal estates where lords protected serfs. Here, force shades over into the strategy of exchange or reward.

In any case, workers who feel coerced would not be committed to the firm, and at every moment would seek to rebel, escape, or sabotage the quality of the shoes that they produce as ways to exercise **subordinate resistance**. Thus, I would need to watch workers' every move, which is a practical impossibility for mortals who need to sleep, travel in search of new opportunities, or whatever other matters might require absence or inattention. One solution to this problem might be to enroll a staff of police who act in my interests in subordinating workers, but the staff itself would be costly insofar as something other than coercion (perhaps money) would be required to make them trustworthy agents. Additionally, a set of surveillance technologies (cameras, alarms, punch-in clocks, architectural design, monitoring of results, audits, etc.) might help to assure compliance, but again the expenses and administrative fatigue associated with such devices are large. If Brown's Shoe Co. expands to new geographic locations, the administration of the enterprise by such means could become quite cumbersome and costly. Similarly, if the functions of the various departments of the company became more complex with expansion (development of separate production, financial, marketing, and sales divisions, for example), it likely would be beyond the capacities of one person to understand, let alone oversee, exactly what amounts to good performance in each division. The lack of adequate knowledge and information about subordinates' duties and activities is a common limitation of authorities' power over others.

The use of sheer force, even where it is available, still engenders numerous problematic social relationships. For this reason, coercion often has a sublime character in organizations—its potential is there, but seldom used to its full extent. It usually is better to save violence as a last resort and rely on less transparent uses of power in the meantime. Exploitation of reward systems is one such opaque power phenomenon.

Economic Exchange: Money Is Power, but Not Absolute Power. If simple force creates administrative difficulties, Brown's Shoe Co. might be well advised to opt for a policy that grants some measure of reward in exchange for workers' diligence. As suggested above, coercive power often tends to be transformed in this direction. Money–in the form of wages, salaries, stock options, retirement pensions, and other liquid assets–and benefits such as health care, education, recreation, housing, food, and protection, are typical forms of rewards that are exchanged for service. The essential idea from a control standpoint is for owners or managers to offer workers sufficient rewards to gain their willing compliance, but not so much money that profits dissipate. In other words, the reward system must remain a means of **exploitation** of workers' efforts. Exploitation is unequal economic exchange. It is a delicate balance that seeks to make workers believe that the exchange is a fair one, but in practice the transparency of the differential value of material rewards versus company profits often reemerges as a source of contentious power relations and worker malfeasance.

The immediate advantages of rewards over brute force seem clear enough. Workers will not so readily revolt, and they will work hard and conscientiously so long as they imagine that the exchange system is fair. Still, there are a variety of distinct disadvantages to reward systems. The most obvious problem is that rewards are costly, and workers tend to demand more and more money and benefits over time in order to satiate their desires for beneficial exchange. If, for example, Brown's Shoe Co. were to pay its workers a minimal wage, what would prevent the employees from organizing themselves and demanding higher wages each year? This is a routine problem that employers face. One common corrective to this tendency is to create a seniority system, or **career structure**, wherein the promise of larger rewards in the future stems demands for compensation in the present. Long-term steps in wage increases and deferred benefits are examples of this system that relies on the social psychology of postponed gratification to gain workers' allegiance.

Even when employees' wages can be held in check, another difficulty arises because rewards alone do not guarantee loyalty to the quality and productivity goals of organizations. On the one hand, workers who are drawn only by their pay will readily leave one workplace for another that offers better compensation. But there is an even more menacing dynamic associated with wage systems. Anyone who has worked in low-wage occupations (or even high-wage jobs, in many instances) realizes that it is very difficult for bosses to monitor workers' performance. To put it bluntly, it usually is easy to cheat employers by collecting a more or less guaranteed paycheck, while putting forth minimal effort or even sabotaging the workplace. Employees are rational actors who, when they are motivated solely by monetary incentives, routinely seek to balance perceived inequities in the reward system by lowering their productivity. In this situation, some type of surveillance again may be utilized in order to assure performance, which constitutes a reversion back to coercive mechanisms that punish cheaters. In addition to the surveillance technologies noted above, authorities may choose to institute a variable reward system that pays according to workers' measurable performance level. At Brown's Shoe Co., for example, it might be possible to start a "piece rate" system that pays workers for each pair of shoes produced. Or, it would be possible to add on a bonus system that provides additional pay for each pair made over some specified minimal level of production. However, even these tactics have drawbacks. Some workers may be content with the pay offered for minimal work, and so not be willing to extend full effort. Then too, there is the problem of managers who actually would need to know what normal performance adds up to in tasks that only workers know how to perform. Brown's workers could collectively limit their normal output to a level that actually is slacking, so that bonuses easily could be achieved with minimal effort. Again, knowledge and information about the minutia of organizational affairs are critical power resources that subordinates can manipulate in their favor.

The old adage that "money is power" appears not to hold up to close scrutiny, at least not in the sense of money as absolute power. Exchange, just as pure coercion, has its limitations. For all the reasons noted above, many authorities try to augment rewards and threats of violence with a third ploy—appeals to subordinates' hearts. That is, bosses seek where possible to create a culture of loyalty among workers that depicts the organizational structure as moral and necessary. Belief systems of this sort are the equivalent of **legitimate authority** in other political domains. A variety of symbolic representations and ritualistic events are the concrete mechanisms that create and sustain such feelings of organizational solidarity and mask differences of power and resources among various actors.

Cultural Legitimacy: Can't We All Just Get Along?   Rodney King's famous emotional cry in reaction to the Los Angeles riots that followed the acquittal of the police who beat him is an apt summation of the moral basis of control in organizations. Where all else fails, calls for allegiance to common cultural values, to feelings of family and "we-ness" instead of "us and them," sometimes can be effective power strategies. Cultural beliefs of this sort essentially define power structures as justifiable, or obscure the very existence of power differences between groups.

Returning to the Brown's Shoes scenario, it is useful to ask what such an owner and his managers might do to generate these apparently illogical loyalty beliefs among workers. Remember that some measure of coercion, and a graduated wage system that potentially creates divisiveness among workers may already be in place. The principle of divide and conquer, where authorities seek to weaken the opposition by creating internal conflict within its ranks (e.g., by pitting men against women or whites against minorities), still requires loyalty from the fragmented opposition. The company may be in dire need of solidarity among its members, and between workers and management, at this point. This is where the interesting work begins, for it takes real ingenuity to devise effective cultural systems that perpetuate power structures. Using dramaturgical sociology, we may explore how cultural legitimacy is created. Consider the following examples of social rituals, and associated symbolism, that seek to paste over power structures with feelings of unity, morality, and necessity.

The most common forms of cultural rituals that reinforce existing power relations are everyday behaviors that signal to and remind participants that they occupy a given place in the power order. For example, distinctive patterns of dress, speech, and tastes tend to emerge between workers and managers, and between age, gender, racial/ethnic, and other segments of organizations. Humor and joking behaviors may differ by group. Different physical quarters and restrictions of physical movement to designated work areas also mark power groups. Managers may get to park their cars in the front row of lots, in designated spots near the factory entry, while workers battle it out for spaces in general lots. Workers may punch time clocks that monitor their promptness, while managers arrive and leave work according to flexible, self-made schedules. All of these examples are elements of the routine of work. The power significance of such rituals lies in the way that, over time, they help bosses and workers alike to view their dominant and subordinate positions as "natural" and "necessarily so." The two groups may even come to see themselves as fundamentally different types of human beings. The multiplicity of these rituals, each symbolically representing power relations, makes alternative power arrangements seem "unthinkable."

Differences between workers and managers, reinforced in cultural practices, also can become problematic in cases where the two parties begin to use their distinctive cultures to create solidarity in their ranks, for example, amid inter-group conflicts. That is, everyday cultures help to separate workers from managers and legitimize reward and other power differences between the two groups, but this very cultural divide potentially is volatile. For this reason, many organizations intentionally develop a second tier, so to speak, of the ritual order that seeks to inculcate organization-wide solidarity and loyalty.

One increasingly common solidarity-building mechanism is teamwork that emphasizes organizational goals over individual aspirations. This organizational model, borrowed from Japanese corporations, uses a variety of rituals that may seem bizarre at first sight. Managers at Wal-Mart stores, for example, conduct an exercise and cheering session for employees each morning prior to opening the doors to shoppers. These ceremonies seek to get workers pumped up with emotions of organizational loyalty that supersede individual interests. Other organizations routinely send their employees to retreats, sometimes in rustic wilderness lodges that feature all manner of odd games, inspirational speakers, award ceremonies, play-acting, and feasts that are geared toward rejuvenating workers' commitment to organizations. Managers for McDonald's restaurants train at Hamburger University, near Chicago, where they too are cultured in the spirit of the organization, which they then are charged to pass on to their workers at individual restaurants (Leidner 1993). These sorts of rituals hold in common the aim to make the visibility of objective organizational power structures fade in the nonrational frenzy of emotional solidarity and "we-ness."

Another tried and true strategy that boosts workers' loyalty to organizations is to entangle their well-being in other aspects of their lives with their fate in the organization. Provision of health care benefits, also a reward tactic, is one such entanglement. In the United States, where people's health is usually dependent on the workplace (rather than on some form of national health coverage, as it is in all other industrialized societies), it becomes difficult to imagine life without the employer. Similarly, employers who offer organization-planned trips, recreation leagues with other workers, health spa privileges, and the like are able to blur the distinction between work and leisure among their employees, thereby increasing organizational dependence. Families, too, can be made into organizational families. Special events for employees' spouses, particularly females, sometimes enjoin them to the workplace. Frequently, dating and courtship as such are a function of the company—when leisure is fully incorporated, potential partners tend to be coworkers. For children, provision of educational benefits or favored treatment in future hiring binds their fate with workers' loyalty to the company. Housing and relocation assistance can be used to concentrate workers' residential lives in the same geographical area in neighborhoods that evince distinctive company cultures. The most surrealistic of these developments involve what Mark Gottdiener (1997) has called "themed environments." One prominent example is Disney World in Florida, which maintains an entire Disney town for employees, replete with streets named after Disney characters. Less audacious examples are widespread in many societies, and indeed in world history.

In all of these cases, savvy organizations are doing things that are analogous to what racial and ethnic groups have done throughout history to build their solidarity—they are providing **institutional completeness** in various areas of workers' lives, such that existence within the organizational enclave becomes second nature. Existence outside the organization becomes nearly unthinkable in workers' consciousness. The organization is a "ghetto" in the nonpejorative, historical sense of a community that provides all needs for its inhabitants. The concept of a "compound" similarly is appropriate, as it implies amalgamation of social functions and psychological existence within the organization.

The significance of cultural manipulations of workers should be clearer now, but we still need to consider strategies that, like theatrical wars between states, seek to bend rebellion and violence toward organizational goals. Cultural anthropologists have long known that social conflicts are not necessarily divisive events, but rather can unite groups. How can this be so? The answer essentially is that such potentially disruptive events may be framed or contained in **social rituals**, so that conflicts actually allow workers to vent frustration rather than cause trouble for organizations. If one is going to boil water, it makes good sense to provide a valve to let off steam—smart bosses know how to make this principle work in social contexts. These rituals take the form of **social dramas** that specify very scripted roles for participants.

The relative power of social actors in workplaces can be measured in terms of who makes decisions and who follows orders—order givers and order takers. Even though most organizations are not participatory democracies (they vary on this dimension, but most are hierarchies of power in the above sense), there are a number of cultural rituals that can help produce the illusion of democracy in the workplace. The notorious suggestion box and its kindred surveys of worker opinions are good examples of practices that ritually provide workers with a "voice." Intelligent managers occasionally will adopt some innocuous suggestion (say, "fix the toilet latches") amid much hoopla about the importance of workers' input. The most important social function of suggestion boxes and similar surveys, though, is the ritual proclamation of democracy in the workplace, and the ritual rebellion it affords against managers. Another very similar practice is the token representation of subordinates on decision-making committees in organizations. Authorities may ask themselves, "Wouldn't it be good to have a [token] worker on that committee?"—realizing that the decisions being wrought will affect workers and that it must not appear that they were left out of the process. Beyond lack of numbers, subordinates may lack voting rights, information, alliances, and all the usual resources that are needed to push an agenda at a meeting. So they normally have little if any power in such contexts. Again, the larger meaning of the ceremony (where it is pulled off effectively) is that it feigns family-like, collegial, intraorganizational relations, while preserving existing structures of power.

For another example of the same sort of ritual, consider something as seemingly benign as a softball game at a weekend company picnic, where workers and managers are pitted against one another on opposing teams. While these kinds of events may indeed be fun for all, they nevertheless can involve serious power relevance. If workers are known to be better at the game, and hence are a shoo-in to win or perhaps even humiliate managers, this victory may spill over for a time into reduced worker frustrations on the job the following week, as they revel over the symbolic defeat of management. This ploy has been a common practice at prisons, where guards and inmates are allowed to compete as equals, if only in the safety of a controlled game. Another typical form of release of tensions has been the open forum "gripe session" (seldom called just that). These periodic airings of grievances rarely lead to serious workplace reforms, but they do a great deal to stem the development of more rebellious behavior among subordinates. In each case, we are seeing rites wherein social actors temporarily play roles that symbolically challenge the prevailing structures of workplace power.

In many cases, these rituals actually demand that social statuses be *reversed* during the event. Workplaces that sponsor a day when bosses do subordinates' jobs and vice versa are good examples of these rituals of status reversal. Authorities then can be seen as regular people competently doing the same jobs as their workers, if only for a day. In more dramatic examples, subordinates may even be encouraged to "boss around" their actual superiors in symbolic disparagement of their positions. This method borrows from the rich variety of status denigration festivals in societies worldwide—Halloween in the United States today is a rather tepid example that lets children make demands ("trick or treat") on adults that otherwise would be unacceptable.

Finally there are rituals of temporary status elevation of subordinates. Secretarys' Day in the United States is designed ritually to uplift the universally lowest paying, female-dominated job in white-collar workplaces to a position of "privilege" (flowers, long lunch breaks, reduced duties, etc.). Labor Day served a similar function at one time, although this meaning largely has faded from popular consciousness into a general holiday. Other examples include the many workplaces that institute rituals that extol the "Employee of the Month" (or "Employee of the Week," if the rotation requires greater volume)—who almost always is a subordinate worker, rather than a manager. The purpose of the ceremony, of course, is not to select the single best worker, or still less to materially reward productivity (there seldom is any compensation for winning), but to make sure that all workers get their recognition. In all such cases, it is increasingly common for organizations to publicize such events in newsletters, websites, and the like in order to further feelings of organizational "belonging" among all workers.

Bureaucratic Organizations and Abstract Social Power

Whether we like it or not, our lives are played out in organizations. Most people are born in medical establishments, learn about the world in educational and religious organizations, work and partake in leisure in a variety of organizations, receive care in nursing homes, and ultimately have our death negotiated by hospitals and the funeral industry. One of the distinctive features of modern organizational structures is that they increasingly are **bureaucracies**. Max Weber (1922) observed several defining characteristics of modern bureaucracies:

1. Means–ends rationality and technical efficiency as guiding principles
2. Standardization, measurement, calculability, and predictability of activities
3. Impersonality and elimination of human error, emotion, and individual and traditional group identities in favor of purely formal positions
4. Hierarchy of authority clearly specified in written rules and permanent files for accurate surveillance of organizational activities
5. Professional, formally educated, expertise among primary decision-making position holders

Schools, for example, have become highly bureaucratized organizations, dominated by rationality, efficiency, impersonality, and hierarchies of authority. Decision making and order giving are allocated to "positions" rather than to "people," and such power is spelled out in procedural rules that grant qualified experts—administrators, professors, coaches—jurisdiction over particular domains of educational activity that others—students, parents, maintenance personnel—are excluded from. Learning is measured in quantifiable grade point averages and credit hours completed. Class sessions are organized in standardized time slots, sometimes with bells that signal people to move to the next class, all in order to optimize efficient use of physical plant and personnel. Standardized exams purport to measure objectively and without human error student performance; the scores then are posted according to impersonal social security numbers. Sequences of courses point the way to supposedly efficient paths to knowledge. In all of these respects, the school has become an object of **scientific management** or **Taylorism**, borrowing from the kindred time and motion studies of efficient, bureaucratic factory operation that Frederick W. Taylor (1911) initiated in the United States in the early twentieth century.

Economic, political, and cultural organizations were in Weber's estimation dominated more and more by the structure and cultural mind-set of bureaucracy. These organizations were in many ways more technically efficient at achieving stated goals, and certainly more consistent and long lasting than their predecessors that were governed by the whims of personal leaders, or by the venerable traditions of various religious and ethnic groups. Nevertheless, Weber shuddered at the darker sides of bureaucratic life and its inexorable march toward control of every dimension of human existence.

Bureaucracies were power structures for Weber, and the winners in these organizations were the administrative and professional experts who monopolized rewarding positions and expanded their spheres of control on the basis of their *claims* to rationality, efficiency, and expertise—in other words, based on a peculiar kind of legitimate authority that he called **legal-rational authority**. We shrink before the power of managers, lawyers, school principals, social workers, engineers, and other bureaucratic and professional authorities who have power over their subordinates based on widely held beliefs that the experts alone deserve the good jobs, promotions, and right to make crucial organizational decisions. Shrouded as much in the mystique of rationality as in its objective outcomes, bureaucratic or legal rational authority was becoming a deep-seated, highly abstract, framework for the establishment of massive social inequalities. Organizational sociologists have come to see the formal structures of bureaucracies as myth and ceremony that block scrutiny of accepted practices (Meyer and Rowan 1977).

People's crippling inability to see through bureaucracies to alternative ways to govern human activities made bureaucracies extremely resilient power structures—"iron cages," as Weber called them in a famous passage from *The Protestant Ethic and the Spirit of*

Capitalism (1905–1906). Bureaucracy itself was a dehumanizing structure that exerted its influence seemingly without human volition to every corner of social life, including, for example, that most human enclave of sexuality, which now has been exposed to rational scrutiny in terms of sex manuals, quantification of sex, and calculative techniques for achieving maximal orgasm efficiency. How bizarre when you think about it—humans are the only animals that have to be instructed about their own reproductive activities. The iron cage of bureaucracy then is two-sided—it is a broker of human power, privilege, and stratification, and yet oddly it is an exploiter of the humanity in its entirety.

The Symbolic Architecture of Organizational Power

Just as in the theater, staged events in bureaucratic and other organizations require a number of "props" that remind actors and audiences of what is going on in the show. This section examines one category of these props—organizational architecture. Have you ever wondered why some bosses have huge desks, lavish offices in secluded suites, and coffee catered in by secretaries, while other employees lack even reasonable privacy in their work, let alone the accoutrements of their superiors? Similarly, have you ever felt hesitant to speak or raise questions at a meeting or event because you imagined yourself out of place in the formal grandeur of the situation? Perhaps these matters pass through your consciousness unnoticed, but they nevertheless are real power issues. In fact, the very taken-for-granted status of power arrangements in such cases is a key component of social power.

We have seen that power often entails a distinctive cultural or moral dimension, insofar as subordinates in a wide array of social contexts may obey others because they have come to accept one or another kind of cultural belief that justifies or legitimizes hierarchical social relations. People also may come to believe in symbols. Symbols of social power are further elements that reinforce cultural legitimacy. Jeffrey Pfeffer (1996) rightly observes that **symbolic power** in organizations takes many forms that correspond to the various structures of power within and between them. Tastes in clothing and everyday language of workers, the glitziness of organizational letterhead, advertisements, and media attention to organizations all carry important symbolic meanings that mark differences between and within organizations. I will focus in the next few pages on some aspects of architectural symbolism in organizations. The following examples are taken from the economy and work, but as you become a more discerning observer of social power it should be possible for you to see and map its presence virtually in other hubs of everyday life.

At the largest scale of architectural-symbolic analysis, we can see power at work in interorganizational relations. For example, as one enters many large cities by automobile, it is common to traverse a beltway road that is lined with corporate offices and headquarters. These buildings tend to be very expensive constructions—mirrored glass exteriors, landscaped grounds with ponds and fountains, spacious interior atriums that feature skylights and tropical plants, and other seemingly needless displays of affluence adorn these facilities. Few of these beltway castles existed prior to 1970, because most corporations still had downtown offices in more modest buildings. The development of beltway headquarters corresponds in part to the incredible growth in U.S. corporate wealth over the past few decades. In part, this change is linked to the desire to locate away from inner-city congestion and poverty, and closer to the airports that shuttle executives around the country and globe to meetings at other beltway corporations. But there is more to it than just technical expediency, as we shall see.

It also may be tempting to suppose that the waste of money involved in such buildings simply is a matter of greed, where executives spend funds on their own quarters (they are "beltway bandits"), rather than improving the lot of workers in affiliated factories, warehouses, and stores, or lowering consumer prices. While greed surely is part of the power involved here, there also are less apparent, symbolic and ritual meanings of the beltway structures, and corporate culture more generally (Deal and Kennedy 2000). On the one hand, a nice workplace symbolizes to the people who work there that they "are somebody" important by virtue of the fact that the corporation chooses to house them in such accommodations. Employees may be more loyal in their duties under these conditions. Also, employees gain cultural prestige vis-à-vis workers in less opulent buildings ("I may be an exploited peon in my castle, but at least my castle is nicer that those dungeons where other peons work").

On the other hand, elaborate accommodations can help entire corporations to symbolize their legitimacy in the market as real players who are worthy of doing business with. Imagine the disgust and defilement feelings of a CEO of a major corporation if she has to walk past homeless people and enter a dingy downtown office in order to meet with a prospective business partner. A very real, symbolic part of being successful is looking successful because appropriate cultural symbolism facilitates smooth interactions between parties (i.e., the cultural similarities help them to perceive that they occupy common ground). In this sense, elaborate offices can be thought of as "power-dressing" writ large.

Symbolic expressions also mirror the divisions of social power *within* organizations. Differences in rank and position, and the relative power and privilege of various departments are culturally represented in the very physical layout and objects of workplaces. Real disparities in decision-making power, and equally hard-nosed differences in wages and benefits, tend to express themselves in this cultural realm of organizations. An important aspect of power is **surveillance**–the ability of authorities to monitor the activities of subordinates. Modern buildings often are set up so that authorities can easily watch subordinates. These arrangements are physical expressions of what philosopher Michel Foucault (1975) called **panopticism**–the culture of surveillance. Borrowing from an early prison design by philosopher Jeremy Bentham (1748–1842) called the panopticon, which had a central tower and a circle of radiating cellblocks, Foucault used this metaphor to describe a disturbing picture of a society obsessed with monitoring human activity.

These tendencies for buildings to express power suggest a case in point from my college days, when I was a security guard at the corporate headquarters of State Farm Insurance Company, a major U.S. insurer. State Farm is a staggeringly wealthy company, despite recent losses in lawsuits over consumer fraud and gender discrimination in its hiring practices. The profits of the corporation are spread unevenly among various types of workers at the corporate headquarters, and these differences were easy to note in the geography of the complex. As a night guard, my job was to meander through the gigantic, multistory building in the dark on a prescribed route that presumably would discourage unwanted intruders. I carried no weapon other than the whistle that I was provided, and to add insult

Deep analogies about the symbolic architecture of power can be drawn from a Hitler Youth dormitory in Nazi Germany during World War II (top left), the guardhouse at the center of a panopticon cellblock at Stateville, Illinois, prison (top right), and a new college dormitory at Georgia Tech University (bottom). Control and surveillance—central goals of these types of organizations—are well reflected in the uniformity of quarters, common baths, ease of observation of people, and fortress-like structures of each example. Perhaps tellingly, the Georgia Tech dormitory was built to house and protect athletes at the 1996 Atlanta Olympic Games, where a terrorist attack occurred. (Top Left: © CORBIS. Top Right: © Bettmann/CORBIS. Bottom: © Kevin Fleming/CORBIS.)

to injury, I had to wear a police uniform and a hat with "Wackenhut," the name of the security outfit, emblazoned on it. I would have run at the first suggestion of trouble, rather than blow my whistle and shout, "Stop in the name of Wackenhut!" Luckily, nothing very exciting ever happened. I carried a black clock-box at my waist and at various locations in the building there were coded keys that I had to insert and turn in the clock-box so that my supervisor would know that I in fact had made my rounds when he came in the next morning (yes, they policed the police). As one can imagine, it was a boring job, but I entertained myself in part by observing the geography of power in a major corporation.

One of the first things that I noticed was that the workstations of State Farm employees on the lower level of the building were quite small, often consisting of row after row of undivided little desks. It appeared that scores of workers readily could be watched by a single person in a strategic central location, or by someone just walking about the area. The departments had wall dividers, but within departments there was little differentiation of quarters. The carpeting in these areas was a typical drab, short-nap, office carpet with little cushioning beneath. All in all, it seemed to me that this floor was a very dreary work environment.

Once I moved up one level, the ambience changed somewhat. This was the area where hundreds of middle managers were located. Here, there was more substantial privacy in work areas, at least for some employees. Larger desks were evident and many of these work areas were divided from one another with removable partitions that stood about at eye level. Some of these cubicles also had a small chair beside their desks, which suggested that the position entailed at least some power over whoever occasionally sat in this seat. Secretaries' desks, typically decorated with objects that suggested female workers, still remained open to general inspection by passersby. Neither the lower level nor this one had much in the way of ornamentation and it appeared to me that it was a very busy area. Escalators along the sides of a wide-open atrium serviced the lower and intermediate floors of the complex and workers would have been visible to all as they went up and down.

An interesting section of the intermediate level was a computer complex that was inaccessible except to those with proper identification passes. A separate State Farm security force monitored all movement in and out of this department, including my own actions. Cameras recorded every move one made in this section. The organizational importance of the central computer files of State Farm was matched by the military-like demeanor of the round-the-clock workers who tended the machines in this surrealistic, sealed and climate-controlled environment. It even smelled different. The floors and walls all had washable white plastic surfaces that lent the entire place an aura of hyper-controlled cleanliness and order.

While the lower and intermediate floors were by far the largest part of the building, the most interesting sectors were in the upper floors that rose in an elevator-serviced tower at the center of the building. This was the executive tower. The elevator itself required a special access key in order to move beyond the first floor or two. As I rose from floor to floor toward the top of the tower, the offices became larger, more ornate, and very secluded from public view. As I stepped off the elevator, each successive floor had deeper, more aesthetically patterned carpeting. Hallways replaced the mazes of cubicles of other levels, and classical oil paintings, overstuffed Victorian chairs, vases full of flowers, pewter coffeepots, and newspaper racks adorned waiting areas in the halls. Many secretaries now appeared to have separate, walled offices that dwarfed even the middle managers' offices of lower floors. Receptionists' areas were stationed in strategic places to intercept people coming off the elevator before they could access interior offices. The waiting areas were luxurious, with catered coffee, newspaper racks, and the like. Even the public rest rooms were on a par with those of exclusive hotels. The very top floor housed the immense office of the CEO, which had a mammoth mahogany desk and matching leather chair that I normally used during my break in a sort of pathetic, symbolic reversal of our power roles. There also was an adjacent health spa and racquetball court that had only a dozen or so private lockers for top executives' use (I saw no female quarters), but I never had time to try the facilities out.

I could well imagine as I passed from one floor to the next the salary and decision-making differences of the workers who occupied them. That much was obvious not only from the luxurious accommodations of the upper levels, but also from the high-level deliberations that were represented in charts and graphs that tended to be left in upper-level meeting rooms. Less transparent, I thought, was how uncomfortable and insignificant a worker from the lower realms of the organization must have felt on the rare occasion (if at all) that he or she might be required to interact directly with an otherwise distant superior in the confines of such extravagant environs. These types of cultural/symbolic differences serve as unerring reminders to bosses and subordinates alike that they differ in organizational power, that some should lead and others follow, and that the bounty of corporate profits will flow more freely to some than others.

It is important to realize that the types of political symbolism I allude to in the above example are found in all sorts of organizations, not just private corporations. A lesson learned is a lesson generalized to other instances. Consider the college campuses that many of us walk about every day. There are architectural differences between the buildings that more and less prestigious departments inhabit. Peripheral programs that are poorly funded tend to occupy geographically peripheral sites and/or less desirable quarters, while core liberal arts departments usually are given symbolic centrality in the campus. Sporting arenas reflect the power of alumni donations, and there are other symbolic differences in the quality and size of facilities for male versus female sports and events, uniforms, and media coverage of men's and women's sports. The availability and proximity of parking spaces to campus varies between power groups at colleges and frequently is a topic of debates (if not violence) over organizational privilege. Student facilities generally contain symbolic representations of an age group's subordinate place in the college hierarchy (lockers versus offices, uncomfortable classroom seats, and prison-like architecture and surveillance in dormitories and classrooms).

Again, it is possible to extend these observations to widespread societal organizations such as restaurants, post offices, hospitals, the military, and so forth. Objective differences between organizational actors' economic and political powers tend to produce symbolic/cultural differences. These symbolic differences, in turn, often validate (legitimize) objective inequalities by making the subjective social meaning of organizational existence (above, the physical traits of organizations) one that is unchallenged, and taken-for-granted by the actors involved.

CONCLUSION

There are, of course, many specific arenas of power that I have not mentioned in this chapter. Inequalities in terms of class, race, gender, age, and many other groupings significantly are the results of power structures in governments, in organizations, and in everyday life. In these, and other cases, a basic analytical approach to deciphering the inequalities observed is to consider the combinative effects of political coercion, economic exploitation, and cultural domination on the people involved. Our ability to cut to the core of these building blocks of power and inequality will serve the cause of justice and equality better than merely describing the extent of inequality in one or another venue of its appearance.

If this chapter has served its intended purpose, it now should be clear that power is a more complex issue than many people suppose it is. I believe that the foremost hidden dimension of social power is the fact that differences in power and related inequalities are often accepted by subordinates as legitimate "business as usual." Social power need not manifest itself in overt conflict to be a significant part of people's lives. Indeed, power structures more often than not take on the appearance of stable, even harmonious, human affairs.

From a moral standpoint, the ability of authorities to conjure up beliefs among subordinates that power does not exist, or if it does that it is justified, may seem just as hideous as power that takes the form of bloody massacres, or power that employs heartless wage exploitation. But here the discussion moves from social analysis into ethics proper, which of course is another field. Yet having one's sociology straight can be an asset to ethical action.

SUGGESTIONS FOR FURTHER STUDY

Dennis Wrong. 1988. *Power: Its Forms, Bases, and Uses.* Chicago: University of Chicago Press.
Probably the best modern discussion of the concept of social power, Wrong's book is very attentive to the many nuances of this idea.

Mario Diani and Donatella Della Porta. 1997. *Social Movements: An Introduction.* Oxford: Blackwell.
An excellent general introduction to the sociology of power and social movements.

C. Wright Mills. 1956. *The Power Elite.* New York: Oxford University Press.
A classic sociological study that first exposed the power alliances among politicians, the military, and industrial leaders.

Robert Bullard. 2000. *Dumping in Dixie: Race, Class, and Environmental Quality.* Boulder, CO: Westview.

Center for Ethics and Toxics (CETOS). Online: www.cetos.org.

People do not generally think of environmental issues as involving social inequalities, but Bullard shows how the disadvantaged receive a disproportionate share of environmental abuse. The social movements that oppressed groups have organized to resist this trend are discussed with great insight. The CETOS website provides up-to-date information on critical issues of this sort.

United Students Against Sweatshops. Online: www.usasnet.org.

Amnesty International. Online: www.amnesty.org.

National Organization for the Reform of Marijuana Laws. Online: www.norml.org.

National Organization for Women. Online: www.now.org.

Mothers Against Drunk Driving. Online: www.madd.org.

Power tends to become highly organized and bureaucratized in successful social movements. Check for evidence of this trend in the above websites of social movements devoted to issues of workers rights, human rights, marijuana legalization, women's equality, and drunk driving. Also, see what alliances of interests each movement appears to meld within the central organization.

Berkeley in the Sixties. 117 min. Directed by Mark Kitchell.

This superb documentary relates the diverse alliances that went into the making of the student movement of the 1960s. You'll learn that hippies and civil rights leaders had less in common than many people suppose.

Matthew Kerbal. 1999. *If It Bleeds, It Leads: An Anatomy of Television News.* Boulder, CO: Westview.

Wag the Dog. 97 min. Directed by Barry Levinson.

The power of mass media to effect the legitimacy of power-holders much rests in an ability to keep common people mesmerized with false issues. Kerbal's examination of news reporting explains how and why this happens, while Barry Levinson's film *Wag the Dog* explores the role of news propaganda in legitimizing the state through the drama of warfare.

Robin Leidner. 1993. *Fast Food, Fast Talk: Service Work and the Routinization of Everyday Life.* Berkeley: University of California Press.

In a fascinating comparison of workers at McDonald's restaurants and salespeople for an insurance company, Leidner shows the subtle ways that bosses control their workers.

Terrance E. Deal and Allan A. Kennedy. 2000. *Corporate Cultures: The Rites and Rituals of Corporate Life.* Cambridge, MA: Perseus.

Charles Derber. 1998. *Corporation Nation.* New York: St. Martins.

A principal center of power in modern societies is large corporations that influence our lives in myriad ways. Derber's book is a superb account of the pervasiveness of this influence, while Deal and Kennedy's work analyzes the cultural meanings and symbolism that corporations promulgate.

Jeffrey Reiman. 1996. *The Rich Get Richer and the Poor Get Prison.* Boston: Allyn and Bacon.

A must-read for anyone who thinks imprisonment is merely what happens to bad people. Reiman forcefully shows the class and racial/ethnic bias that is behind the record levels of imprisonment that America is undertaking today in the name of social justice.

Angela Davis. 2000. *The Prison Industrial Complex.* CD-ROM. 54 min. BAK Press.

Davis, a formerly imprisoned member of the Black Panther party, is a moving speaker who discusses her path to activism and the alarming case of the modern "prisons for profit" initiative of corporate capitalism in this speech.

CHAPTER 5

Globalization

Conceptualizing Twenty-First-Century Social Change

When the classical social theorists of the nineteenth century stepped back to take a look at changes that were underway in the social fabric of their societies, many of them embarked on that endeavor with a great deal of uncertainty and confusion, for they were not quite sure what the future held in store. The capitalist economy and the nation-state were too new on the social scene to make much of a confident assessment of them. Some analysts waxed nostalgic for bygone days, some foresaw unending social progress, while still others criticized the social ills that accompanied these developments. We are in much the same situation today with regard to our understanding of the acceleration of global social relations, but we surely stand to benefit from the lasting insights that these thinkers bestowed upon us about the mechanisms that shape the social world. "Globalization" is the buzzword of our age, but its exact meaning is the object of much contention. Most people would agree that the term implies a compression of physical space and time on a global scale, but beyond that there is much to be sorted out. This final chapter addresses the issue of globalization with a sociological eye to the enduring usefulness of key concepts and theories that have been discussed in earlier chapters.

INTRODUCTION

Many people feel put on the defensive when global issues are discussed. Perhaps their lack of international travel makes them feel they have little familiarity with the subject. It is ironic that Americans are among the world's greatest travelers and yet they are highly insulated from global issues by the sparse attention that American mainstream media coverage gives to most global happenings. At the outset, I will advise you that neither of these facts in themselves are reasons to feel ignorant, or still less to feel oneself incapable of gaining an understanding of the issues at hand. Being a tourist is but a small part of experiencing globalization.

The fact of the matter is that we are all more "global" in our lives now than ever before, whether we like that situation or not. The Ford and Volkswagen cars we drive are products of global assembly processes, the Gap and Old Navy clothes we wear may be stitched in foreign sweatshops, the chocolate we eat and the coffee and soda we drink come from plants that may be harvested by global workers who themselves are on the brink of starvation, and the jobs we hold or hope to hold may no longer exist if they are exported to distant lands. Oddly enough, K-Mart sells as many global goods as Pier One Imports, and the General Motors labor force is more global than American. We also experience global affairs instantaneously and simultaneously with distant peoples. The September 11, 2001, attacks on New York were known in Japan as quickly as they were in Boston. Stock markets react instantly to minute changes in global circumstances. Risks of all sorts are increasingly shared globally as a consequence of interdependence (Beck 1999). Midwestern farmers who grow genetically modified corn, European consumers who reject the product as unsafe "Frankenfood," and Mexican farmers who produce an alternative product are all linked in their actions. What we do affects people in other places, as well. If we support wars that ravage innocent people, we are global actors. Our policies and practices toward immigrants drastically influence the character of other countries. The cultural icons that people embrace—from Mickey Mouse to the Marlboro Man—are increasingly the same ones that other societies find at their doorsteps. Perhaps most importantly in the case of the American and other citizens of wealthy countries, our inattention to the plight of fellow humans affects them because our governments and economic policies are implicated in their problems. The task then, is to begin thinking critically about current trends, even if they seem remote, frightening, or beyond our control.

GLOBALIZATION: HOW GLOBAL, HOW NEW?

It may be helpful to think of globalization as a variable, rather than as an accomplished fact. That is, some areas of human activity have been more globally linked than others, some nations have been more influential in defining global matters than others, some of these linkages are stronger between certain nations, and some connections are of more recent origin than others. Globalization certainly involves social power, but as we saw earlier, power is seldom absolute and its exercise and reception take on different forms.

An important debate concerns the extent to which changes associated with globalization are the result of the emergence of a mutually interpenetrating *global* society, or are merely an indication of an increasingly *Americanized* world. There can be little question that U.S. economic, political, and cultural influence on other societies today exceeds that of any other nation. U.S. corporations dominate global economics, the United States is the undisputed and sole military superpower on the planet, and American culture has profoundly penetrated even remote societies. Other countries such as Japan and Germany similarly have extended their economic influence through their large corporations, but hardly influence global culture in the manner that American sports heroes such as Michael Jordan or Hollywood films have done. In politics, the proclamations of the Brazilian president or Canadian prime minister are weighty, but hardly command as attentive a global audience as those of an American president.

On the other hand, America itself must adjust to global economic and political realities, and foreign cultures continue to exercise strong influences in what has always been a melting pot American culture. The U.S. economy was rocked by the September 11, 2001, attacks by foreigners, but its subsequent invasion of Iraq was harshly criticized by global audiences. The U.S. failure to ratify the Kyoto, Japan, environmental summit accords in 1997 and prior U.S. boycotting of the Rio de Janeiro conference in 1992 similarly cost the United States dearly in terms of world opinion. The American music scene—from jazz to reggae to hip-hop—continues to derive from diverse global contributions. The lesson to be drawn from these observations is that one should neither underestimate nor exaggerate the part played by the United States in globalization.

Wherever globalization stems from, if anywhere in particular, a further consideration is the relative novelty of these forces. It is not as though crossing time and space boundaries began in the late twentieth century. The expansion of world empires—Roman, Ottoman, Ming, Dutch, British, Spanish, Russian, and others—is quite simply the fabric of world history (Arrighi 1999). In each case, some of the elements of modern globalization were present, for example, economic exploitation by global business such as the British East India Company, political domination by foreign armies, and cultural imperialism as in the case of the spread of Christianity by Western European missionaries. One thing that may be new in the case of modern globalization, as world-system analyst Immanuel Wallerstein (1974–1989) has argued, is the downplaying of direct political/military force in favor of more abstract economic exploitation as the driving force of globalization (the U.S. invasion of Iraq being an exception, of course). The sheer number of powerful economic actors and the interconnectedness of economic markets have vastly increased in the past few decades. The means for rapidly spreading information and culture have improved from the at one time revolutionary printing press and clock, to radio, television, and now the Internet in fairly quick succession. As access to these most recent inventions rises, so too globalization processes surely will advance.

Earlier, I discussed C. Wright Mills' (1959) advocacy of attentiveness to the nuances of social structural and historical forces as lynchpins of the sociological imagination. We would be well advised with respect to this strange, but in some ways familiar, matter of globalization not to mistake current global experiences for being utterly uniform or entirely unique in history.

ECONOMIC AND POLITICAL GLOBALIZATION

Globalization is a notoriously broad concept that entails a number of interrelated social processes. For clarity of presentation, I will organize this discussion of globalization around its economic, political, and cultural manifestations, along with a number of important subdivisions of these three realms. Figure 5.1 serves as a guide to some of the more important facets of globalization that are discussed in this chapter. While the three dimensions are analytically separable, they often are entangled in complex ways in global realities. Therefore, many of the examples that I will discuss reflect this intermingling of economic, political, and cultural domains of globalization.

The economic dimensions of globalization are as critical to the livelihood of the world's majority working and poor populations as they are to the wealth of the minority who benefit from globalization. Who are the poor and the rich of the global economy, and

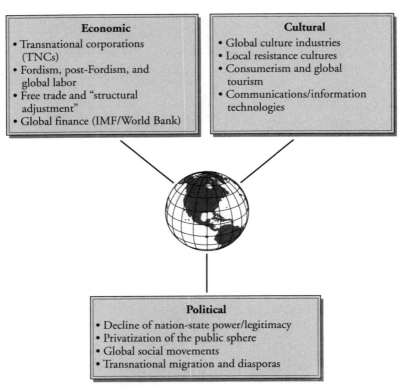

Figure 5.1 Essential Economic, Cultural, and Political Globalization Processes

what makes them that way? The most simple matters of who eats and who does not, who gets health care and who suffers debilitating illnesses, and who toils long hours for meager pay and who enjoys the fruits of stupendous salaries are all economic issues. Today, the disparities in the above categories are increasing at alarming rates, even while new technologies of production and distribution promise a world of plenty. Inequalities within the richer, developed countries of the globe are deepening, but even more dramatic are the inequalities between regions of the world where sub-Saharan Africa, Central and South America, and many parts of Asia live in deepening poverty that dwarfs even the worst conditions in Europe and North America. I begin this consideration of global society with a focus on economic and political issues because these material conditions ultimately are the largest life and death matters. Cultural globalization forces are critical and closely related issues that I will deal with in turn.

The Ideological and Policy Basis of the New World Order: Neoliberalism and Its Critics

Economic globalization is not merely the end result of some inevitable unfolding of the logic of economic development, although that is what some advocates of the system would have us believe. The most forceful arguments in favor of economic globalization are based on claims that globalization is good for humanity as a whole. This strand of economic thought has a very long history. The "liberal" theory in classical economics that this set of policies is based on is hardly what modern people typically think of as liberalism—in fact, it is in many ways just the opposite of what liberal politicians of the twentieth century fought for. The eighteenth-century economist Adam Smith was the chief sponsor of the early liberal theory of laissez-faire, free market economic policy—the idea that the economy obeyed laws of its own that ought not be impeded by government or other regulations, and that the market itself was a self-balancing mechanism that led to the greatest public good. The "liberal" aspect of this theory argued that markets needed to be "free," that is, liberated from government and other nonmarket fetters like trade unions that "artificially" propped up wages. **Classical liberalism** revolves around these central ideas. In the latter part of the twentieth century, this meaning of liberalism gave way to new and critical economic ideas based in the work of economist John Maynard Keynes (1883–1946) about the necessity for liberal social benefits (welfare, health, education, unemployment insurance, etc.) to citizens from government intervention that tempered the ills of inherent unemployment crises associated with capitalist development. These ideas are called **Keynesian economics**. Hence, the renewed support for free markets and government nonintervention in the current phase of economic policy is called "neoliberalism," so as not to confuse its objectives with twentieth-century liberalism.

Globalization enthusiasts embrace the ideas of liberalism in its classical rendition. There is more, though. Observing that the great surge in industrial production and improvement in human material conditions first occurred in Western Europe and North America, the proponents of globalization assume the same practices that happened in these regions must be the key to development in poorer regions of the globe. Modernization theory, a close relative of evolutionary functionalist thought, which dominated thinking about international relations in the immediate post–World War II era, asserted that the poorer nations of the world needed to follow the lead of the developed nations if they were to improve their circumstances. They would need to industrialize, democratize governments, and above all adapt themselves to open trade in the world economy—and any excess riches would then spill over to their societies. Free trade arguments are a direct extension of modernization thought.

The opposite of "free trade" in this understanding of economic processes is **protectionism**. Protectionism is the intervention of government in the establishment of barriers to free markets—things such as tariffs on imported goods that give domestic industries advantages over foreign competitors, price controls, minimum wage laws and unions that raise the costs of labor for foreign investors, government-run industries and services (railways, utilities, water purification, education, etc.) that are not open to market competition, and more recently environmental regulations that raise the costs of production of goods. Free trade, not protectionism leads to development, or so the story goes. What educated critics see as missing in this narrative, of course, is the fact that countries that developed did so by establishing strong protections from foreign competition where and when needed—the United States did this with regard to Britain and other global powers in terms of steep tariffs, and the more successful Asian economies were guided by strict governmental policies in more recent times. Economic success stories typically have borrowed only selectively from the advice of neoliberal economists.

The idea of free markets in economics is nothing new, then. What has changed is the balance of national and global economic policies toward the principles of classical liberal economics, and away from economic Keynesianism. It all accelerated in the 1980s with the leadership of the United States and Britain under President Reagan and Prime Minister Thatcher, respectively. These leaders spoke in rosy terms of a "new world order" that would mean prosperity for all. In the United States, this was the dawn of conservative Republicanism (forging free market capitalism and cutting social programs) that has persisted to the present, and made the differences between Republicans and Democrats negligible in terms of broad domestic and foreign policies. The collapse of the Soviet Union in the early 1990s gave neoliberals new ammunition in their arguments that government-run economies were inherently inefficient and doomed to failure. The impact of neoliberalism on global economics has been immense and by and large unimpeded since 1980. Its essential and interrelated principles can be summarized as follows:

1. **Free markets** for the flow of capital, goods, services, and labor in the business sector
2. **Deregulation** of all business activity by government and other organizations, and reduction of government size and influence in general
3. **Government Social Benefit Cuts/Reductions** (e.g., in social welfare programs, unemployment benefits, free health care, public education, public transportation, postal service, public parks and other recreation sites)
4. **Privatization** (selling off to private investors) of government-run industries and services (e.g. public utilities, highways and railways, hospitals, schools, and prisons)

These ideas have already been implemented in many domestic and foreign policies, and more extensive measures loom on the horizon. Social security and welfare have been under attack in the United States, the electricity and other industries have been deregulated, public schools and prisons have been privatized to some extent, labor organizing and minimum wage increases have been suppressed, North American trade with Mexico and much of the rest of the globe has been opened, generous European welfare states have seen slashes in their programs, and global economies have seen their doors swung wide open to foreign investment.

Who are the critics of neoliberalism? On the one hand, there are liberals in developed countries who long for a return to domestic policies that favor workers and the poor in their home countries. These critics are not always so concerned about global inequalities. Other critics see the plight of global peoples as an additional issue. Then, of course, there are the masses of global peoples themselves who have seen the results of globalization policies in their own lives and have mobilized to combat these forces. I shall have more to say about these global resistance movements later as elements of political globalization. Nearly all critics of neoliberalism are disturbed by the lack of government-sponsored social "safety nets" for the many people who are not benefiting, and indeed are suffering more than ever before, as a result of the globalization of the economy. Neoliberalism answers that "individual responsibility and freedom" are part and parcel of this system, that is, the poor are left out only by their own choice and/or lack of ambition to take advantage of the market system. The Western philosophical principle of individualism is thus deeply embedded in the globalization movement, whereas the notion of policies that directly promote societal or public good is submerged under the supposed social efficiency of markets themselves and the supposed failure of socialism worldwide.

Globalization critics have strong evidence to marshal against any naïve notions that recent policies unambiguously benefit the whole world. Much as Karl Marx judged the problem with capitalism not to be its productivity but its exploitation of workers, many of these critics see the globalization problem not so much as a problem with the world becoming more interconnected, but as a problem with the conditions surrounding this weaving together of the world's people—who wins and who loses? Both capitalism and its globalization have in principal great potential for human betterment in this view, but the distribution of rewards from such an endeavor is the key. So what has been the result of now decades of neoliberal global economic policies? For this, we might turn to James Wolfensohn, the former head of the leading financial motor of economic globalization, the World Bank, who admitted that "at the level of people" globalization has been a failure (Faux and Mishel 2000). What else could one say when faced with the fact that after near full implementation of neoliberal policies, the poorest people on Earth are poorer than before, everyday workers of the developed world have lost ground, and a small cadre of the rich have grown phenomenally richer? Consider some disturbing indicators:

• In the United States, 75 percent of the workers are worse off economically now than in 1980.
• The wealthiest 1 percent of U.S. citizens controls more wealth than the lower 92 percent of citizens as a whole. Average CEO salaries in Fortune 500 companies are 170 times the compensation of the lowest paid workers in those companies.

- Corporate profits have skyrocketed. About half of the world's largest "economies" now are not nations but private corporations, most of them based in developed nations and operating in other countries (comparing national gross domestic products versus corporate annual sales). Ninety-nine out of 100 of the world's largest "multinational" corporations are based in the developed world.
- The top 200 corporations undertake 28 percent of all global economic activity, while employing less that 1 percent of the global labor force.
- Global environmental problems of many types have grown worse. Deforestation and fossil fuel emissions have depleted the ozone layer, leading to a consensus in the world scientific community that global warming is a serious and worsening problem with dire consequences.
- Global poverty has increased, not decreased, since 1980.
- In economically "liberated" Mexico, 75 percent of the population now lives in deep poverty, compared with 49 percent in 1981.
- Poor countries as a whole have paid five times as much in interest on debts to the developed world as they have received in foreign aid loans since the 1980s. Overall, their debt has more than doubled since 1980, while their poverty has increased.
- In sub-Saharan Africa, site of extensive neoliberal policy implementation, debt repayment is four times what it was in 1980, and exceeds spending on health care by 400 percent. Foreign debt per capita is almost 20 percent higher than gross domestic product per capita.
- Women and children have suffered most acutely from increased globalization and poverty worldwide. Seventy percent of the world's poor are now women.
- Global consumption of Western culture (as represented in the movie, music, sport, and fashion industries) has increased, while material hardships in poverty-stricken regions remain.
- The introduction of market economies to former socialist states, and of democratic government to former dictatorships, has not led to improvement of economic conditions in these countries.

While it is true that global poverty existed before 1980, and while there are some isolated cases of economic improvement, the undeniable fact is that things are now worse for the vast majority of the global poor, worse for average workers in many developed countries, and yet strangely much better for a small fraction of humanity. "At the level of people" Wolfensohn was surely right about the failure of globalization, but what other level matters? For an answer to that question, we need to take a closer look at the actors and mechanisms guiding current economic globalization initiatives and the way that so few win and so many lose.

The Global Power of Transnational Corporations

General Motors Corporation (GM) makes cars and trucks, such as Chevrolets, Buicks, and Cadillacs. Headquartered in Detroit, Michigan, GM is the largest business in the world and has been for some time now. Mass production of autos in domestic factories where workers were unionized, loyal, long-term workers in well-paid jobs marked much of the company's history until the late twentieth century. The United Auto Workers (UAW) union was formed in a GM plant in Flint, Michigan, in the 1930s, and, as Michael Moore's famous documentary *Roger and Me* (1987) suggests, both company and workers prospered for many decades. Today, GM and many other large corporations worldwide such as Wal-Mart, Sony, Hewlett-Packard, and Nestle no longer confine their economic activities to one nation. GM, for example, still maintains a Detroit home office but assembles cars globally. Production facilities in Canada, Mexico, Europe, and Asia make the cars from parts that likewise are made the world over by other companies whose headquarters are in particular countries, but who manufacture globally. The auto industry is not unique in this regard, for other industries do the same thing—Coca-Cola and Pepsi in soft drinks and bottling, Philips and Samsung in electronics, DuPont and Dow in chemicals, Anheuser-Busch and Heineken in beer, Shell and Exxon in petroleum, and so on with nearly every major economic good or service. It has become trite to say that our goods are made elsewhere, but serious reflection on the extent and larger consequences of this fact is revealing.

GM and similar corporations are "multinational corporations," or as they now are called in an effort to emphasize their relative independence from the rule of particular governments, **transnational corporations** (TNCs). TNCs are economic organizations that *own and operate production and/or service facilities* in more than one, and often many, countries (on average, ten, but some have many more). Note that they do not merely sell goods and services globally, buy foreign parts, invest in foreign stocks, or have representatives who sit on boards of directors of foreign companies, none of which alone make a company a TNC—TNCs fundamentally *are* transnational because they fully control global economic production entities. They are engaged in what is known as **foreign direct investment** (FDI), or investment where the TNC has a controlling share of ownership in an enterprise, as opposed to a simple stock portfolio investment (Weisbrot 1999).

The growth of TNCs in the late twentieth century and into the present has been astronomical in terms of numbers, wealth, control of basic economic markets, and political and cultural influence. There are about 63,000 such businesses today. The vast majority of TNCs are based in the richest of the developed countries. The United States leads in this regard, but Canada, Western Europe, Japan, and Australia have their fair share of TNCs.

Why do TNCs operate across national boundaries? Some of the reasons are simple technical matters, as for example when it is more profitable and efficient to produce closer to where raw materials are available, or nearer to where products will be consumed. Transportation costs drive globalization in this case. Transnational business has a long history of such practice. The risks and feasibility of distant economic activity were often complicated by unpredictable and/or hostile global circumstances (strikes, revolts, piracy, and volatility in laws and customs, for example) on the one hand, and by communications and transportation technology difficulties on the other. For these reasons, early transnational activity often was militarily reinforced and limited to relatively simple endeavors that required little and infrequent communications with home offices. The expansion of postal, radio, telephone, and now Internet services to remote areas have radically enhanced the technical feasibility of global economic enterprise, which is another reason for the rise of TNCs.

Globalization advocates tend to laud these technical efficiency bases of global trade, along with the cornucopia of productivity that supposedly will spill over to the world's poor. However, there are other reasons for globalizing production that critics argue center on social power, exploitation, and growing inequality. TNCs seek out cheap global labor and actively endeavor to keep it cheap. An electronic circuit maker or sewing machine operator in Juarez, Mexico, or Singapore costs much less in wages than the same worker in Cleveland, Ohio, or Boston, Massachusetts, because the workers in the former countries tend to be poorer, nonunionized (often legally barred from organizing), more plentiful due to high unemployment rates, and thus willing to settle for lower wages. The same idea is true for costly workers in Canada, Germany, Japan, Sweden, and other developed nations compared to cheaper workers in much of Africa, South America, Asia, and the Middle East. Labor in the "global north" currently is more costly than it is in the "global south." Labor in the developed countries also is more militant and demanding that its interests be served. TNCs often desire female and youth labor in poorer countries because these workers' relative powerlessness in their own societies makes them more easily manipulated than grown males. A further consequence of this pursuit of cheap global labor is job loss and falling wages among workers in the developed countries themselves, as they stand in competition with global workers. Thus, job losses in Ohio or California are intimately tied to "development" in the global south. Neoliberal economists make no bones about their expectation that wages in the developed world will continue to fall until they reach parity with the global labor force. This prediction assumes, of course, that workers will not undertake and succeed in the difficult task of organizing and resisting exploitation globally, as opposed to nationally.

Global labor is now characterized by its "flexibility" (a kind term, to say the least) and disposability in the hands of TNCs. In the decades following World War II, unionized jobs in developed nations generally paid well, guaranteed a retirement income and other benefits such as health care, and involved performance of a specialized task that workers did for a lifetime in the same company and community. This mode of work organization is called **Fordism**, named after the way Ford Motor Company and many other businesses treated their workers. The transformation of work in the late twentieth century into the present is called **post-Fordism** and has become a dominant feature of the global economy and of TNC labor policy. The new flexibility of global labor in both developed and poor regions means that work and compensation are now offered on an "as needed" basis, with little expectation from workers or employers that one will do the same job for a lifetime, few if any guaranteed retirement or other benefits, and a general recognition that companies owe workers nothing beyond the wages they offer on a "take it or leave it" basis. Work long hours for regular pay, without overtime bonuses, is the new rule. Companies can move to new global locations without remorse for communities or nations that are devastated by their departures. By the same token, labor is expected to physically relocate to where businesses offer work. This movement creates vast streams of **transnational migration** of peoples. The combined effect of labor displacement and refugees from global political upheavals has resulted in the formation of far-flung geographic **diasporas** (communities of people dispersed globally, such as Turks in Istanbul, Madrid, and New York) of displaced national and ethnic groups that struggle to maintain coherent identities in the face of these disruptive forces.

It is very costly for businesses to care about their employees' welfare and still make optimal profits. It likewise is unprofitable for them to have concern about the environment and the long-term effects of their conduct of business for the future of humanity. In the twentieth century, the developed countries almost universally established legal restraints on business practices that unduly exploited labor, and at later points in time, the environment. Social movements involving primarily domestic environmental issues arose all over the developed world in the late twentieth century (global environmental movements are more recent phenomena). In the United States, the Environmental Protection Agency (EPA) was established and charged with a host of regulatory tasks to protect air, water, and land from the plunder of business and consumer practices. Although its charge was really unmanageable given its insufficient funding and staffing, EPA did bring about some swift and sweeping changes in environmental quality in the 1970s. Water toxicity was greatly reduced in many instances. Lake Erie, all but dead to aquatic life and actually flammable as a result of industrial pollution in its worst ports, was revived. Smog in cities such as Los Angeles, Denver, Chicago, and New York was drastically reduced by emission and fuel regulations. Agricultural pesticides and herbicides were scrutinized, resulting in removal from the market of a number of dangerous chemicals such as Dow Chemical's DDT. Forests and wetlands were partially saved, along with a number of animal species that were on

Global corporate homicide? In 1984, lethal gases from a defective Union Carbide Corporation pesticide plant in Bhopal, India, exposed 500,000 people to the gases. Three thousand people died immediately, about the number killed in the September 11 attacks on the United States. Another 5,000 died in the months that followed, and perhaps as many as 20,000 have died since then of poison-related complications. Eighty thousand people remain chronically ill and unable to work. Groundwater and soil still are highly toxic in the absence of a cleanup. The Indian government filed murder charges against Union Carbide and its CEO Warren Anderson, but both refused to appear for trial. Instead, the company convinced the Indian government that murder charges would create a bad climate for future investment and got the charges reduced to criminal negligence. The settlement gave affected survivors about $500 each on average. In 2001, Dow Chemical bought Union Carbide, forming the world's largest chemical company. Dow refuses any further liability in the case, while at the same time refusing to release vital information on the nature of the gases involved. Amazingly, in 2002, Dow's CEO was invited to sit at the World Summit on Sustainable Development in Johannesburg as Bhopal survivors protested outside (CorpWatch 2002c). (© Reuters NewMedia Inc./CORBIS)

the verge of extinction. Oil production and mining industries were required to clean up their operations to limited degrees.

Many industries, of course, continued to pollute, finding the fines imposed for violations cheaper than the costs of changing production practices. But the costs were there, either way. Meanwhile, the environmental movement had hardly touched the poverty-stricken global south at that time, so few if any regulations on business activity existed. For some industries, the savings in environmental costs were decisive in their decisions to globalize production. For others, the move to globalize was guided by a variety of technical, labor, and regulatory issues. Add to these incentives the relief from relatively high taxes and tariffs that existed in developed countries, and the willingness of foreign governments and global financiers to provide start-up money for global ventures, and it is no wonder that TNCs have multiplied and their profits grown enormously. Still, one wonders why poor countries have been so open to TNC entry. To understand that issue, it will be useful to consider the role of global finance and quasi-governmental organizations and their relationships to poor nations and their economic policies.

International Governmental and Nongovernmental Organizations: International Monetary Fund, World Bank, World Trade Organization, and G-8

It may be tempting to think that since rich countries have helped poor countries in the past (e.g., with food aid, money, and sharing of technologies) and continue to do so in the present with little alleviation of poverty, it is time to cease helping and let poor nations handle their own problems. After all, even employment in developed nations now is exported to the global poor. Unfortunately, this line of reasoning fails to come to terms with the nature of foreign assistance and its relationship to global economics.

The truth of the matter is that foreign aid to the global poor has always come with many strings attached. Food aid, health care assistance, and other amenities have gone mainly to those countries whose wider political and economic policies are in line with the desires of foreign aid givers, or more precisely with the most powerful actors in donor nations, such as TNCs. The primary form of assistance that developed countries provide to poor countries today is loans rather that gifts, and these loans have many conditions associated with them that some analysts say tend to perpetuate rather than alleviate world poverty. These same conditions may make for a highly profitable investment climate for TNCs that are eager to mine the resources—material and human—that are abundant in places such as Brazil, Indonesia, Nigeria, and the global south in general.

The primary lenders to poor nations in recent decades are the International Monetary Fund (IMF) and the World Bank Group (WB), two financial powerhouses with nearly identical lending policies that embrace the principles of neoliberalism as conditions of economic reform in the countries that they lend to. The IMF and the WB are international nongovernmental organizations (INGOs). Established in 1944 at the Bretton Woods Conference to rebuild the battered economies of Europe, the IMF and the WB now are heavily concerned with lending and economic policy reforms in poor countries of the global south (Eichengreen 1996). The money goes to the countries themselves and to TNCs for the projects they undertake. The IMF and the WB work very closely with international governmental organizations (IGOs), such as the World Trade Organization (WTO, formerly the General Agreement on Tariffs and Trade or GATT), the G-8 (formerly G-7, a global policy-making body composed of representatives from the world's eight richest nations), and the Organization for Economic Cooperation and Development (OECD), and various international development divisions of the United Nations (UN). The IMF and the WB are funded by subscriptions from 177 member nations and their taxpayers. While membership includes rich and poor nations, voting and policy making are based on how much money member nations contribute. Rich nations contribute most and thereby dominate IMF and WB policy making. It is customary for an American and a European to be president of the WB and the IMF, respectively. Thus, the richest nations of the G-8, led by the United States, dominate policy at the IMF and the WB and see to it that the interests of the TNCs that are headquartered in their territories are well served.

After decades of IMF and WB loans, poverty and associated health, nutritional, mortality, and educational problems of poor nations are inseparable from their debt problems. In fact, some commentators argue that debt now drives poverty in these nations. There are no bankruptcy provisions regarding IMF and WB loans, so debts from decades past continue to mount no matter the corruption that may have instigated such loans in the first place. Many poor countries spend large portions of their national income servicing interest on IMF and WB debts, to the neglect of desperately needed improvements in national health, education, and infrastructure improvements such as roads and bridges, water supply and sewers, and basic power and communications systems. In other words, they are unable to establish the basic preconditions of development because they are paying out interest on debts that supposedly would bring about development—a vicious circle, indeed. In some cases, early loan funds were siphoned from the people to corrupt rulers who worked in collusion with powerful economic and political interests of the developed world to keep conditions of foreign investment ripe. In Indonesia, dictator General Suharto, whose administration murdered millions of citizens, may have absconded with up to a third of all money loaned. Other funds sometimes were squandered on similarly corrupt, ill-advised, and ultimately unhelpful infrastructure projects that mainly lined the pocketbooks of the firms from developed nations who built them. With no other sources of funding, and faced with understandable internal unrest, leaders of poor nations today reluctantly are more dependent than ever on new external loans to provide at least the illusion of economic improvement to their citizens.

Additional loans are granted only once countries accept terms for reorganization of their economic and political policies in compliance with IMF and WB demands. These **structural adjustment programs** (SAPs), as they are called, set out a familiar neoliberal mantra that often spells ongoing poverty for poor nations, and continued profits for TNCs:

- Eliminate tariffs that protect local producers in favor of free trade, thereby giving TNCs unfettered access to all national markets.
- Privatize government industries and services so that foreign investors can take control of them at a profit.
- Eliminate minimum wage supports and trade unions for workers so that foreign investors will be attracted by cheap labor.
- Cut social programs for health and education, substituting "user fees" to raise money to pay back debts, even while depriving citizens of basic needs.

- Focus the economy on exports that will raise money to pay back debts, even though local business and agricultural production for domestic needs will be eliminated in the process.
- Raise interest rates to create recession, unemployment, wage decline, and small business failures, all of which will draw investment by profit-seeking TNCs.

The "SAP" acronym perhaps is appropriate, as one poor country after another has seen wealth ooze if not gush from its borders to the developed world. Even the most spectacular success stories of economic development policies led by the IMF and the WB—the Southeast

In Malaysia, tropical rainforests were cleared with assistance from developed world interests, exotic lumber and mineral deposits sold to Western markets, and the rest slashed, burned, and bulldozed to make way for mass export agriculture, again to Western markets. Similarly huge-scale developments in the Amazon basin in South America, in the rich forests of Chiapas, Mexico, and elsewhere threaten drastic reduction of biodiversity. Moreover, scientists find that deforestation reduces Earth's capacity to process carbon dioxide, which when coupled with increased fossil fuel heat and emissions results in depletion of the outer protective ozone layer of the planet and heat-trapping buildup of the inner ozone layer (the greenhouse effect) that contributes to global warming. (© Sally A. Morgan; Ecoscene/CORBIS)

Asian economies of South Korea, Indonesia, Malaysia, Thailand, and the Philippines (the "Asian Tigers" as they were called in their heyday)—collapsed in the late 1990s under the weight of overzealously optimistic private banks in developed nations that lent liberally to speculative real estate and other ventures that got caught up in a currency panic that quickly spread throughout the region (Volcker 2000). Having created the bubble of investment opportunity through its own lending policies, the IMF then implored these nations to do more of what the IMF always recommended in order to get bailout assistance. The results were doubly disastrous for the poor nations involved (save for Malaysia, which had seen enough IMF and WB advice and wisely declined on further loans), as unemployment and poverty rose. Meanwhile, the IMF bailed out the private bankers whose wild speculations contributed to the collapse as well, freeing them up to do more of the same kinds of investing in Russia, Brazil, and elsewhere throughout the world. It remains to be seen if the East Asian economy will reemerge as a challenger or successor to the long history of European- and American-centered global economics (Frank 1998).

Bittersweet Chocolate: Child Slave Labor in West Africa

The global economy of TNCs has some very ugly sides. The global market for chocolate is a case in point. Americans love chocolate, so much so that they spend about $13 million as consumers each year, more than any other country. Chocolate is a sweet reward, Americans learn as children, and later they find it is a sensuous gift between lovers. Two corporations—Hershey's and Mars—control two-thirds of the U.S. chocolate industry. Unfortunately, these chocolate "kisses" and whatnot may be products of child slave labor.

Chocolate is made from the cacao plant, which is a native shade-growing tree of Latin American forests. Today, most cacao is commercially produced from sun-growing hybrid trees that have been planted in rows where rainforests once stood. About two-thirds of the world crop now comes from West Africa, where countries such as Ivory Coast and Ghana have up to 40 percent of their exports wrapped up in chocolate, so to speak. All in all, about 14 million people are involved in the making of this luxury food, with the typical farmer earning only about one cent of the sixty-cent value of a candy bar and farm laborers making much less than that (Global Exchange 2002). Many cacao plantation workers have never tasted chocolate, the end product. Farmers sell their crops to governments who in turn use export proceeds to pay off foreign debts.

World tourists now visit the grim historical remains of coastal West African slave encampments that once housed slaves awaiting transport to the New World. Little do most of these sightseers realize that slavery continues in these countries. West Africa is very poor today, but even more poor are neighboring countries to the east, such as Mali, Burkina Faso, Benin, and Togo, where destitute parents pay from $14 to $140 for child traffickers to take their children away to what most believe will be better circumstances in a new household where they will get education, vocational training, and kind treatment (International Labor Organization 2001). They also are told that any wages the children earn will be transferred back to the needy family. The sad truth is that many traffickers sell children outright into slave labor on cacao and cotton plantations and diamond mines, or confiscate their wages as street vendors and prostitutes, never sending money or word of the children's fate back to parents. Some children wind up as commodities in the European sex trade or as ritual objects.

The numbers of children involved are difficult to estimate, but even conservative reports are horrifying—in Burkina Faso alone 80,000 children are placed through third parties to unknown fates; 15,000 Malian children work on Ivory Coast plantations alone; 4,000 Nigerian children were subjects of known trafficking in 1996; and 1,000 per year are known of in Benin. Claiming ignorance of the matter for years, only in 2001 did the chocolate industry take even token recognition of the problem. By 2002, an estimated 284,000 child workers were still involved in West African cacao production.

So Long Nation, Hello Corporation?

The largest TNCs are wealthier and more influential in global affairs than many highly modernized countries. These corporations are far richer and more powerful than poorer countries, no matter how large these countries' territorial boundaries, how abundant their natural resources, or how populous they are. The usual comparison here is corporate annual sales versus the value of a country's total economic production or gross national product (GNP). That measure makes GM a larger economy than either Denmark or Norway.

Wal-Mart's economy is about the same size as that of the world's fourth most populous nation, Indonesia. Nestle is bigger than Egypt, and Unilever (which you may never have heard of) is larger than Pakistan with its 126 million people. The power of TNCs is even more staggering when one begins to think of their additive influence, which often is exercised in political alliances concerning global policy making. The five largest TNCs alone are economically greater than all of the Middle East and North Africa combined. Global corporate coalitions are more powerful than not just countries, but entire continents. Needless to say, this power dwarfs that of workers in particular countries. These workers rarely mobilize across national borders as TNCs do, and workers frequently struggle with one another over available jobs within nations.

A key point about TNCs and the global economy that derives from their having greater economic power than countries is their *political independence* from particular nations and their simultaneous *political influence* over national governments. These seem like contradictory notions, but they are not. The idea simply is that TNCs are free from many of the legal constraints of territorial governments, while at the same time TNCs exert extraordinary control over these governments in terms of policy making. The geographic mobility of TNCs means that they are not bound by the labor laws, tariffs, environmental legislation, interest rates, and other policies of particular locales—they can simply move where they want to maximize their interests. At the same time, they may not have to move if they can influence governments to serve their interests. TNCs' wealth gives them extraordinary access to politics in their home countries by way of election campaign contributions, lobbying, and mass media control (Derber 1998). Their political influence in host nations where they produce is based on these same mechanisms, plus others such as control of international finance.

The political power of TNCs and nongovernmental organizations of national (NGOs) and international (INGOs) scope, along with the dense interconnectedness of global economics, politics, and culture has diminished the abilities of nation-states to act alone in global affairs. Even the United States, as sole superpower, finds itself hesitant to wage warfare in the absence of broad global coalitions against enemies, as the case of U.S. courting United Nations "approval" of two wars with Iraq suggests. The military impotency associated with recent historical losses in Vietnam and Korea, and with U.S. susceptibility to domestic attacks (September 11), led Immanuel Wallerstein (2002) to argue that the United States can either accept its gradual decline in global economic preeminence or accelerate its own fall by continuing to try to act alone in global political affairs, thereby generating worldwide resentment and hostility. These are sobering thoughts in light of recent U.S. global aggression in the "War on Terror."

On domestic fronts, TNC influence over politics has contributed to voting apathy in developed nations where corporate interests are served over those of citizens as a whole, who desire better social welfare in terms of health, education, and relief from economic woes. Increasingly, people reason that party politics are irrelevant to their needs. Oddly enough, this decline in fundamental democratic processes has occurred at the same time as waves of democracy have swept newly independent nations of the global south and Eastern Europe (Markoff 1996). The **Balkanization**, or fragmentation of prior nation-states such as Yugoslavia and the Soviet Union into distinct ethnic nationalisms is itself a further decentering force in some older nation-states.

The precarious future of the nation-state remains a hotly contested issue. Some commentators see little future for nation-states and instead envision the inevitable emergence of new global governance organizations (Ohmae 1995; Strange 1996). Saskia Sassen (1991, 1998) views the geography of globalization in terms of the emergence of global city and regional economic and political centers that will supplant traditional national boundaries and regulatory bodies. Other scholars, such as Anthony Giddens (2000), maintain that changes and erosion of some nation-state influences does not suggest the demise of the nation-state as such. From this standpoint, nation-states will continue to be important players in interaction with newly emerging global political actors.

International Social Movements

If political and economic power and authority have moved significantly beyond national borders to become global phenomena, it is equally true that political resistance to these powers is moving in the same direction—social movements remain relevant to globalization (Hamel, Lustinger-Thaler, and Mahen 1999). Social movements protesting the effects of economic free trade policies, labor conditions, environmental devastation, human rights abuses such as the exploitation of women and sexual minorities, deficient health care, and wars have taken on global dimensions that oppose or seek to influence organizations such as the IMF, the WB, and the United Nations.

The spectacular protests of the meeting of the World Trade Organization in Seattle, Washington, in December 1999 brought nearly 50,000 people in confrontation with police who sought to control the crowd and keep the meeting going. Other global protests of WTO, IMF, WB, and G-8 meetings occurred in Washington, Los Angeles, Quebec City, London, Prague, Barcelona, Genoa, Gothenburg, Buenos Aires, Okinawa, Bogota, Doha, and wherever the organizations sought to conduct their affairs. These protests sometimes brought forth up to a half a million people. During the July 2001 G-8 meeting in Genoa, for example, 150,000 protesters confronted upwards of 20,000 police and military personnel armed with tanks, SAM missiles, fighter jets, battle ships, mine sweepers, and water cannons. Rail, road, air, and sea links to the city were closed off and a "red zone" wall of steel I-beams and concrete was built to block the area surrounding the convention center. One of the G-8 delegates—President George W. Bush of the United States— was housed on an aircraft carrier in the bay, rather than at the convention center. One protester was killed and more than 500 were injured as arrests were made for possessing a knife. Future G-8 delegations would be cut in size from 900 to 35 in order to facilitate security and cut expenses (it cost $110 million to host the Genoa meeting).

The largest globalization protests such as those in Genoa and Seattle have involved alliances of free trade opponents, feminist organizations protesting the effects of globalization on women, labor and environmental activists, AIDS/HIV prevention movements, gay and lesbian rights groups, and other groups casting their demands at global economic and political powers. There were more than 700 organizations represented at Genoa, for example. Smaller protests have been aimed at specific policy conferences (e.g., environmental summits and United Nations commissions on the rights of women) and involved proportionally smaller numbers of organized participants.

McDonald's restaurants have spread to virtually every major city in the world and somewhat tailored their menus to variations in national cuisine. This influence has not happened without local resistance, however. Here, protesters at an Istanbul, Turkey, McDonald's demand closure of the restaurants in their country in 2000. A year later, in September 2001, an explosion ripped through another McDonald's in that city. In December 2002, a Makassar, Indonesia, McDonald's exploded. As Benjamin Barber argues in his Jihad vs. McWorld *(1996), the cultural conflict between Islam and Western society runs deep. The Islamic world is not alone in challenging this global icon of American culture, though. In France, for example, a social movement under the leadership of Jose Bove called the Peasant's Confederation formed, charging that McDonald's threatens the demise of a significant element of French culture—its slow, sociable, appreciation of fine food and conversation. Global McDonald's have become "dangerous places," at least in people's perception of them as centers of cultural conflict. (© Reuters NewMedia Inc./CORBIS)*

Nearly all of these movements have made extensive use of the Internet and World Wide Web to communicate to affiliates and to get word out of their causes where traditional media and political forums ignore their issues. Social justice movements are hampered, however, by the utter absence of computer-based information access among the majority of the world's poor population, and by still quite limited access among citizens outside North America and Western Europe where the technology has had its greatest reach thus far. Nevertheless, these technologies have enabled greater global organization of movements than ever before. The dispersion of movements across cyberspace has also lent such movements the advantage of being more difficult for their opposition to target with destabilizing attacks than traditional, geographically based movements with physical centers of operations, human spokespersons, and activities that take place at specific times.

In many cases, economic and cultural globalization has had the ironic consequence of strengthening people's allegiance and willingness to fight for nonglobal or "local" customs, identities, institutions, and other causes. **Glocalization**, the odd term for this process, involves the development of strong new attachments to local matters as a form of resistance to globalization. It is a form of **globalization from below**, as opposed to globalization at the hands of powerful economic and political actors "above" (Brecher 2000). The resurgence of Islamic fundamentalism is a case in point, where renewed vigor for the most non-Western aspects of the religion (e.g., the covering of women) among people disaffected with globalization is fueled by globalization itself. The same processes have fostered renewed ethnic and national loyalties the world over.

Mexico: Poverty and Protest in a "Model" Free Trade Nation

Mexico exhibits a number of interrelated globalization processes that may be worth exploring in some detail. Like many Americans, my knowledge of Mexico was very limited at first. My first trip to Mexico came in fourth grade. In a sort of "Beverly Hillbillies" affair, my parents moved the family from rural Illinois to Los Angeles, where it was nearly obligatory to wander south across the border to Tijuana. I recall the mayhem of tourists searching for souvenirs, and the indignity of a family photo atop donkeys painted with zebra stripes, each of us sporting sombreros bearing captions like "Kiss Me" and "El Drunko." Much like a trip to a high-rise hotel in Cancun today, it was a dubious educational experience. As I grew up, the only other things I knew about Mexico were the migrant agricultural workers who came in the summer to work in Illinois fields (we couldn't handle southern California, and moved back in less than a year), tales from travelers of the prostitution and drug trade, and stories in the early 1980s that a Chicago public school teacher told me of cheap travel to the beautiful, then remote, beaches of Cancun and Cozumel. I still hadn't learned much, so inspired by the $-35°$ F winter in a Wisconsin city where I was a professor at the time, I returned to the state of Guererro in Mexico in 1994 to warm up and assess things for myself. Mexican poverty was very real, and remained that way in 2003 when I made a subsequent visit. I had a better experiential familiarity of Mexico but still needed a sociological lens to interpret what I saw.

Mexico is an enigma for advocates of neoliberal globalization. Rich in oil and other natural resources, industrialized, open to global markets, export-oriented, and neighbor of the most prosperous nation on Earth, Mexico nevertheless is desperately poor, with over half its population living in official poverty. How could this "model student" of economic and political structural adjustment, as the IMF and the WB called it at the outset of the North American Free Trade Agreement (NAFTA) in 1994, be failing so miserably? Maybe it is understandable that neither U.S. presidential candidate in 2000 called much attention to NAFTA in their campaigns.

Mexican markets were almost completely opened to U.S. and Canadian markets by NAFTA, but this was not the first such restructuring. Mexico has been following IMF and WB prescriptions since the early 1980s. Mexicans call the 1980s the "lost decade" for good reason—wages fell 75 percent; consumer prices rose; government spending on education and other social welfare was cut; lowered tariffs on corn produced a 45 percent price drop that, coupled with similar change in the coffee market, drove farmers off their lands; and more than 1,000 public enterprises were sold off to private investors (e.g., the Telmex public phone system that Southwestern Bell bought, resulting in a sevenfold increase in the cost of local calling) (Global Exchange 2001).

In the 1990s, economic crisis forced Mexico into further IMF and WB loans and reforms, and compliance with NAFTA policies. Unemployment doubled and 12,000 more local businesses filed for bankruptcy. The Mexican Constitution, which once protected communal property (*ejidos*), was altered by NAFTA to facilitate removal of financially ruined people from their last and most cherished resource—their land. Every major quality of life indicator declined, yet Mexico's President Vincente Fox, a former Coca-Cola executive whom the U.S. business community much supported, still saw further adherence to IMF, WB, and other foreign investment recommendations as the key to the country's future.

The newest and in many ways boldest "development" plan targets, among other places, the poorest and most remote of Mexican regions, the state of Chiapas in the extreme south along the Guatemalan border. Chiapas is the home of the lush Lacandon jungle, the last surviving tropical rainforest in North America. Half of all Mexican rainfall is there, making it a target for water resource development. Biodiversity, oil, and fishing are other resources planned for development. Mayan ruins are abundant in Chiapas, and the many indigenous Indian peasants with diverse languages and cultures who live there trace their roots to a Mayan culture that has survived two centuries of European colonization and domination.

Plan Puebla Panama (PPP), proposed by President Fox and the international investment community, would transform Chiapas and the strip of land running southward through Guatemala to the Panama Canal into a vast region for lucrative foreign investment (CorpWatch 2002a, 2002b). There are a number of prongs to the plan. The creation of *maquila* assembly industries similar to those in the north is already underway and would expand under the plan (Sklair 1993). Oil would be developed to supply the increasing U.S. dependency on Mexican oil as its major source. Water resources would be harnessed by twenty-five major dams that would privatize water supply for use in commercial export agriculture (e.g., Monsanto), for factories (e.g., Coca-Cola bottling interests), and for hydroelectric power generation to be used in the factories and to be sold to the U.S. market for power. Railways, roads, bridges, and communications facilities would be improved to facilitate these industries and to bring in more tourists. The rainforests would be taken from the Indians and made into a string of "bioreserves." Critics argue that this later provision of PPP is merely **greenwashing** its economic policies, in other words, creating minimal but highly publicized environmental concessions to appease environmentalists. The bioreserves still would be open to exploitation by foreign bioprospectors in lumbering, agricultural seed industries, pharmaceutical and beauty products, and other industries. At least 780 companies already have been drawn to informational conferences on PPP opportunities.

One problem for PPP, of course, is that for all of this supposed development to happen, the Chiapas peasants on the land have to be removed. That may not be so easy because these diverse Indian populations have created a united identity in the past decade to form a **resistance movement** that targets the corrupt and exploitative Mexican government and foreign domination as their—and other people's—oppressors. This initiative, call the Zapatista movement, seeks democracy, human rights, and self-determination in Chiapas and Mexico as a whole. They are supporters of the peasant Indian's cause. The Zapatistas are at least nominally a guerilla warfare organization, well known for their trademark black ski masks. They live in the forests of the Montes Azul region of the Lacandon jungle. Indian rights to land in this region were taken away in 1992 by the Mexican government under a pretext that built on the publicity of the Rio de Janeiro Conference on the Environment—the Indians were "destroying the environment." It was only at that point that the movement took on a military character. Two years later, NAFTA went into effect and the Zapatista guerillas briefly overran several Lacandon villages, only to retreat back to the forests when the Mexican army arrived.

The Mayan history of colonization and oppression and the Zapatistas' rebel leadership under an urban intellectual called Subcomandante Marcos augurs well with popular Mexican political and cultural themes, even outside Chiapas. Zapatista support from Bishop Samuel Ruiz of the Catholic Church and from other liberation theologians likewise strikes a sympathetic chord with the Mexican people. The surprising strength and visibility of the Zapatistas has not only protected them from outright military elimination by the army, which fears public image problems, but also has made the Zapatistas an important element of Mexican national politics. The rebels are heroes among many of Mexico's poor who see little legitimacy left in their government.

The Zapatistas' real military power is negligible, and their actual mobilization of Chiapas peasants themselves has not been impressive. Still, their extraordinary ability to shape media and other cultural imagery has prompted Manuel Castells (1997) to label them the world's first "informational guerilla movement." The takeover of the villages was carefully orchestrated to gain maximum media coverage, prior to a hasty, low casualty withdrawal. The Zapatistas knew that the social drama surrounding war was as important as war itself. Their cause was promoted with Internet publicity on websites that gave them instant access to a wide array of global allies and sympathizers. This type of **globalization from below** unites resistance against powerful global economic and political actors ("globalization from above") (Brecher 2000). This cyber-awareness also limited the Mexican government's ability to destroy the Zapatistas with overt force. Plan Puebla Panama, a more abstract and invisible economic instrument, may be in part a new strategy for removal of Chiapas' Indians.

CULTURAL GLOBALIZATION

The number 23 has a worldwide meaning, even in countries that don't use Arabic numerals, as "Michael Jordan's number." Professional basketball player Michael Jordan, with a career spanning the Reagan, Bush Sr., Clinton, and Bush Jr. presidencies, is one of the best known persons on the planet. Closely associated with the Jordan mystique is another sign, that of the transnational Nike Corporation "swoosh" that is branded on shoes, T-shirts, baseball hats, and other fashion wear that also can be found in every global enclave. Spawned by a powerful combination of transnational corporate sponsorship, advertising, and global telecommunications, the Jordan/swoosh image is the epitome of cultural globalization processes (LaFeber 1999).

Beyond economic and political transformations, human experience of the world has changed. Cultural meanings, beliefs, and practices associated with objects, events, and places have taken on an astonishingly new global significance in the past few decades. These changes have occurred in close concert with similarly globalized economic, political, and organizational structures. Many cultural topics covered thus far in this book have global dimensions. McDonald's restaurants are routinized workplaces that have gone on from a single hamburger stand outside San Bernadino, California, to become global economic and cultural forces. The Red Hot Chili Peppers rock band was number one on the charts in nineteen countries. Money, such as the Euro, and credit cards are now global currencies that one "can't leave home without," as the American Express credit card advertisement goes. Hollywood films, CNN news, and Disney theme parks have captured a large share of global leisure activity.

The Internet and cell phones generate global flows of information and commerce that people engage in from their homes—something that was inconceivable just thirty years ago. Exotic pets such as tigers, pythons, and llamas are now traded in global markets for mass entertainment among diverse global audiences. Social problems such as terrorism and oil tanker spills at sea attain global proportions overnight by virtue of the spread of mass media outlets. Global television viewers review the progress of wars nightly. Affluent tourists interact with increasing regularity with the global poor, while massive influxes of transnational migration produce hybrid national identities for people involved in these processes.

The examples just cited are only a snapshot of cultural changes that one could go on and on with. Everyone knows at some level of cognition that cultural globalization is happening. Yes, cars and clothing are made globally, but as we have already seen economic globalization is a complex matter. The same is true for cultural globalization. The goal here is not merely to chronicle these changes, but to derive some analytical insights about what is going on. Cultural globalization as a sociological phenomenon can be better understood with the aid of the rich conceptual tradition that invokes ideas such as social power, social structures, organizations, classes and status groups, individuality and identities, the social construction of realities, history, and of course the culture concept itself. Culture at once defines, unites, and divides human groups, and global culture is no different. In the sections that follow, we shall begin with a consideration of the uniqueness of contemporary cultural globalization, and proceed to a look at the field of its greatest flowering—the notion of global consumer society.

Limiting Factors Concerning Cultural Globalization

The worldwide proliferation of Christianity was a highly consequential cultural revolution that obviously predates modern examples of cultural globalization. Western European cultural forms ranging from the clock and printing press to maps, clothing, and culinary habits were likewise strewn across the globe by the political and economic colonization initiatives of Britain, France, Spain, Germany, the Netherlands, and other nations. Moreover, a two-way street existed, where Chinese silk, African ivory and diamonds, Caribbean sugar, Japanese architecture, Indian spices, and other elements of global culture infiltrated and creatively meshed with cultures of the Western world. And of course, other world religions such as Buddhism, Hinduism, Islam, Judaism, and Taoism made their way across vast territories. My point here is that cultural globalization is not utterly new, any more than economic and political globalization are complete novelties. Cultural globalization is indeed a variable, meaning that it is important to gauge the *extent* of the process across time and geographical space.

The interpenetration of global cultures has displayed spurts of intensity throughout history, for example, during the sixteenth-century expansion of global exploration and commerce, over the course of the industrial revolution in Europe and America, and now with the growth of telecommunications (television, the Internet, cell phones) and mass global transportation networks (jet travel) and the extension and improvement of ground transportation in previously remote areas (Arrighi 1999). So, while we are most concerned with the contemporary phase of globalization, it is well to bear in mind that other humans have had to grapple with what were equally incomprehensible changes in their worlds.

The Global and the Local. Experience of many forms of global culture was until recently largely limited to elites and to military personnel of powerful nations who were engaged in various types of imperialist warfare and policing. Costly foreign luxury goods and travel to distant lands marked social status divisions between elites and the masses whose experience of global culture came only in limited interactions with immigrant ethnic groups, transported slaves, and some international shopkeepers and employers. This situation was the case in the United States until the late twentieth century. The United States was certainly a culturally diverse country, but not a global culture in the sense of its citizens as a whole experiencing extensive interaction with global realities. An increasing volume of consumption of global goods and services, particularly among the middle class but also among working-class and poor people, has defined modern cultural globalization. Access to the agents of cultural globalization remains highly stratified, but all are exposed, willingly or not. Home Internet access, for example, is an expensive undertaking that has created a **digital divide** between the affluent who can afford such service and the poor who must use limited public access to such technologies.

This point about unequal access to technologies, goods, and services associated with globalization is even more germane with regard to divisions between developed and poor nations, where chairs, bicycles, and clean water are luxuries in many places. One of the tragic and politically volatile ironies of globalization is that global media create tensions for the global poor between *knowing about* global wealth and cultural accoutrements—say through limited access to a community television, old-fashioned magazines, or by serving tourists—and *possessing* their fair share of it. The outpouring of cultural products from the United States has led some analysts such as George Ritzer (2000) to view the process as primarily one of "Americanization," but other cultural producers, such as those in Japan and Western European nations, deserve due consideration. The movement of culture from poor nations to developed ones also is an important aspect of this process, even if it is less pronounced. In both directions of cultural movement, globalization frequently mixes with local cultures to create new and seemingly strange hybrid cultures in what is known as **creolization**. American adaptation of Japanese pagodas and goldfish ponds alongside garages and decks in suburban homes, minus the other parts of Japanese culture that surrounded and made meaningful these gardening elements, is an example of this trend. Even the hot dog, the quintessential "all-American" food, emerged much earlier as an unexpected mix of German cuisine and peculiarly American circumstances.

Another critical issue that has tempered the effects of cultural globalization has been **global resistance**. In heavily Islamic societies, centuries of tension between religious tolerance and the effects of outside religions have now been augmented by resistance on the part of some sectors of these societies to the spread of Western cultural influences such as McDonald's restaurants, clothing such as the business suit/tie, and women's apparel that exposes the body—even while other foreign cultural products such as telephones and computers are readily embraced; global resistance is full of nuance. The meanings of "serious" American television shows are sometimes turned into "comedic and derisive" ones by laughing viewers in other parts of the world, rather than taken with the intended meanings given by the producers of the shows, again suggesting the limits and vicissitudes of cultural globalization. In some instances, the introduction of global cultures has engendered renewed allegiance to and fervor for local customs (ethnic, racial, and religious), national group solidarities, and organized social movements that seek to oust global culture or limit its influence. In virtually every society, "the global" has had to contend with and very often strike compromise with "the local" in forging distinctive new cultural landscapes.

Cultural globalization then, is an uneven and often interpenetrating process between social groups subject to its historical fluctuations in intensity. It is not the task of sociology to make ultimate judgments about whether this phenomenon is a good or bad thing, but we can discuss and debate the factual consequences that attend its development. Bearing in mind that there are many facets of this transformation that deserve independent assessment, there are analysts who see either broad prospects of hope for humanity or deeply disturbing damages resulting from this trend.

Much as neoliberals see economic globalization as a liberating policy for the world's people, some observers view cultural globalization as a move toward greater "global understanding." In a similarly positive vein, there are arguments that cultural globalization unleashes human creativity as more and more people are allowed to participate in global consumption, making choices from an infinite array of product differentiation and wistfully concocting new global identities for themselves (Featherstone 1991). This **bricolage** view of newly melded global cultural elements is an argument that cultural autonomy and freedom exist for global consumers, in other words, that they are relatively uninhibited by large social structures that determine their choices and lifestyles. In short, cultural globalization represents for these commentators human freedom from the heavy chains of prior commitment to limited territorial social structures such as nations, communities, families, and occupations and the class, racial/ethnic, gender, and sexual orientation groups within them.

Critics of this view of unbridled global cultural creativity point to the obvious limitations that wealth imposes on this fanciful notion of identity choice and regard the idea that universal access to global cultural amenities is merely a matter of time as chimerical. Global consumption patterns are stratified, thus creating worldwide status groups, not a cornucopia of choices. Additionally, the idea of choice in consumption has been ruthlessly challenged by commentators such as George Ritzer (2000) who, following Weber's lead about the rationalization of societies, argues that the "McDonaldization" of products and services under largely American auspices has artificially standardized culture and severely limited our choices. This cookie cutter character of global culture is devoid of the mystery, uncertainty, and difference that previously enchanted the world. Indeed, Ritzer and other critics of **consumerism** charge that global consumption and its advertising machinery are in effect a mandate to buy more needless things and services, not a rational decision made by individuals seeking to satisfy needs that they have identified on their own. Global consumption is a major area of current research and intellectual debate that incorporates and extends a number of central conceptual and theoretical concerns, so a closer look at the issues is appropriate here.

Global Consumerism: You Gotta Shop Around, Even If It's All the Same

In the months following the September 11, 2001, attacks on the World Trade Center and the Pentagon, the U.S. economy accelerated a downward spiral that began somewhat earlier. Stock values plummeted as corporate crime in the grisly Enron Corporation case became clear to Americans. The public had been robbed and bombed and there was no reason to think the worst was over. In highly uncertain times people tend to clam up and hold tight to their resources, but President George W. Bush had a different idea—he urged Americans to get out and shop in defiance of terrorism as the Christmas season approached, as though nothing was wrong. It was advice that dumbfounded even Bush supporters and that he undoubtedly regrets making, but it nevertheless is telling of how central consumption has become to capitalist economies. In a sort of hackneyed way, Bush was right—without shopping, the whole house of cards would come crashing down (although shopping itself obviously depends on a sound economy with adequate wages, job security, and a trustworthy investment climate). A good opening question to ask oneself is, how important is the consumption of goods and services to contemporary societies, particularly relative to the world of work?

From Worker to Consumer Exploitation.   While increasing consumption beyond human needs is a global phenomenon in all developed countries, Americans are among the most incredibly wasteful global consumers. Just think of wardrobes, where people may own ten or more pairs of shoes, a dozen or so sweaters, drawers full of underwear and T-shirts, and so on. Large clothes closets requiring "organizers" and extra capacity washers and dryers that waste space and energy are "needed" to satisfy desires for fashionable clothes that get discarded long before their usefulness expires. Our food is wasteful, too. Feed costs make meat a wasteful food compared to grains and vegetables, yet Americans eat almost five times as much of it as Chinese people do, and fifty times as much as the people of India. Americans' energy consumption is double that of Germans, ten times that of Chinese, and thirty times that of Indians and Indonesians (Durning 1992). The majority of U.S. households have air conditioning, color televisions with VCRs, and microwave ovens today, whereas thirty-five years ago these goods were nonexistent or present only in rich people's homes. Kitchen appliances in American homes exceed what was present in restaurants only a couple of decades ago, as indeed the "commercial" look has captivated the consumer market for these products. Americans have more private automobiles and consume more gasoline to run them than do the people of any other country, although Germans are not far behind now. It is not that consumer products are utterly absent in poor countries—it is the lack of mass access that differentiates these countries from rich ones. Compared to the global poor, Americans and other members of the consumption elite have it all—cell phones and fax machines, computers, big screen plasma televisions and satellite dishes, restaurants and supermarkets, exercise machines and diet programs, shopping malls and ATMs, antiques and artwork, garages for SUVs and boats, manicured lawns and mowers, soda pop and liquors, toys and games, cosmetics and tooth whiteners, pools and sprinkler systems, gourmet pet foods and grooming, psychiatric counselors, and of course legal and insurance services to protect their stuff. Americans also have more garbage cans and trash compactors per capita than any other nation, and a waste management industry that builds dumps that are second to none in volume, even if their environmental protection adequacy is less than state of the art.

So, why do people consume so much in the developed world—what is the meaning of these goods and services? Put differently, what makes people consume? In order to answer these questions, it is helpful to think of three distinct forms of "value" that goods and services may have. First, of course, is practical or **use value**, where food provides for a nutritional need, or wool provides insulation from nature's harshness. Karl Marx, who again focused on class issues, noted that work and production in traditional societies centered on use values. People directly produced what they needed and saw the fruits of their own labor in the satisfaction of these needs. Capitalism as an economic system changed the meaning of things (and of workers) from having use value to having money or **exchange value** as **commodities** in economic markets—capitalist's profits came partly from getting more money for products than they were worth in terms of use value. Marx also hinted at how capitalists could make abstract things that were produced by workers and consumed by others the objects of near religious consumer desires. He called this phenomenon **commodity fetishism**, meaning that the consumers lost sight of needs in favor of wants, and failed to see the essential character of commodities as results of the exploitation of labor. What Marx was getting at with the notion of commodity fetishism was something that later social scientists came to see as symbolic of the **sign value** of things—their cultural meanings to consumers. Max Weber's ideas about status groups who developed distinctive consumption lifestyles was likewise based on a rudimentary notion of sign values, as would be Pierre Bourdieu's later ideas about cultural capital and habitus. Emile Durkheim's work on the role of sacred objects in creating a unifying, collective consciousness also rested on the idea of sign values.

A turn-of-the-twentieth-century American intellectual named Thorstein Veblen (1857–1929) was undoubtedly the most astute early critic of consumption though. His *The Theory of the Leisure Class* (1899) outlined how wasteful consumption of useless commodities, services, and leisure had become the defining characteristic of the new **leisure class**, quite apart from their wealth and control of industry. Veblen's leisure class had much in common with Weber's idea of status groups but went a bit further. The main traits of this class were abstention from useful work, combined with what Veblen termed **conspicuous consumption** (public flaunting of their waste of goods and services) and **conspicuous leisure** (public shows of their slothful avoidance of work). For Veblen, consumption culture spread throughout the class structure of societies as the have-nots engaged in **pecuniary emulation** as they strove as best they could for the lifestyles of the rich. The leisure class was a gluttonous minority atop a symbolic pyramid of status hierarchy whom the rest of society had come to admire, envy, and ultimately mimic. Mass industries were growing to satiate and service the wasteful desires of the leisure class and its wanna-be followers—travel and tourism, pets, nonphysical sports, movies, automobiles, beauty, fashion, and the rest of a now very familiar set of conveniences. Long before the Toys "Я" Us retail chain existed, children became for the first time commodities of consumer parents' adoration and competition in early twentieth-century America as toddler fashion and toy industries, catalogue sales, and advertising agencies emerged to sell to parents ideas about perfect children, and to set children themselves on early paths to becoming consumers (Cook 2000). These industries included high-, middle-, and low-end consumer goods and services to address the pocketbooks of various social strata, much as there are today different sizes and qualities of televisions, or different prestige levels of golf course memberships.

Veblen's work was far ahead of its time. Most sociology in the twentieth century continued to focus on the world of work as the central societal institution that defined people's identities and saw work as the hub of exploitation that spilled over to other forms of social inequality. In developed countries today though, consumption plays perhaps as large a role in the formation of group identities as work, and the exploitation of consumers stands alongside the exploitation of workers as a major basis of domination and inequality. In Fordism, employers appeased workers with paternalistic benefits such as health care, job safety, and a reasonable number of hours in the workday. In post-Fordism, many of these advantages are being eaten away and replaced only by workers' appeasement with consumer goods as tokens of appreciation for their labor. Work may be utterly unrewarding, anxiety-ridden, and exploitative, but workers reason that at least they can afford a cell phone.

As we know, work in the most advanced societies is increasingly concerned with provision of services and management of information, as opposed to the production of goods that increasingly takes place in global poor regions. Poor nations produce but don't consume; rich nations consume but don't produce. We also know that the post-Fordism workplace is one of temporary, impermanent, and in many ways unrewarding employment that fails to capture people's loyalty and identity in the way that working for one paternal company for a lifetime once did. The widespread availability of credit cards and the increasing social acceptability of debt have transformed the United States from a nation of savers to one where the average American is at once a consumer and a debtor. Small wonder then that consumption takes on such added meaning for individuals in postindustrial societies, and emulation of Western consumption habits is common in the poorer regions of the world. New York and Washington get bombed—we shop; people graduate or get married—we shop; our birthday arrives—we shop; depression sets in—we shop some more.

Many people define themselves and boundaries between their groups and others through their consumption patterns: "Abercrombie is really me"; "I'm happiest when I'm with my Harley [Davidson] friends"; "I hate people who drive SUVs." Shopping itself—where and how people shop—is as important to some people as the objects and services consumed, which often are not even rationally planned purchases: "I like Borders better than Barnes and Noble, don't you?" Feelings of self and ecstasy thus emerge in consumption of products and services, where the "real me" is as likely to surface at the shopping mall as at work. There remains a certain hollow character to these new kinds of consumption identity, owing to structural features that produce them. Consumption identities are quite transient, as people's tastes change by their own volition or through the varied influences of fashion and advertising industries (Crane 2000). Unlike traditional community-based identities where people interact on a regular basis in the confines of geographical space and time, consumption identities may consist of loose networks of dissociated individuals who are united only by relatively abstract market, media, and advertising forces. Perhaps it is for this reason that places of consumption like shopping malls are so important to consumers as proxies for other kinds of communal experience.

The Eclipse of Authenticity. The **themed environments** of stores sometimes are as much a part of the consumption and identity-forming experience as the goods and services offered (Gottdiener 1997). The Mall of America in Minneapolis, Minnesota—the most visited site in the country—is the ultimate example of this phenomenon, with its "Lego" display, cyber NASCAR raceway, "Camp

Snoopy," parks, aquarium, and other attractions. The same developers who made this mall earlier made a Canadian one in Edmonton, Alberta, with essentially the same product lines along with another replica, a scale model of Christopher Columbus' ship, the *Santa Maria*. Disneyland, Disney World, and their global extensions offer similar fantasy consumption experiences, as do many chains such as the Hard Rock Cafe, Planet Hollywood, and the Harley Davidson Cafe. The line between truth/reality and reproduction/fantasy in these places sometimes blurs to the point where people experience copies that seem to have no point of reference to an original. Authenticity gives way to its commodified form. Jean Baudrillard (1983) called this global trend the experience of **simulacra**, or things that exist outside of time and space as simultaneous phenomena. Reenactments and replicas are as real, if not more so, as the originals. It doesn't matter where or when you see Mickey Mouse, eat a Big Mac, or watch the Gulf War, for they are in many ways "hyperrealities" that are unbound by conventions of time and space. Global culture is significantly influenced by these kinds of standardized, replicating commodities. A Las Vegas casino done up in "Egyptian" motif may seem to consumers more like Cairo, the country's capital city, than the actual place, which might itself seem more like New York. Tijuana is not Mexico but its commodified form. Hannibal, Missouri, becomes an image of Mark Twain books. Living rooms are made more "Victorian" with available reproduction products than most Victorian homes in fact were. Patchouli fragrances, bell-bottom jeans, beads, and body-piercing jewelry are remarketed to make twenty-first-century youths into replicas of 1960s "hippies." Historical movies evoke more emotion for viewers than the history they are documenting in fact did among past peoples.

It is a comparatively bizarre world with an absence of objectivity and permanence that consumption culture creates for its participants. Nowhere are the traits of consumer culture more evident than in the growth and character of world travel, which is the final topic I will discuss in this regard.

Global Tourism: Cultural Freedom, Structural Constraints, and Exploitation

In addition to the rapid movement of goods, services, and information, globalization entails an acceleration of the physical movement of bodies across territories. Increasing numbers and types of global tourists account for one part of this flow of people, along with international migration that stems from changing regional economic and political circumstances. An analytical distinction may be drawn between **global tourism** as the experience of global phenomena for their own sake, and global military service for political purposes, or global exploration for economic gain. While there clearly is overlap among these types of global experience, my focus here is on global

The world has witnessed an unprecedented growth in tourist movement in recent decades, but the very wealth and technology that has enabled this change has also altered tourists' experience of global realities. The strangeness, danger, and excitement of being in the Sahara desert surely is reduced by the ability to speak on a cell phone to people at home or at work. This search for adventure without leaving behind the comforts of home has encouraged the growth of an accommodating and lucrative tourism industry that offers facsimiles of foreign experiences to mass tourists. (© Stuart Hughes; Photex/ CORBIS)

tourism. Sociologically, global tourism is many things. It is an organized form of global production and consumption, and a way that cultural meanings get forged and contested. Global tourism is a type of social interaction between groups and a basis for individual identity formation. Power, inequality, and exploitation are closely associated with the topic, as well. Global tourism thus serves as a fitting final topic for this book.

Much like globalization in general, global tourism is not entirely new. Religious pilgrimage, for example, has a lengthy history involving tourist travel to holy sites (Shoval 2000). Aristocrats of medieval and early industrial Europe routinely toured neighboring countries and even distant colonies as part of their "cultivation" as cosmopolitan elites.

In the nineteenth and twentieth centuries, wealthy Americans likewise sought cultural enlightenment in trips to the Old World where many of them studied in universities. Arabian sultans, Chinese mandarins, Indian Brahmans, and other global elites took part in similar activities. Global travel offered a desirable mixture of difference, danger, and excitement to privileged travelers as they were confronted with the challenge of interacting with global peoples and their unfamiliar practices and institutions. The artifacts that these tourists brought back from distant places combined with similar relics gathered by missionaries, colonists, and explorers to form the basis of a museum culture that entertained gawking audiences at home in an early example of the commodification of global culture.

What is unquestionably new is the scale of a number of types of tourism in the late twentieth and early twenty-first centuries. In 1950, there were fewer than 30 million international tourists annually. By 2000, there were more than 600 million such travelers each year (Cohen and Kennedy 2000). Contemporary tourists are engaged in many activities, including exposure to foreign cultural places, icons, people, and events; the appreciation of environmental diversity in so-called ecotourism; the experience of disasters, slavery, battlefields, genocide, and other sullen affairs in human tragedy tourism; and commercial sex tourism that offers consumers the satisfaction of sexual fantasies with prostitutes in distant lands. Most of the tourist flow today consists of "mass tourists" who are involved in highly orchestrated, commercial travel to well-known attractions. A much smaller number of other tourists take more individualized, noncommercial paths to global travel.

Global tourism has far-reaching economic, political, and economic implications. It has become a key element of the global economy, rivaling the oil and automotive industries in terms of money generated. Politically, tourism is fostered by host states that seek to create appealing tourist sites and climates of hospitality among their citizens. Terrorists have targeted tourists for attacks that create publicity for terrorist causes and challenge the legitimacy of governments that seek to accommodate tourists. As a cultural force, global tourism is involved in the creation of new meanings of objects, events, places, and people, as well as in the alteration or destruction of prior meanings of phenomena.

Why are there so many more global tourists in recent decades? Simple. Availability of cheap mass transport to global destinations and enhanced tourist amenities at these places have increased in the late twentieth century. Lowered costs have opened opportunities for global travel to a much wider spectrum of the economic class structure of the world. Much like the diffusion of color televisions before, the spread of global travel to new groups marks status divisions between them and less fortunate poor people who cannot afford this kind of travel. Global travel has also become a safer undertaking than it was in previous eras, both in the technical and political senses of safety. Reliable information about destinations has proliferated via advertising and the Internet, and through personal networks of travelers themselves.

Given this growth of tourist movement, two sociological positions have arisen to explain rather opposing views of the significance of this change. One view sees tourism (and globalization in general) as an example of the increasing freedom and cultural autonomy of individual tourists who are released from the binding social structural constraints of nations, classes, racial and ethnic groups, families, occupations, and other groups as they travel aloof from these forces. John Urry (1990), for example, uses the metaphor of the "tourist gaze" to refer to what he sees as tourists' ability to freely and playfully construct meanings of travel experiences for themselves, quite independent of the meanings that sites, events, and other things have for locals or for promoters of travel. Urry and some other "postmodernist" thinkers, such as Jean Baudrillard (1983) and Umberto Eco (1986) see no sense in debating the virtues of authenticity versus reproductions in tourism or elsewhere in society. For them, replicas of colonial Williamsburg are no less "real" than the historical town itself was, and to claim otherwise is to enact arbitrary power in defining reality. These postmodernist observers believe that the world now is one where truth and the cultural authorities that assert it lack the objective validity they had in the "modern" industrial era, and indeed that such claimed truths can and should be subjected to challenges by other social actors who can assign alternative meanings to experiences. These analysts view tourism as an activity that allows people to develop creative new identities for themselves, much as they see shopping as an unencumbered pursuit of individual freedom and identity.

The whimsical imagery of the tourist as individual identity entrepreneur and agent of cultural autonomy has been criticized by scholars who see tourism more as a sphere of social structural determinism, power, inequality, and exploitation. A baseline criticism is that not everyone is touring the globe, only the relatively affluent are. Given this fact, critics see the notion of the dawn of a new age of global identity seekers as premature, if not blind to the sedentary poverty and work-a-day drudgery of the vast majority of the world's people. But even those fortunate people who do trot the globe hardly are realizing freedom in their adventures, according to critics of the postmodern perspective. George Ritzer (2000), for example, argues that mass tourism has become such a packaged commodity that the hallmarks of bureaucratic, rationalized society accompany mass tourists wherever they go. Predictability and sameness are built into planned tours as tourists complain if things aren't just as they are at home. Meanings of experiences are framed by predigested orientation snippets that tour guides provide to onlookers. Efficiency reigns as tourists are herded through sites, and quantity of experience eclipses quality as tourists scurry about to see as much as possible within the time and money constraints of their vacations. For structural determinists, the failure of mass tourists to protest this rationalization of travel does not alter the fact that they are being controlled any more than a goldfish's contentment in a fishbowl is a sign of its freedom. The rogue tourist who shakes off these structural influences is rare, indeed.

Another prong of critique of the postmodern account of global tourism charges that tourism destroys local traditions and subordinates many locals to wealthy tourists in direct servitude as maids, waiters, cooks, guides, and so forth. In some poor countries, tourism is a vital part of the economy in which many residents make their living. Other locals not directly employed in the trade nevertheless must interact with arrogant tourists and tolerate them as part of the tourist economy. While tourism generates money and can even revitalize local traditions, there remains a deep tension for locals between being honored and being demeaned as their values, norms, customs, places, and friends are made objects of commercial tourist spectacle.

A vivid example wherein the benign tourist gaze interpretation seems unconvincing is the case of the global sex tourism industry, which has greatly expanded in recent decades in places such as Cambodia, Thailand, India, the Philippines, Peru, Brazil, the Caribbean islands, and elsewhere. Now easily accessible through Internet advertising and even package deals for air, hotel, and sex, mass sex tourism draws males and females (heterosexuals and homosexuals) to destinations where they enjoy the "exotic" services of usually poverty-stricken sex workers who range in age from young children to older adults (Rojek 2000). Some prostitutes contract their own services, but a much larger number are marketed by pimps in the streets or assigned to brothels. In the most severe cases of exploitation, sex workers are slaves of owners and reap no monetary return at all for their services. Beverly Mullings (2000) reports that among Caribbean sex tourists fantasy fulfillment and "relief" from the experience of gender equality in developed countries are motives that lure men to what they perceive as erotic and highly domestic Third World women. These relationships are not experiments in identity liberation for destitute females who sell such services and servitude in order to survive. It seems inappropriate to trivialize these encounters under the lofty and playful idea of global identity freedom, much as tourist travel to the Auschwitz gas chambers of Nazi Germany and trips to the ruins of Hiroshima, with its burn marks of vaporized Japanese children, present dilemmas to proponents of the idea of tourism as mere fun.

CONCLUSION

It has been a daunting task to introduce essential elements of sociological thinking in this book. There is so much more that I would like to convey but cannot in the interest of keeping the book brief.

I will combine concluding remarks on globalization and the field of sociology as a whole in what follows.

Globalization issues are in many ways a leading edge in sociology today, although the vast accumulation of prior sociological knowledge over the past century and a half surely makes possible the insights that sociologists have about this unfolding transformation of societies. Karl Marx could not have come to such a piercing understanding of the great changes that were swirling about him in Western Europe during the early industrial age without a firm grasp of existing philosophical, economic, and political thought. We share a similar situation with regard to globalization tendencies today, where any serious understanding of the changes taking place will have to be well steeped in foundational, conceptual, and theoretical contributions from the past.

"Globalization" is one of those catchy words that tend to become more vacuous as they circulate in public discourse. The foregoing chapter suggests that at a minimum it is advisable to differentiate economic, political, and cultural elements of the process, however intertwined these dimensions may be in concrete realities. There are further distinctions that are worth drawing between various social actors and processes within each of these three strands of globalization. Economic globalization, for example, means different things to multinational corporations, to workers in developed countries, and to peasant workers in the global south, even though these social actors are bound up in the same process. Political globalization may limit the power of states in some respects, while making them crucial global actors in other regards. Cultural globalization entails simultaneous processes leading to identity liberation for some, and spelling further exploitation for others. Such are the complexities and contradictions of globalization and of social life in general.

One of the dangers about new fields of inquiry such as globalization is the temptation to jump on the bandwagon of newfangled thinking without fully understanding the long history of analogous and cumulative social processes that led up to and produced the seeming novelty of current events. It would make comprehension of the world easier if all we had to do was size up what is going on today. Unfortunately, the task is more difficult than that. The Renaissance, the industrial revolution, and other watershed events in world history were not utter breaks with past events and social arrangements, and neither is globalization. It still is hard to say exactly how far globalization will tread in changing the world as we know it, but one thing is certain–the conceptual and theoretical tools that sociology has developed over the years will still be crucial for coming to any serious understanding of what is going on today. Social inequality, power, and legitimate authority; social structures such as nations, organizations, and classes; racial, ethnic, gender, and age groups; and the associated bundles of cultural meanings that groups develop simply do not go out of date, if recorded human history is any indication. New variations within these basic categories of social life are not only possible, but are assured as history unfolds. The task of the sociology of globalization will be to track changes in these familiar domains of the social.

Sociology is and always had been a highly provocative and contested discipline. The political volatility of sociological renderings of worldly events is perhaps unrivaled among academic fields. The empirical bases of these observations make them all the more troubling for people who might prefer to overlook uncomfortable facts. For all of its vitality and novelty though, sociology remains fairly circumscribed in terms of its overall influence on popular thought. Bits and pieces of sociological thought abound, but systematic thinking along sociological lines is still rare in human civilizations. Part of the reason for this isolation undoubtedly is political, but another reason may be the relatively small number of "public intellectuals" within the field who carry sociological reasoning to wider audiences in popular media, as opposed to the limited readership that academic journals generate. This book is part of my own efforts to move further in the direction of public sociology, and I will be gratified if its contents encourage you to share insights with others. I am inclined to believe that revolutions in thought ultimately take place at the level of expanding networks of acquaintances that do this kind of mindful conversing about new perspectives.

If these pages are the last sociological work that you read, my goal in writing the book will only partially have been met. Education is about enabling people to learn more on their own. The substantive topics that sociological writing explores far exceed the ones discussed in this book, since my primary aim has been to provide a template of basic sociological ideas that will enhance the understanding and critical capacities of readers who go on to engage in other more comprehensive studies of sociological issues. No matter what topical interests you hold, chances are that sociologists have put their distinctive mark on it in books that offer dramatically different perspectives from those put forth by others.

Beyond undertaking further reading, sociological awareness means putting thoughts into action. This practice may be as simple as coming to understand your own life events in new ways, sharing knowledge with others, or contesting ill-conceived utterances in everyday conversations. Most people who are sociologically trained do not formally teach or otherwise employ their knowledge in schools and universities, although some individuals obviously do so. Beginning students of sociology often ask me what one can do with sociology besides teach it. My answer is normally a long one, but here suffice it to say that sociology, like other liberal arts education, is broadly useful training for a wide range of research and practical careers in nonprofit and for-profit organizations, in government agencies at all levels, in social service organizations, and most generally in vocations that seek to make a difference in the world.

In the late 1950s, sociologist C. Wright Mills, who was always a thorn in the side of the powerful and the complacent, wrote in his great work *The Sociological Imagination* (1959) that

> Ours is a time of uneasiness and indifference—not yet formulated in such ways as to permit the work of reason and the play of sensibility. Instead of troubles—defined in terms of values and threats—there is often the misery of vague uneasiness; instead of explicit issues there is often merely the beat feeling that all is somehow not right. Neither the values threatened nor whatever threatens them has been stated; in short, they have not been carried to the point of decision. Much less have they been formulated as problems of social science.

Things haven't changed much in terms of people's deep sense that things are askew in twenty-first-century societies. Belief in inevitable social progress has long since waned and widespread pessimism has taken its place. Even so, social science has come a long way in identifying the nature of social problems. It remains to be seen if the diagnoses of social science, the values of moral institutions, and public consciousness can come together to surmount the economic, political, and cultural powers that so relentlessly perpetuate such problems. Mills saw this convergence as the promise of sociology, and it seems to me that it remains a viable strategy for restoration of a sense of meaning and purpose in social life.

SUGGESTIONS FOR FURTHER STUDY

David Held, Anthony McGrew, and David Goldblatt. 1999. *Global Transformations*. London: Polity.

Anthony Giddens. 2000. *Runaway World: How Globalization Is Reshaping Our Lives*. New York: Routledge.

Manuel Castells. 1996. *The Rise of the Network Society*. Oxford: Blackwell

——. 1997. *The Power of Identity*. Oxford: Blackwell.

John Beynon and David Dunkerley (eds.). 2000. *Globalization: The Reader*. New York: Routledge.

The above ensemble of books serves as a good introduction to key globalization issues. Giddens and Held, McGrew, and Goldblatt provide excellent overviews of economic, political, and cultural dimensions of globalization, while Castells' work covers the influence of information technology and global social movements in detail. Beynon and Dunkerley's reader contains a wealth of nicely excerpted materials from leading globalization authors.

Alan Durning. 1992. *How Much Is Enough? The Consumer Society and the Future of the Earth*. New York: W. W. Norton.

Mark Gottdiener (ed.). 2000. *New Forms of Consumption: Consumers, Culture, and Commodification*. Lanham, MD: Rowman and Littlefield.

Durning's book is a highly readable, well documented, and still very pertinent early work on global consumerism that includes discussion of the environmental consequences of consumer waste. Gottdiener's edited volume has essays on a wide variety of consumer society topics, ranging from themed environments to tourism.

Global Exchange. Online: www.globalexchange.org.

A comprehensive global awareness website founded in 1988. Promotes environmental, political, and social justice.

Global Trade Watch. Online: www.citizen.org/trade/.

This website is devoted to study and education about the impact of economic globalization on work, environment, health, and democracy.

Global Policy Forum. Online: www.globalpolicy.org.

A helpful clearinghouse of information on a variety of global initiatives and their consequences.

International Monetary Fund. Online: www.imf.org.

World Bank. Online: www.worldbank.org.

World Trade Organization. Online: www.wto.org.

United Nations. Online: www.un.org.

Organization for Economic Cooperation and Development. Online: www.oecd.org.

These websites provide essential information on the undertakings and philosophies of these leading actors in global change.

The New Rulers of the World. 2001. 53 min. Directed by John Pilger.

Pilger's provocative look at the history and contemporary effects of globalization on Indonesia is one of the finest documentaries available on the topic. It documents the horrific genocide conducted under the leadership of General Suharto with international cooperation.

REFERENCES

Anderson, Margo and Stephen Feinberg. 1999. *Who Counts? The Politics of Census-Taking in Contemporary America.* New York: Sage.

Arrighi, Giovanni. 1999. "Globalization and Historical Macrosociology." Pp. 117–133 in Janet Abu-Lughod (ed.), *Sociology for the 21st Century.* Chicago: University of Chicago Press.

Ayers, Bill. 2001. *Fugitive Days.* Boston: Beacon.

Barber, Benjamin R. 1996. *Jihad vs. McWorld: How Globalism and Tribalism Are Reshaping the World.* New York: Ballantine.

Baudrillard, Jean. 1983. *Simulations.* New York: Semiotexte.

——. 1995. *The Gulf War Did Not Take Place.* Bloomington: Indiana University Press.

Beck, Ulrich. 1999. *World Risk Society.* Cambridge: Polity Press.

Becker, Howard S. 1963. *Outsiders: Studies in the Sociology of Deviance.* New York: Free Press.

——. 1982. *Art Worlds.* Berkeley: University of California Press.

Beisel, Nicola. 1997. *Imperiled Innocents.* Berkeley: University of California Press.

Bellah, Robert N., Richard Madsen, William M. Sullivan, Ann Swidler, and Steven M. Tipton. 1985. *Habits of the Heart: Individualism and Commitment in American Life.* Berkeley: University of California Press.

Berger, Peter and Thomas Luckmann. 1966. *The Social Construction of Reality.* Harmondsworth, UK: Penguin Books.

Bernstein, Basil. 1971–1975. *Class, Codes, and Control.* London: Routledge and Kegan Paul.

Bielby, Denise. 1995. *Soap Fans: Pursuing Pleasure and Making Meaning in Everyday Life.* Philadelphia: Temple University Press.

Bierstedt, Robert. 1950/1974. "An Analysis of Social Power" in *Power and Progress.* New York: McGraw-Hill.

Blumer, Herbert. 1969. *Symbolic Interactionism.* Englewood Cliffs, NJ: Prentice-Hall.

Bourdieu, Pierre and Jean-Claude Passeron. 1970/1990. *Reproduction in Education, Society, and Culture.* London: Sage.

Bourdieu, Pierre. 1979/1984. *Distinction: A Social Critique of the Judgment of Taste.* Chicago: University of Chicago Press.

Brecher, Jeremy, Tim Costello, and Brendan Smith. 2000. *Globalization from Below: The Power of Solidarity.* Cambridge, MA: South End Press.

Brown, David K. 1995. *Degrees of Control: A Sociology of Educational Expansion and Occupational Credentialism.* New York: Teachers College Press.

Bullard, Robert. 2000. *Dumping in Dixie: Race, Class, and Environmental Quality.* Boulder, CO: Westview.

Butler, Judith. 1989/1999. *Gender Trouble: Feminism and the Subversion of Identity.* London: Routledge.

Carruthers, Bruce and Sarah Babb. 2000. *Economy/Society: Markets, Meanings, and Social Structure.* Thousand Oaks, CA: Pine Forge Press.

Castells, Manuel. 1996. *The Rise of the Network Society.* Oxford: Blackwell.

——. 1997. *The Power of Identity.* Oxford: Blackwell.

Cerulo, Karen. 1995. *Identity Designs: The Sights and Sounds of a Nation.* Piscataway, NJ: Rutgers University Press.

Clark, Candace. 1997. *Misery and Company: Sympathy in Everyday Life.* Chicago: University of Chicago Press.

Cohen, Robin and Paul Kennedy. 2000. *Global Sociology.* New York: New York University Press.

Coleman, James. 1990. *Foundations of Social Theory.* Cambridge, MA: Harvard University Press.

Collins, Patricia Hill. 1991. *Black Feminist Thought.* New York: Routledge.

Collins, Randall. 1975. *Conflict Sociology: Toward an Explanatory Science.* New York: Academic Press.

——. 1979. *The Credential Society.* New York: Academic Press.

——. 1986. *Weberian Sociological Theory.* Cambridge: Cambridge University Press.

——. 1994. *Four Sociological Traditions.* New York: Oxford University Press.

Cook, Daniel. 2000. "The Rise of 'The Toddler' as Subject and as Merchandising Category in the 1930s." Pp. 111–129 in Mark Gottdiener (ed.), *New Forms of Consumption.* Lanham, MD: Rowman and Littlefield.

Cooley, Charles H. 1902. *Human Nature and the Social Order.* New York: Scribner.

CorpWatch (www.corpwatch.org). 2002a. "The Lacandon Jungle's Last Stand Against Corporate Globalization." September 26, 2002.

——. 2002b. "PPP: Plan Puebla Panama, or Private Plans for Profit?" September 19, 2002.

——. 2002c. "Bhopal Survivors Protest Dow's Presence at the World Summit on Sustainable Development." August 28, 2002.

Coser, Lewis. 1956. *The Functions of Social Conflict.* New York: Free Press.

Crane, Diana. 2000. *Fashion and Its Social Agendas.* Chicago: University of Chicago Press.

Croteau, David and William Hoynes. 2000. *Media/Society: Industries, Images, and Audiences.* Thousand Oaks, CA: Pine Forge Press.

Dahrendorf, Ralf. 1967. *Society and Democracy in Germany*. New York: W. W. Norton.

Davis, Fred. 1992. *Fashion, Culture, and Identity*. Chicago: University of Chicago Press.

Deal, Terrance E. and Allan A. Kennedy. 2000. *Corporate Cultures: The Rites and Rituals of Corporate Life*. Cambridge, MA: Perseus.

Derber, Charles. 1998. *Corporation Nation*. New York: St. Martins.

Diani, Mario and Donatella Della Porta. 1997. *Social Movements: An Introduction*. Oxford: Blackwell.

Douglas, Mary. 1966. *Purity and Danger: An Analysis of the Concepts of Pollution and Taboo*. London: Routledge and Kegan Paul.

DuBois, W. E. B. 1903/1989. *The Souls of Black Folk*. New York: Bantam.

Dunier, Mitchell. 1992. *Slim's Table*. Chicago: University of Chicago Press.

——. 1999. *Sidewalk*. New York: Farrar, Straus, and Giroux.

Durkheim, Emile. 1895/1982. *The Rules of Sociological Method*. New York: Free Press.

——. 1915/1965. *The Elementary Forms of the Religious Life*. New York: Free Press.

Durning, Alan. 1992. *How Much Is Enough? Consumer Society and the Future of the Earth*. New York: W. W. Norton.

Eco, Umberto. 1986. *Travels in Hyper Reality*. London: Picador.

Edin, Kathryn and Laura Lein. 1997. *Making Ends Meet*. New York: Sage.

Ehrenreich, Barbara. 1989. *Fear of Falling: The Inner Life of the Middle Class*. New York: Pantheon.

Eichengreen, Barry. 1996. *Globalizing Capital: A History of the International Monetary System*. Princeton, NJ: Princeton University Press.

Elkind, David. 1997. *All Grown Up and No Place to Go: Teenagers in Crisis*. Cambridge, MA: Perseus.

Epstein, Jonathon S. 1997. *Youth Culture: Identity in a Postmodern World*. Oxford: Blackwell.

Etzioni, Amatai. 1961. *A Comparative Analysis of Complex Organizations*. New York: Free Press.

Fantasia, Rick. 1988. *Cultures of Solidarity*. Berkeley: University of California Press.

Faux, Jeff and Larry Mishel. 2000. "Inequality and the Global Economy." Pp. 93–111 in Will Hutton and Anthony Giddens (eds.), *Global Capitalism*. New York: New Press.

Featherstone, Mike. 1991. *Postmodernism and Consumer Culture*. New York: Sage.

Fifty Years Is Enough: U.S. Network for Global Economic Justice (www.50years.org). 2002. "The World Bank and International Monetary Fund."

Fine, Gary Alan. 1987. *With the Boys: Little League Baseball and Adolescent Culture*. Chicago: University of Chicago Press.

——. 1996. *Kitchens: The Culture of Restaurant Work*. Chicago: University of Chicago Press.

——. 1998. *Morel Tales: The Culture of Mushrooming*. Cambridge, MA: Harvard University Press.

Fischer, Claude, Michael Hout, Martín Sánchez Jankowski, Samuel R. Lucas, Ann Swidler, and Kim Voss. 1996. *Inequality by Design: Cracking the Bell Curve Myth*. Berkeley: University of California Press.

Foucault, Michel. 1975/1995. *Discipline and Punish*. New York: Vintage Books.

Frank, Andre-Gunder. 1998. *Re-Orient: Global Economy in the Asian Age*. Berkeley: University of California Press.

Gamson, Joshua. 1994. *Claims to Fame: Celebrities in Contemporary America*. Berkeley: University of California Press.

Gans, Herbert. 1995. *The War Against the Poor: The Underclass and Antipoverty Policy*. New York: Basic Books.

Garfinkel, Harold. 1967. *Studies in Ethnomethodology*. Englewood Cliffs, NJ: Prentice-Hall.

Giddens, Anthony. 1984. *The Constitution of Society: Outline of the Theory of Structuration*. Berkeley: University of California Press.

——. 2000. *Runaway World: How Globalization Is Reshaping Our Lives*. New York: Routledge.

Gitlin, Todd. 1980. *The Whole World Is Watching*. Berkeley: University of California Press.

Glassner, Barry. 1999. *The Culture of Fear: Why Americans Are Afraid of the Wrong Things*. New York: Basic Books.

Global Exchange (www.globalexchange.org). 2001. "How the IMF and World Bank Undermine Democracy and Erode Human Rights: Five Case Studies."

——. 2002. "The Chocolate Industry: Slavery Lurking Behind the Sweetness."

Goffman, Erving. 1959. *The Presentation of Self in Everyday Life*. Chicago: University of Chicago Press.

——. 1961. *Asylums*. Chicago: Aldine.

——. 1967. *Interaction Ritual*. New York: Doubleday.

——. 1974. *Frame Analysis*. Cambridge, MA: Harvard University Press.

——. 1979. *Gender Advertisements*. Cambridge, MA: Harvard University Press.

——. 1981. *Forms of Talk*. Philadelphia: University of Pennsylvania Press.

Gottdiener, Mark. 1997. *The Theming of America: American Dreams, Media Fantasies, and Themed Environments*. Boulder, CO: Westview.

—— (ed.). 2000. *New Forms of Consumption: Consumers, Culture, and Commodification*. Lanham, MD: Rowman and Littlefield.

Granfield, Robert. 1991. "Making It by Faking It: Working Class Students in an Elite Academic Environment." *Journal of Contemporary Ethnology* 20: 331–351.

Griswold, Wendy. 1994. *Cultures and Societies in a Changing World*. Thousand Oaks, CA: Pine Forge Press.

Gusfield, Joseph. 1963. *Symbolic Crusade: Status Politics and the American Temperance Movement*. Urbana: University of Illinois Press.

——. 1981. *The Culture of Public Problems: Drinking-Driving and the Symbolic Order*. Chicago: University of Chicago Press.

Halle, David. 1993. *Inside Culture: Art and Class in the American Home.* Chicago: University of Chicago Press.

Hamel, Pierre, Henri Lustinger-Thaler, and Louis Maheu. 1999. "Is There a Role for Social Movements?" Pp. 165–180 in Janet Abu-Lughod (ed.), *Sociology for the 21st Century.* Chicago: University of Chicago Press.

Haraway, Donna. 1989. *Primate Visions.* New York: Routledge.

Harrington, C. Lee and Denise Bielby (eds.). 2001. *Popular Culture: Production and Consumption.* Oxford: Blackwell.

Heiner, Robert. 2002. *Social Problems: An Introduction to Critical Constructionism.* Oxford: Oxford University Press.

Herrnstein, Richard and Charles Murray. 1994. *The Bell Curve.* New York: Free Press.

hooks, bell. 1989. *Talking Back: Thinking Feminist, Talking Black.* Boston: South End Press.

——. 2000. *Where We Stand: Class Matters.* Boston: South End Press.

International Labor Organization. 2001. "Combating Trafficking in Children for Labor Exploitation in West and Central Africa." Geneva, Switzerland: International Labor Organization.

Kantor, Rosabeth Moss. 1977. *Men and Women of the Corporation.* New York: Basic Books.

——. 1979. "Power Failure in Management Circuits." *Harvard Business Review* 57: 65–75.

Kerbal, Matthew. 1999. *If It Bleeds, It Leads: An Anatomy of Television News.* Boulder, CO: Westview.

Kingston, Paul. 2000. *The Classless Society.* Stanford, CA: Stanford University Press.

Kozol, Jonathan. 1992. *Savage Inequalities: Children in America's Schools.* New York: HarperCollins.

Kuhn, Thomas. 1970. *The Structure of Scientific Revolutions.* Chicago: University of Chicago Press.

Labaree, David. 1997. *How to Succeed in School Without Really Trying: The Credentials Race in American Education.* New Haven: Yale University Press.

LaFeber, Walter. 1999. *Michael Jordan and the New Global Capitalism.* New York: W. W. Norton.

Lamont, Michelle. 1992. *Money, Morals, and Manners: The Culture of the French and American Middle Class.* Chicago: University of Chicago Press.

Lamont, Michelle and Marcel Fournier (eds.). 1992. *Cultivating Differences: Symbolic Boundaries and the Making of Inequality.* Chicago: University of Chicago Press.

Leidner, Robin. 1993. *Fast Food, Fast Talk: Service Work and the Routinization of Everyday Life.* Berkeley: University of California Press.

Liebow, Elliot. 1967. *Tally's Corner.* Boston: Little, Brown.

Lipset, Seymour Martin. 1996. *American Exceptionalism.* New York: W. W. Norton.

Luker, Kristen. 1984. *Abortion and the Politics of Motherhood*. Berkeley: University of California Press.

———. 1996. *Dubious Conceptions: The Politics of Teen Pregnancy*. Cambridge, MA: Harvard University Press.

MacLeod, Jay. 1995. *Ain't No Makin' It: Aspirations and Attainment in a Low-Income Neighborhood*. Boulder, CO: Westview.

Markoff, John. 1996. *Waves of Democracy: Social Movements and Political Change*. Thousand Oaks, CA: Pine Forge.

Marx, Karl and Friedrich Engels. 1846/1947. *The German Ideology*. New York: International Publishers.

———. 1848/1948. *Manifesto of the Communist Party*. New York: International Publishers.

Mead, George Herbert. 1934. *Mind, Self, and Society*. Chicago: University of Chicago Press.

Merton, Robert. 1949. *Social Theory and Social Structure*. Glencoe, IL: Free Press.

Meyer, John W. and Brian Rowan. 1977. "Institutionalized Organizations: Formal Structure as Myth and Ceremony." *American Journal of Sociology* 83: 340–363.

Mills, C. Wright. 1959. *The Sociological Imagination*. New York: Oxford University Press.

Moore, Barrington. 1966. *Injustice: The Social Origins of Obedience and Revolt*. New York: M. E. Sharpe.

Morris, Aldon. 1984. *The Origins of the Civil Rights Movement*. New York: Free Press.

Mullings, Beverly. 2000. "Fantasy Tours: Exploring the Global Consumption of Caribbean Sex Tourisms." Pp. 227–250 in Mark Gottdiener (ed.), *New Forms of Consumption*. Lanham, MD: Rowman and Littlefield.

Nock, Steven. 1993. *The Costs of Privacy: Surveillance and Reputation in America*. New York: Aldine de Gruyter.

Ohmae, Kenichi. 1995. *The End of the Nation State: The Rise of Regional Economics*. London: HarperCollins.

Olson, Mancur. 1965. *The Logic of Collective Action*. Cambridge, MA: Harvard University Press.

Patillo-McCoy, Mary. 1999. *Black Picket Fences: Privilege and Peril Among the Black Middle Class*. Chicago: University of Chicago Press.

Peterson, Richard (ed.). 1976. *The Production of Culture*. Beverly Hills, CA: Sage Publications.

———. 1997. *Creating Country Music: Fabricating Authenticity*. Chicago: University of Chicago Press.

Pfeffer, Jeffrey. 1996. *Managing with Power: Politics and Influence in Organizations*. Cambridge, MA: Harvard Business School Press.

Pickering, Andrew. 1999. *Constructing Quarks: A Sociological History of Particle Physics*. Chicago: University of Chicago Press.

Probyn, Elspeth. 2000. *Carnal Appetites: Food/Sex/Identities*. London: Routledge.

Quadagno, Jill. 1994. *The Color of Welfare: How Racism Undermined the War on Poverty.* New York: Oxford University Press.

Reiman, Jeffrey. 1996. *The Rich Get Richer and the Poor Get Prison.* Boston: Allyn and Bacon.

Ritzer, George. 2000. *The McDonaldization of Society.* Thousand Oaks, CA: Pine Forge.

Rojek, Chris. 2000. "Mass Tourism or the Re-enchantment of the World? Issues and Contradictions in the Study of Travel." Pp. 51–69 in Mark Gottdiener (ed.), *New Forms of Consumption.* Lanham, MD: Rowman and Littlefield.

Rubin, Lillian. 1994. *Families on the Fault Line: America's Working Class Speaks About the Family, the Economy, Race, and Ethnicity.* New York: HarperCollins.

Sahlins, Marshall. 1976. *Culture and Practical Reason.* Chicago: University of Chicago Press.

Saïd, Edward. 1978. *Orientalism.* New York: Pantheon

Sassen, Saskia. 1991. *The Global City: New York, London, Tokyo.* Princeton, NJ: Princeton University Press.

——. 1998. *Globalization and Its Discontents: Essays on the New Mobility of People and Money.* New York: New Press.

Schudson, Michael. 1984. *Advertising: The Uneasy Persuasion.* New York: Basic Books.

Seidman, Steven (ed.). 1994. *Contested Knowledge: Social Theory in the Postmodern Era.* Oxford: Blackwell Publishers.

——. 1996. *Queer Theory/Sociology.* Oxford: Blackwell.

Shoval, Noam. 2000. "Commodification and Theming of the Sacred: Changing Patterns of Tourist Consumption in the 'Holy Land.'" Pp. 251–263 in Mark Gottdiener (ed.), *New Forms of Consumption.* Lanham, MD: Rowman and Littlefield.

Simmel, Georg. 1908/1955. *Conflict and the Web of Group Affiliations.* New York: Free Press.

Skinner, B. F. 1948/1966. *Walden Two.* New York: Macmillan.

Sklair, Leslie. 1993. *Assembling for Development: The Maquila Industry in Mexico and the United States.* San Diego: Center for U.S.–Mexican Studies, University of California.

Smith, Adam. 1776/1975. *The Wealth of Nations.* Chicago: University of Chicago Press.

Smith, Dorothy. 1990. *The Conceptual Practices of Power: A Feminist Sociology of Knowledge.* Toronto: University of Toronto Press.

Stephens, W. Richard. 1998. *Careers in Sociology.* 2nd ed. Boston: Allyn and Bacon.

Strange, Susan. 1996. *The Retreat of the State: The Diffusion of Power in the World Economy.* Cambridge: Cambridge University Press.

Taylor, Frederick W. 1911. *Scientific Management.* New York: Harper and Brothers.

Tilly, Charles. 1978. *From Mobilization to Revolution.* Reading, MA: Addison-Wesley.

——. 1998. *Durable Inequality*. Berkeley: University of California Press.

Urry, John. 1990. *The Tourist Gaze*. London: Sage.

Vaughan, Diane. 1996. *The Challenger Launch Decision: Risky Technology, Culture, and Deviance at NASA*. Chicago: University of Chicago Press.

Veblen, Thorstein. 1899. *The Theory of the Leisure Class*. New York: Macmillan.

Volcker, Paul. 2000. "The Sea of Global Finance." Pp. 75–92 in Will Hutton and Anthony Giddens (eds.), *Global Capitalism*. New York: New Press.

Wagner-Pacifici, Robin. 1987. *The Moro Morality Play: Terrorism as Social Drama*. Chicago: University of Chicago Press.

Wallerstein, Immanuel. 1974–1989. *The Modern World-System*. 3 vols. New York: Academic.

——. 2002. "The Eagle Has Crash Landed." *Foreign Policy* July: 60–68.

Weber, Max. 1904–1905/1996. *The Protestant Ethic and the Spirit of Capitalism*. Los Angeles: Roxbury Publishing.

——. 1922/1968. *Economy and Society*. 3 vols. Berkeley: University of California Press.

Welch, Michael. 2000. *Flag Burning: Moral Panic and the Criminalization of Protest*. Hawthorne, NY: Aldine de Gruyter

Weinstein, Deena. 2000. *Heavy Metal: The Music and Its Culture*. Cambridge, MA: Perseus.

Weisbrot, Mark. 1999. "Globalization: A Primer." Washington, DC: Center for Economic and Policy Research.

Willis, Paul. 1977. *Learning to Labor: How Working Class Kids Get Working Class Jobs*. New York: Columbia University Press.

Wilson, Pamela. 1995. "Mountains of Contradictions: Gender, Class, and Region in the Star Image of Dolly Parton." *South Atlantic Quarterly* 94: 109–134.

Wright, Will. 2001. *The Wild West: The Mythical Cowboy and Social Theory*. Thousand Oaks, CA: Pine Forge Press.

Zelizer, Viviana. 1985. *Pricing the Priceless Child: The Changing Value of Children*. New York: Basic.

——. 1994. *The Social Meaning of Money*. New York: Basic Books.

INDEX

A

Abbey Road E.P., The (RHCP), 135
Abortion, 158
Affirmative action, 21
Africa, 198, 203, 206
African Americans. *See* Blacks
Aggregates of people, 33
Aguilera, Christina, 132
AIDS/HIV prevention, 217
Alcohol use, 125
Alda, Alan, 25
American Kennel Club, 139
American Revolution, 150
Analytical categories of people, 33
Anderson, Margo, 18
Anderson, Warren, 208
Anheuser-Busch, 204
Arby's, 10
Asia, 198, 206
Asian Tigers, 213
Audience interpretation, 127–40
Auschwitz gas chambers, 238
Australia, 205
Authenticity, eclipse of, 232–33
Authoritarian regimes, 160–63
Authority
   charismatic, 90, 151, 161
   legitimate, 90, 146–47, 184
   organizational power and, 172,
     185
   rational-legal, 90, 184
   social movements and, 159
   of the state, 163–71
   traditional, 90
   in the workplace, 177–83
   See also Legitimate authority
Automobiles
   attachment to, 8–9
   consumer behavior and, 53–55
Ayers, Bill, 155–56
Azul, Montes, 222

B

Back to the Future, 135
Bad as I Wanna Be (Rodman), 12
Baghdad, 169, 171
Balkanization, 216
Balzary, Michael ("Flea"), 133, 134
Banks, Annie, 12
Barber, Benjamin, 218
Baseball, 113
Baudrillard, Jean, 169, 233, 236
Baywatch, 12
Beanie Babies, 127
Beatles, 135
Becker, Howard S., 67, 69–70, 75
Beethoven, Ludwig van, 15
Behavioral psychology, 31
Bell Curve, The (Herrnstein and
   Murray), 38
Benatar, Pat, 25
Benin, 214
Berger, Peter, 68

Berlin Wall, 167, 168
Bernstein, Basil, 91
Berry, Halle, 15
Bhopal, India, 208
Bierstedt, Robert, 144
Bin Laden, Osama, 170
Bioreserves, 221
Black Panthers, 153
Blacks, 3–4, 114
   as a caste, 89
   double consciousness in, 26,
      27–28
   IQ test controversy, 38
   welfare system and, 21, 123–24
   See also Minority groups; Race
BloodSugarSexMajik (RHCP), 136
Blumer, Herbert, 67
Borneo, 27
Bourdieu, Pierre, 90, 103, 112,
      114–17, 230
Bourgeoisie, 80, 81
Bove, Jose, 218
Brazil, 210, 213, 238
Breaching experiments, 68
Brentham, Jeremy, 187
Bretton Woods Conference, 210
Bricolage, 227
British East India Company, 197
Bureaucracies, 150–51, 183–85
Burger King, 10
Burkina Faso, 214
Bush, George, 20, 59, 168–71, 223
Bush, George W., 17–18, 20, 59, 217,
      223, 228
Butler, Judith, 28
By the Way (RHCP), 136

C

Cacao plant, 213–14
Californication (RHCP), 136
Cambodia, 160, 238
Canada, 201, 204, 205, 206, 220

Capital
   cultural, 91–92, 114–17, 139, 230
   economic, 115–17
   social, 115–17
Capitalism, 109
   functional theories on, 59
   Marxist theory on, 79–84, 202,
      230
   rational choice theories on, 52, 56
   Weberian theory on, 84–85,
      102–3
Cardigans, 132
Career structure, 176
Carey, Mariah, 128
Caribbean islands, 238
Carnegie, Andrew, 161
Cartels, 19
Carter, James, 166–67
Castells, Manuel, 26, 222
Castes, 89
Castro, Fidel, 167
Celebrities
   identity selection in, 25
   sociology of, 11–16
Cellular phones, 9, 224, 234
Census, U.S., 18
Central America, 198
Central Intelligence Agency (CIA),
      168
Challenger Launch Decision, The
      (Vaughan), 37
Charismatic authority, 90, 151, 161
Chiapas, Mexico, 221–23
Chicago Bulls, 12, 14
Child labor, 213–14
China, 56, 103, 168
Chocolate production, 213–14
Christian Dayaks, 27
Christianity, 109, 127–28, 197, 224
Civil rights movement, 158
Class
   conflict theories on, 94
   cultural differences and, 112–14,
      116, 119

double consciousness and, 28
educational inequality and, 90–93
everyday expressions of, 119–22
Marxist theory on, 80, 81–82, 101
symbolic interactionism/
  constructionism on, 65
Weberian theory on, 85–88
Class-consciousness, 81
Classical economic theory, 19–21
Classical liberalism, 199
Class struggles, 80
Clinton, Bill, 59, 82, 164, 171, 223
Clinton, Hillary, 15
Coca-Cola, 204, 220, 221
Cocaine, 70, 126
Coercive power, 145, 147, 163
  of groups, 33
  in organizations, 172–73
  in the workplace, 174–75
Cold War, 166
Collective consciousness, 33–34
Collective representation, 105
Collins, Patricia Hill, 27
Collins, Randall, 41, 145
Color of Welfare, The (Quadagno), 21
Commodities, 230
Commodity fetishism, 230
Communism, 41, 79, 81, 166
Competence, appearance of, 72
Conceptual Practices of Power, The
  (Smith), 40
Conflict theories, 48–49, 50, 64, 71,
  75–94, 124
  interplay with other theories,
    77–79
  pessimism vs. realism in, 93–94
  See also Marx, Karl; Weber, Max
Confucianism, 103, 128
Conspicuous consumption, 230
Conspicuous leisure, 230
Constructing Quarks (Pickering), 39
Consumerism
  globalization and, 227–33
  nonrational choice in, 53–55

Consumption identities, 232
Cooley, Charles Horton, 66, 85
COPS, 19
Corrective practices, 73–74
Coser, Lewis, 77
Counter-movements, 148
Crack cocaine, 70
Credentialing, 92
Credit, 109, 111
Credit cards, 232
Creolization, 226
Crew (rowing), 113
Crime, 4, 126
  conflict theories on, 75
  individual blame for, 19
  labeling theory of, 69–71, 127
  primary and secondary, 70
  war on, 59
Croatians, 26–27
Croteau, David, 129
Cuba, 79, 168
Cultural autonomy, 102, 108, 236,
  237
Cultural capital, 91–92, 114–17, 139,
  230
Cultural construction of social
  problems, 122–27
Cultural discourse, 151
Cultural distribution, 127–40
Cultural globalization, 223–38,
  239
  consumerism and, 227–33
  limiting factors concerning,
    224–28
  the local and, 225–28
  tourism and, 233–38
Cultural issues, 158
Cultural legitimacy. See Legitimate
  authority
Cultural meanings, 65, 137
Cultural production, 127–40
  example of, 132–37
  model of processes, 129–32
Cultural resources, 150–52

Cultural rituals, 178–79. *See also* Social rituals
Cultural turn, 78
Culture, 50, 97–142
  defined, 100
  functional theories on, 63
  high, 117–19
  individualism in, 16–17
  Marxist theory on, 81
  popular, 117–19
  social power and, 112–27
  social problems and, 122–27
  social structures and interactions distinguished from, 98–101
  structural determinist views of, 101–12
  Weberian theory on, 84–86, 88–89
Culture groups. *See* Status groups
Curie, Marie, 15

D

Dahrendorf, Ralf, 162
Dalai Lama, 136
Daley, Richard J., 153, 155, 157–58
Daly, Chuck, 14
Dammett, Blackie, 133
Darwin, Charles, 60
Davis, Fred, 118
DDT, 207
Deductive reasoning, 47–48
Deforestation, 203, 212
Degradation rituals, 72
Democratic National Convention, 153–55
DeNiro, Robert, 164–65
Deregulation, 201
Desires, 53–56
Detroit Pistons, 14
Deviance, labeling theory of, 69–71, 127
Diasporas, 207

Dietary taboos, 105–6, 140
Digital divide, 225
Disney theme parks, 180, 223, 233
Distinction (Bourdieu), 114
Dogs, differing views of, 137–40
Donations, 110
Double consciousness, 26–28
Douglas, Kirk, 25
Douglas, Mary, 140
Douglas, Michael, 7–8, 9, 11
Dow Chemical, 124, 204, 207, 208
Dramaturgical sociology, 71–74, 178. *See also* Social drama
Drug abuse, 59, 126
DuBois, W. E. B., 26, 27
Dunier, Mitchell, 4
DuPont, 204
DuPont, Pierre, 161
Durkheim, Emile, 22, 61, 63, 71, 102, 108, 230
  on groups, 32–34
  on religion, 103–7
Dursban, 124
Dylan, Bob, 25

E

Earnhardt, Dale, 113
East Timor, 27
Ebert, Roger, 161
Eco, Umberto, 236
Economic capital, 115–17
Economic determinism, 81
Economic exchange, 145, 147
  in authoritarian regimes, 163
  workplace power and, 172, 175–77
  See also Money
Economic globalization, 197–223, 239
  finance and, 209–13
  Fordism and post-Fordism in, 206, 231–32
  free trade and, 56, 200, 219–23

structural adjustment programs
 and, 211–12
transnational corporations and,
 204–9, 210, 211–12, 214–16
Economic issues, 158
Economics
 individualism in, 19–21
 rational choice theories in, 52
Economy and Society (Weber), 84, 85
Ecotourism, 235
Ecstasy (drug), 126
Edin, Kathryn, 41
Education
 bureaucratic organization in,
  183–84
 compulsory, 28–29, 173
 functional theories on, 61–63
 individualism in, 16–17
 organizational power and, 172–73
 privatization of, 201
 stratification theory on, 90–93
Ehrenreich, Barbara, 59
Einstein, Albert, 15
Ejidos, 220
Electra, Carmen, 12
*Elementary Forms of the Religious Life,
 The* (Durkheim), 103–4
Elkind, David, 29
Embarrassment as a social ritual,
 73–74
EMI America, 134, 136
Empirical phenomena, 32–33
Engels, Friedrich, 80
Enron Corporation, 20, 168, 228
Environmental movements, 125,
 207
Environmental problems, 203,
 207–9
Environmental Protection Agency
 (EPA), 207
Epstein, Jonathon, 29
Equilibrium state, 63
Ethnocentrism, 114
Ethnomethodology, 68–69

Eugenics, 38
Evolutionary functionalist thought,
 200
Exchange value, 230
Exploitation, 145, 176
 consumer, 228–32
 Marxist theory on, 80
Exxon Corporation, 204

F

Factual statements, 34–38
Falling Down, 7–9, 11
False consciousness, 81
Family values, 59
Fashion, 112, 118–19
Fast food restaurants, 9–11
Feinberg, Stephen, 18
Fields, social, 115
Fine, Gary Alan, 68, 70
First Gulf War, 168–71
Fischer, Claude, 38
Fitzgerald, Ella, 15
Flag, symbolic importance of, 107–8
*Flag Burning: Moral Panic and the
 Criminalization of Protest*
 (Welch), 107
Flexibility of global labor, 206
Food stamps, 111
Fordism, 206, 231
Ford Motor Company, 206
Foreign direct investment (FDI), 205
Foreign loans/debt, 203, 209–13
Foucault, Michel, 187
Fox, Vincente, 220–21
Frames, situational, 71, 72
Franco, Francisco, 162
Free market economic policies, 52,
 59, 199, 200, 201
Free-rider problem, 56–58, 87, 152
Free trade, 56
 Mexico as model of, 219–23
 modernization theory on, 200

Freud, Sigmund, 127
Frontstage and backstage behavior, 71–72
Frusciante, John, 135
Fugitive Days (Ayers), 155
Functional explanation, 59
Functional integration, 61
Functional theories, 48–49, 58, 59–64, 94
  basic imagery, 60–63
  conflict theories and, 77–78
  social inequality in, 63, 64, 76
Functions of social conflict, 77–78

G

G-8, 154–55, 210, 217
Gadhafi, Mu'ammar, 160
Gamson, Joshua, 11
Gandhi, Mahatma, 15, 90
Gans, Herbert, 21, 124
Garfinkel, Harold, 67–69, 73
Gas prices, 20
Gated communites, 76
Gatekeepers, 130, 133
Gates, Bill, 15, 64, 82, 83, 161
Gautama Buddha, 128
General Agreement on Tariffs and Trade (GATT), 210
Generalized other, 67
General Motors Corporation (GM), 195, 204, 214
Genocidal ethnic cleansing, 26–27
Georgia Tech University, 188
German Ideology, The (Marx and Engels), 80
Germany, 196, 206, 229
Ghana, 213
Giddens, Anthony, 103, 216
Gifts, 110
Gill, Andy, 135
Gitlin, Todd, 156
"Give It Away" (RHCP), 136

Globalization, 194–242
  from below, 219, 223
  cultural, 223–38, 239
  economic, 197–233, 239
  Marxist theory applied to, 82–83
  political, 197–223, 239
Global north, 206
Global resistance, 202, 226–27. *See also* Resistance movements
Global south, 206, 209, 210, 239
Global tourism, 233–38
Global warming, 203, 212
Glocalization, 219
Goffman, Erving, 68, 71–74, 75, 164
Gonzalez, Elian, 126
Gore, Al, 17–18
Goth look, 29, 30
Gottdiener, Mark, 180
Government social benefit cuts, 201
Granfield, Robert, 25
Great Britain, 200
Greenhouse effect, 212
Greenpeace, 99, 151
Greenwashing, 221
Grenada, 167
Gripe sessions, 182
Griswold, Wendy, 129
Groups
  rational choice theories on, 55–56
  as social facts, 32–34
  as social structures, 99
Guerilla warfare, 150
Gulf War. *See* First Gulf War; Second Gulf War
Gusfield, Joseph, 125

H

Habitus, 115, 230
Halle, David, 116
Hamburger University (McDonald's), 10, 179
Haraway, Donna, 40

Hard Rock Cafe, 233
Harley Davidson Cafe, 233
Heche, Anne, 164
Hegel, Georg, 15
Heineken, 204
Hendrix, Jimi, 133
Herrnstein, Richard, 38
Hershey's Corporation, 213
Hewlett-Packard, 204
High culture, 117–19
Hippies, 153
Hiroshima, 37, 238
Historical context, 5
Hitler, Adolf, 90, 160, 161–63,
     165–66
Hitler Youth dormitory, 188
Hoffman, Dustin, 164
Hogan, Hulk, 12
Homosexuals, 40, 217, 238
Honesty, rational choice theories
     and, 56–58
hooks, bell, 27
Hoynes, William, 129
Human agency, 102, 103, 108
Humor, 74
Hussein, Saddam, 160, 168–69, 170,
     171
Hyper-realities, 233

I

Identities, 22–30
   consumption, 232
   labeling theory on, 70
   social, 25–30, 40
Identity liberation, 237, 238, 239
Identity repertoires/selection, 25–26
Ideology, 81
IMF. *See* International Monetary
     Fund
Immigrant groups, 25
Impression management, 72–73
India, 238

Individualism, 5–22, 41–42, 128
   celebrities and, 11–16
   in culture, 16–17
   in economics, 19–21
   globalization and, 202
   in politics, 17–19
   of psychology, 31–32
   rational choice theories and, 50
   science and, 38
   social facts vs., 34
   teenagers and, 29
   webs of group affiliation vs.,
      22–24
Individual vs. social problems, 7–11
Indonesia, 27, 210, 211, 213
Inductive reasoning, 47–48
Industrial revolution, 79, 225, 239
Infrastructure, 81
Inside Culture (Halle), 116
Institutional completeness, 180
Institutionalized power, 162
Institutions, 61, 99
Interaction processes, 159
International governmental
     organizations (IGOs), 209–13
International Monetary Fund (IMF),
     210–13, 217, 220, 221
International nongovernmental
     organizations (INGOs), 209–13
International social movements,
     216–19
Internet, 197, 205, 218–19, 223, 224,
     225, 238
Interplay of theories, 47
IQ tests, 38
Iran-Contra affair, 167
Iran hostage crisis, 166–67
Iraq, 160, 168–71, 196, 197
Iron cages, bureaucracies as, 184, 185
Irons, Jack, 133
Islamic fundamentalism, 219, 226
Istanbul, 218
Ivory Coast, 213, 214
Iwo Jima, 107

J

Jackson, Jesse, 161
Jackson, Phil, 14
Japan, 56, 179, 196, 205, 206
Jennings, Peter, 169
Jesus Christ, 90, 128
Jewel, 132
Jews, holocaust and, 163, 165–66
John Paul II, Pope, 161
Johnson administration, 123
Jordan, Michael, 12, 14, 161, 196, 223
Juries, decision making among, 69

K

Kant, Immanuel, 15
Kantor, Rosabeth Moss, 143–44
Keeping Up Appearances, 72
Kennedy, John F., 160
Kennedy, Robert F., 153
Kent State University, 155
Kentucky Fried Chicken, 10
Keynes, John Maynard, 199
Keynesian economics, 199, 200
Khmer Rouge, 160
Khomeini, Ayatollah Ruhallah, 166
Kiedis, Anthony, 133, 134, 135, 136
Kilmer, Val, 117
King, Martin Luther, 151
King, Rodney, 178
King of the Hill, 132
K-Mart, 195
Koppel, Ted, 107
Korea, 139–40. *See also* South Korea
Korean War, 166
Kubrick, Stanley, 128
Kuhn, Thomas, 46
Ku Klux Klan, 99
Kurds, 160
Kuwait, 168–71
Kyoto conference, 196

L

Labeling theory of deviance/crime, 69–71, 127
Labor force, global, 206–7
Lacandon jungle, 221, 222
Laden, Osama Bin. *See* Bin Laden, Osama
Lake Erie, 207
Language, as cultural capital, 91–92, 116
Leadership, 151
Legal-rational authority. *See* Rational-legal authority
Legitimate authority, 90, 146–47, 184
    organizational power and, 172, 185
    social movements and, 159
    of the state, 163–71
    in the workplace, 177–83
    See also Authority
Leidner, Robin, 9
Lein, Laura, 41
Leisure class, 230–31
Levinson, Barry, 164
Leviticus, Book of, 140
Lewinsky, Monica, 82, 164
Libya, 160
Liebow, Elliot, 4
Life magazine, 156
Listerine, 131
Loans
    foreign debt and, 203
    international organizations and, 209–13
    social distinctions and, 111
Logic of Collective Action, The (Olson), 57
Looking-glass self, 66
Lost decade, 220
Luckman, Thomas, 68
Luker, Kristen, 47–48

M

MacLeod, Jay, 93
Macro-sociological theories, 49–50
  conflict, 76
  symbolic interactionism/
    constructionism and, 64–65,
    74–75
Madonna, 12
Malaysia, 212, 213
Mali, 214
Mall of America, 232–33
Management theory, 56
Manifesto of the Communist Party
    (Marx), 80, 84
Maquila industries, 221
Marcos, Subcommandante, 222
Marijuana use, 69–70
Market position, 87
Markets, 19. *See also* Free market
  economic policies
Mars Corporation, 213
Marx, Karl, 22, 79–84, 93, 94, 101,
    102, 107, 202, 230, 239
  basic argument of, 80–84
  Weber compared with, 84–87
*M*A*S*H*, 116
Mass tourism, 235, 237
Mass transit, 8, 124
Master statuses, 25
Materialism, 84–85
Material resources, 148–50
Mayan culture, 221, 222
McCarthy, Eugene, 153
McCarthy, Joseph, 166
McDonaldization of society, 10, 228
McDonald's, 9–10, 179, 218, 223,
    226
Mead, George Herbert, 66–67, 71, 85
Means of material production, 80,
    86–87
Media
  globalization and, 226

legitimate authority claimed by,
    147
  Marxist theory on, 81, 82
  social movements and, 155,
    156
  social problems and, 125
  Zapatista movement and, 222
Mental patients, 72
Merton, Robert K., 67
Mexico, 201, 203, 204, 219–23
Micro-sociological theories, 49–50
  conflict, 76
  rational choice, 53
  symbolic interactionist/
    constructionist, 65, 74
Microsoft Corporation, 82, 83, 99,
    124, 161
Middle East, 206
Military resources, 149–50
Mills, C. Wright, 5–7, 75, 197, 241–42
Mind, 66–67
Minimum wage standards, 200, 201,
    211
Minority groups
  imprisonment of, 19, 75
  teenage pregnancy in, 48
  See also Blacks; Race
Modernization theory, 200
Money
  globalization and, 223
  social power and, 149, 160–61
  sociology of, 108–12
  See also Economic exchange
Monsanto, 221
Moore, Barrington, 163
Moore, Michael, 137, 204
Moral issues, 158
Morel Tales (Fine), 70
Morisette, Alanis, 136
Mother's Milk (RHCP), 135
Mullings, Beverly, 238
Multidimensional stratification,
    85–93

Murray, Charles, 38
Muslim Madurese, 27
Mussolini, Benito, 160, 162
My Own Private Idaho, 135

N

NASCAR racing, 112, 113
National Association for the
    Advancement of Colored
    People (NAACP), 110, 151, 153
National identities, 26
National Organization for the
    Reform of Marijuana Laws
    (NORML), 151
National Organization for Women
    (NOW), 99, 110, 151, 153
Nations, 99
Nation-states, 107, 109, 214–16. *See
    also* States
Nazi Germany. *See* Hitler, Adolf
Nelson, Willie, 164
Neoliberalism, 199–204
    principles of, 201
    transnational corporations and, 206
    in World Bank and IMF, 210
Nestle, 204, 215
New world order, 200–201
Nicaragua, 167
Nigeria, 210, 214
Nike Corporation, 223
Nirvana, 136
Nock, Steven, 9
North American Free Trade
    Agreement (NAFTA), 124, 220,
    222

O

Oil
    in Iraq, 168–169
    in Mexico, 220, 221
    pricing and, 20, 55, 87
    social problems and, 209, 224
Ologopolies, 20–21
Olson, Mancur, 57
One Hot Minute (RHCP), 136
OPEC, 55
Organizational innovation, 131
Organizational power, 171–91
    bureaucratic organizations and,
        183–85
    symbolic architecture of, 185–91
    workplaces and, 173–83
Organizational recruitment, 172
Organizational resources, 133,
    150–52
Organization for Economic
    Cooperation and Development
    (OECD), 210
Organizations, 61, 99
Orientalism (Said), 39
Outsiders (Becker), 69
Ozone layer depletion, 203, 212

P

Panopticism, 187
Paradigms, 35, 46–47
Parties, political, 85, 89–90
Parton, Dolly, 28
Passeron, Jean-Claude, 91
Pearl Jam, 12, 136
Peasant's Confederation, 218
Pecuniary emulation, 231
Pentagon, September 11 attack on,
    108, 150, 170, 196, 228
Pepsi, 204
Peron, Eva, 15
Persian Gulf War. *See* First Gulf War;
    Second Gulf War
Persson, Nina, 132
Peru, 238

Pfeffer, Jeffrey, 185
Philippines, 213, 238
Philips Electronics, 204
Phoenix, River, 133
Pickering, Andrew, 39
Piece rate system, 177
Pier One Imports, 195
Pink flamingos, cultural significance
    of, 119–21
Pippen, Scottie, 12
Planet Hollywood, 233
Plan Puebla Panama (PPP), 221–23
Point Break, 135
Political alliances, 152, 153, 162
Political coercion. *See* Coercive
    power
Political construction of social
    problems, 122–27
Political globalization, 197–223,
    239
    diasporas and, 207
    nation-state decline and, 214–16
    privatization and, 201, 211
    social movements and, 216–19
    transnational migration and, 207
Political issues, 158
Political parties, 85, 89–90
Political processes, 147
Political protests, 152–59
Politics
    individualism in, 17–19
    Marxist theory on, 81
    of social knowledge, 38–41
    Weberian theory on, 85–86,
        89–90
Polo, 112, 118
Pol Pot, 160
Popular culture, 117–19
Post-Fordism, 206, 231–32
Postmodernism, 236–37
Poverty, 2–4, 123–24
    facts vs. myths, 123
    global, 198, 203–4

individual blame for, 21
in Mexico, 219–23
Power. *See* Authority; Charismatic
    authority; Coercive power;
    Institutionalized power;
    Legitimate authority;
    Organizational power; Power
    prism; Rational-legal authority;
    Social power; Symbolic power;
    Traditional authority
Power prism, 144–47
Pregnancy, teenage, 47–48
Presley, Elvis, 127
Pretty Woman, 135
Preventive practices, 73
Primary deviance/crime, 70
Primate Visions (Haraway), 40
Prisons
    privatization of, 19, 201
    symbolic architecture of, 188
Privacy, 9
Privatization, 19, 201, 211
Probyn, Elspeth, 140
Profane phenomena, 104, 105
Prohibition movement, 125
Proletariat, 80
Props, organizational, 185
Protectionism, 56, 200
*Protestant Ethic and the Spirit of
    Capitalism, The* (Weber), 84–85,
    102–3, 184–85
Protestant work ethic, 102–3
Psychology, 31–32, 66
Public goods, 57
Public sentiments, 155

Q

Quadagno, Jill, 21
Quateman, Bill, 132
Queer Theory/Sociology (Seidman),
    40

R

Race, 3
  double consciousness and, 26,
    27–28
  IQ controversy and, 38
  See also Blacks; Minority groups
Rainforests, 221
Rational choice theories, 48–49,
    50–59, 69, 94
  conflict theories and, 77
  desires in, 53–56
  free-rider problem in, 56–58, 87
  social inequality in, 58–59
Rationality, 50–51
Rational-legal authority, 90, 184
Reagan, Ronald, 59, 160, 167–68,
    200, 223
Reagonomics, 59
Reality
  social construction of, 78–79
  Thomas theorem on, 67
Red Hot Chili Peppers (RHCP),
    132–37, 223
Red Scare, 166
Region behavior, 71–72
Religion, 109, 224–25
  as an emblem of society, 103–8
  Marxist theory on, 81
  Weberian theory on, 84–85, 102–3
Resistance movements, 222–23. *See
    also* Global resistance
Resource mobilization, 148–52
RHCP. *See* Red Hot Chili Peppers
Richardson, Mark ("Rooster"), 133
Rio de Janeiro Conference on the
    Environment, 196, 222
Rites of passage, 29, 110
Rituals
  cultural, 178–79
  degradation, 72
  sacred, 105–6
  social, 69, 73–74, 181–83
  sociology of, 71

Ritzer, George, 10, 226, 227–28, 237
Road rage, 8
Robert Taylor housing project, 3
Rockefeller, John D., 161
Rodman, Dennis, 12–15
Roger and Me, 137, 204
Rousseau, Jean-Jacques, 52
Ruiz, Samuel, 222
Run-DMC, 133
Russell, Kurt, 117
Russia, 167–68, 213
Ryder, Winona, 25

S

Sacred phenomena, 104–6, 230
Sahlins, Marshall, 140
Said, Edward, 39
Samsung, 204
San Antonio Spurs, 14
Sandanista rebels, 167
Sassen, Saskia, 216
Savings and Loan (S&L) Crisis,
    168–69
Schools
  bureaucratic organization in,
    183–84
  compulsory attendance and,
    28–29, 173
  functional theories on, 61–63
  individualism in, 16–17
  organizational power and, 172–73
  privatization of, 201
  stratification theory on, 90–93
School vouchers, 17
Schumacher, Joel, 7
Science
  factual vs. value statements in,
    34–38
  functional theories and, 60
  politics of, 38–41
  social construction of, 39
  truth in, 46

Scientific management, 184
Secondary deviance/crime, 70
Second Gulf War, 107, 169
Seidman, Steven, 40
Self, 66–67, 85
Self-fulfilling prophecy, 67, 71
Self-interest, 50, 77. *See also* Rational
  choice theories
September 11 terrorist attacks, 107,
  108, 150, 170, 195, 196, 228
Serbs, 26–27
Service workers, 10–11
Sex tourism, 238
Shakespeare, William, 117
Sheen, Martin, 25
Shell Corporation, 204
Sidewalk (Dunier), 4
Siegel Schwall Band, 132
Sierra Club, 110
Sign value, 230
Simmel, Georg, 22–24, 25, 26, 32,
  34, 77
Simpson, O. J., 126
Simpsons, The, 132
Simulacra, 233
Situational frames, 71, 72
Skinner, B. F., 31
Slave labor, 213–14
Slim's Table (Dunier), 4
Slovakand, Hillel, 133
Smashing Pumpkins, 12
Smith, Adam, 52, 80, 199
Smith, Dorothy, 40
Smoking, 6, 70
Snipes, Wesley, 15
Social capital, 115–17
Social class
  conflict theories on, 94
  cultural differences and, 112–14,
    116, 119
  double consciousness and, 28
  educational inequality and, 90–93
  everyday expressions of, 119–22
  Marxist theory on, 80, 81–82, 101

symbolic interactionism/
  constructionism on, 65
  Weberian theory on, 85–88
Social construction
  of reality, 78–79
  of science, 39
  of state legitimacy, 163–71
Social constructionism. *See*
  Symbolic interactionist/
  constructionist theories
Social contracts, 52
Social Darwinism, 60
Social drama
  U.S. military history as, 166–71
  warfare as, 164–66
  in the workplace, 181
  See also Dramaturgical sociology
Social facts, 32–34
Social identities, 25–30, 40
  double consciousness and, 26–28
  repertoire selection in, 25–26
Social inequality
  conflict theories on, 76
  culture and, 112
  functional theories on, 63, 64,
    76
  rational choice theories on, 58–
    59
  Weberian theory on, 85
Social interactions, 50, 65, 97–101,
  141
  culture and social structures
    distinguished from, 98–101
  defined, 97
Socialism, 79, 202
Social Meaning of Money, The
  (Zelizer), 109
Social movement organizations, 151
Social movements
  defined, 148
  international, 216–19
  resource mobilization in, 148–52
  social power and, 147–59
Social positions, 119–22

Social power, 48, 143–93
  in authoritarian regimes, 160–63
  conflict theories on, 50, 76, 77
  culture and, 112–27
  dramaturgical sociology on, 71,
    72
  institutionalized, 162
  Marxist theory on, 82
  of money, 111
  rational choice theories on, 58–59
  social movements and, 147–59
  sociological perspective on,
    143–47
  the state and, 159–71
  symbolic interactionism/
    constructionism on, 75
  Weberian theory on, 85
  See also Organizational power
Social problems
  cultural and political construction
    of, 122–27
  individual problems vs., 7–11
Social progress, 38–41
Social reproduction, 91, 103, 115
Social rituals, 69, 73–74, 181–83. See
    also Cultural rituals
Social security, 201
Social solidarity, 50, 87, 94, 102,
    105, 110
Social stratification, 76. See also
    Multidimensional stratification
Social structures, 50, 97–112, 141
  culture and social interactions
    distinguished from, 98–101
  defined, 97
  symbolic interactionism/
    constructionism on, 65, 66, 67,
    75
  See also Structural determinism
Social systems, 61
Social theories, 45–96
  conflict theories, 75–94
  functional theories, 59–64
  interplay of, 47

nature and relevance of, 45–50
as paradigms, 46–47
rational choice theories, 50–59
symbolic interactionist/
  constructionist theories, 64–
  75
theoretical reasoning and, 47–48
types of, 48–50
See also Classical economic
  theory; Conflict theories;
  Functional theories; Labeling
  theory of deviance/crime;
  Macro-sociological theories;
  Management theory; Micro-
  sociological theories;
  Modernization theory;
  Multidimensional stratification;
  Rational choice theories;
  Structuration theory; Symbolic
  interactionist/constructionist
  theories; World system theory
Social trust, 109
Societal forces, 5
Society
  culture distinguished from, 100
  in symbolic interactionism/
    constructionism, 66–67
Sociological imagination, 5–22, 40,
  75
  description of theory, 5–7
  individual vs. social problems in,
    7–11
  sociology of celebrities in, 11–
    16
Sociological Imagination, The (Mills),
  241
Sociology
  of celebrities, 11–16
  contested terrain of, 30–41
  dramaturgical, 71–74, 178
  of identities, 22–30
  of money, 108–12
  of power, 143–47
  psychology vs., 31–32, 66

of rituals, 71
standpoint, 40
Solidarity. *See* Social solidarity
Somalia, 167, 168
Sony, 204
Sound moral character, appearance
of, 72
South America, 198, 206
South Korea, 56, 213
South Park, 132
Southwestern Bell, 220
Soviet Union, 26, 41, 107, 201, 216
Spears, Britney, 132
Spencer, Herbert, 60
Spice Girls, 132
Sports, 112, 113
Spring, McKendree, 132
Stalin, Joseph, 160, 162
Standpoint sociology, 40
State Farm Insurance Company,
187–91
States, 159–71, 172
authoritarian, 160–63
defined, 160
See also Nation-states
Statuses
master, 25
organizational, 61, 100
Status groups, 85, 88–89, 227, 230
Stewart, Martha, 15
Stratification theory. *See*
Multidimensional stratification
Structural adjustment programs
(SAPs), 211–12
Structural determinism, 101–12
defined, 101
mass tourism and, 237
on money, 108–12
on religion, 103–8
Structuration theory, 103
Structure of Scientific Revolutions, The
(Kuhn), 46
Student movement, 153–56, 157–58,
159

Students for a Democratic Society
(SDS), 153
Subordinate resistance, 175
Sub-Saharan Africa, 198, 203
Suggestion boxes, 181
Suharto regime, 27, 211
Super Bowl, 107
Superstructure, 81
Supply and demand, 19–21, 52, 80
Surveillance, 9, 175, 177, 187
Sweden, 206
Symbolic interactionist/
constructionist theories, 48–49,
64–75, 94, 124
conflict theories and, 78–79
mind, self, and society in, 66–67
strengths and weaknesses, 74–75
Weber and, 85
Symbolic issues, 158
Symbolic power, 185–91
Symbolic violence, 117
Symbols, sacred, 105–6

T

Taco Bell, 10
Taiwan, 56
Tally's Corner (Liebow), 4
Tariffs, 200, 211, 220
Taylor, Frederick W., 184
Taylorism, 184
Teamwork, 179
Teenagers
identity crisis in, 28–30
pregnancy in, 47–48
Telecommunications, 225
Television, 226
Telmex, 220
Terrorism
September 11 attacks and, 107,
108, 150, 170, 195, 196, 228
social power and, 150
tourists targeted by, 236

Thailand, 213, 238
Thatcher, Margaret, 200
Themed environments, 180, 232–33
Theory of the Leisure Class, The
    (Veblen), 230
Thomas, William I., 67
Thomas theorem, 67
Tilly, Charles, 144, 147
Titanic, 127
Togo, 214
Tombstone, 117
Tonnies, Ferdinand, 22
Tourism, 233–38
Tourist gaze, 236, 238
Trade
    in kind, 109
    rational choice theories on, 56
    See also Economic globalization;
        Free market economic policies;
        Free trade; North American
        Free Trade Agreement
Trade barriers, 79
Traditional authority, 90
Transnational corporations (TNCs),
    204–9, 210
    defined, 204–5
    impact on nation-states, 214–16
    structural adjustment programs
        and, 211–12
Transnational migration, 207
Trickle-down economic policy, 168
Twister, 136

U

Unilever, 215
Union Carbide Corporation, 208
Unions, 200, 206, 211
United Auto Workers (UAW), 204
United Nations (UN), 210, 215, 217
University of California at San
    Diego, 68

Uplift Mojo Party Plan, The (RHCP),
    133
Urban, Walter, 133
Urry, John, 236
User fees, 211
Use value, 230

V

Value statements, 34–38
Vaughan, Diane, 37
Veblen, Thorstein, 230–31
Ventura, Jesse ("The Body"), 11–12
Vietnam War, 153, 158, 166, 171
Vocationalism, 173

W

Wages, 110, 176
    globalization and, 206–7
    in Mexico, 220
    minimum, 200, 201, 211
    organizational power and, 172
    social power and, 145
    for women, 111
Wag the Dog, 164–65
Walden Two (Skinner), 31
Wallerstein, Immanuel, 82, 197, 216
Wal-Mart, 82, 83, 179, 204, 215
Warfare, 79, 149–50
    construction of state legitimacy
        in, 163–71
    as social drama, 164–66
Warner Brothers, 136
War on Poverty, 21, 123–24
War on the Poor, 21, 124
Weather Underground, 153, 156
Weber, Max, 22, 58, 78, 79, 84–93,
    94, 102–3, 227–28, 230
    on bureaucracies, 183, 184–85
    Marx compared with, 84–87

on multidimensional
  stratification, 85–93
on social power, 144, 159–60
Webs of group affiliation, 22–24, 26
Welch, Michael, 107
Welfare system, 21, 41, 48, 201
  facts vs. myths, 123
  Reagonomics and, 59
  social power and, 111
  as a social problem, 123–24
Willis, Paul, 93
Wolfensohn, James, 202, 204
Women
  degradation rituals and, 72
  double consciousness in, 27–28
  globalization and, 203, 206, 217
  money and, 111
  standpoint sociology and, 40
Workplace, 172, 173–83
  coercive power in, 174–75
  economic exchange in, 175–77
  legitimate authority in, 177–83
World Bank (WB), 202, 210–13, 217,
  220

WorldCom, 168
World system theory, 82
World Trade Center, September 11
  attacks on, 108, 150, 170, 195,
  196, 228
World Trade Organization (WTO),
  156–57, 210, 217
World War I, 162, 163
World War II, 37, 107, 160. *See also*
  Hitler, Adolf

Y

Yippies, 153
"You Oughta Know" (RHCP), 136
Youth culture, 29–30
Yugoslavia, 26–27, 171, 216

Z

Zapatista movement, 222
Zelizer, Viviana, 109